EXCEL for Engineers
and Scientists

EXCEL for Engineers and Scientists

Second Edition

S. C. BLOCH

University of South Florida

WILEY

ACQUISITIONS EDITOR	Joseph Hayton
SENIOR MARKETING MANAGER	Katherine Hepburn

This book was set in Times Roman by the author and printed by Malloy Inc. The cover was printed by Phoenix Color Corporation

This book is printed on acid free paper.

ISBN 0-471-25686-2

Printed in the United States of America

10 9 8 7 6 5 4

To my parents

Preface

The essence of knowledge is, having it, to apply it.
Confucius (K'ung Fu-tse, about 551 BC – 479 BC)

EXCEL is the most popular spreadsheet for scientific, engineering and technical applications because of its powerful features and universal availability. EXCEL is a complete spreadsheet application that lets you analyze, organize, interpret, and present data quickly and easily.

Engineering and science require imagination, insight, reasoning, and calculation. They mutually reinforce each other, so if you can get help with one of these things you have more than a 25 percent advantage at the start. This book will help you with the easiest one, calculation. The other three are up to you.

Goal of this book

The goal of this book is to help you with numerical calculation and data analysis. Calculation is easier than imagination, insight, and reasoning, but calculation is not always easy to accomplish and it is often tedious. This is a "how to" book intended to give you some of the survival skills that you need to get you through. However, there are many advanced topics that you will have to learn later.

This book is designed to fit in a backpack. It should be used interactively with your notebook or desktop PC. Turn your computer on and insert the CD. Explore EXCEL and the workbooks on the CD as you read the chapters.

- I hear, I forget.
- I see, I remember.
- I do, I understand.

Who needs it?

This book is for engineers and scientists, a person who wants to be an engineer or a scientist, and anyone else who wants to know some of the things that they know. This book is basically for beginners, students who are probably struggling with courses in calculus, chemistry, biology, and physics, and are starting up the incline to statics, dynamics, thermodynamics, molecular biology, a.c. circuits, electrodynamics, quantum mechanics and more specialized courses.

What's inside?

- 90 example workbooks on the CD, grouped by their chapters.

- Simple, straightforward explanations in text and graphics. All graphics in the chapters are in the workbooks on the CD, where they are displayed in color.

- How to do structured, efficient, documented workbook composition with data entry cells, summary results and statistics cells, and commented cells.

- Tips and tricks for using EXCEL for engineering and scientific applications.

- Pedagogical strategies to assist beginners.

- Emphasis on graphical presentation of data in standard technical formats.

- Web site for updates to the text and CD.

- Links to the Internet. Appendix 2 and the Bibliography are on the CD in HTML for access with your web browser.

- Clear explanations and comparisons of numerical differentiation methods and simple numerical integration techniques.

- Thorough treatment of Analysis ToolPak features useful in technology.

- Exercises to apply skills learned in each chapter.

- Applications of EXCEL's matrix operations.

- Using EXCEL to import, analyze, and export data to a word processor.

- Inserting an active worksheet in a word processor.

- Including video clips and screen cam clips in a worksheet.

- Using EXCEL for automatic data acquisition and control of local and remote experiments.

- Using EXCEL with popular student lab hardware and software.

- Acquiring experimental data in EXCEL through the serial or parallel port without a data acquisition board.

- Acquiring experimental data in EXCEL through a USB port.

- A tutorial on using the Fast Fourier Transform in EXCEL.

- A tutorial on engineering and scientific applications of the Fast Fourier Transform using EXCEL's functions and operators.

What's new in the Second Edition

- More workbooks to demonstrate EXCEL's features.
- Frequently-asked questions (FAQs) with answers.
- More examples from across engineering and scientific disciplines.
- Expanded explanations of integration methods.
- More matrix methods and examples.
- Added emphasis on documenting worksheets using Comment notes.
- More examples and explanations for solving differential equations.
- Use of new features in EXCEL 2002 (Microsoft OFFICE XP).

Student laboratories have evolved from the read-the-meter format to computer-assisted data acquisition. Excel is ideal for laboratories at all levels because it is easy to use and it is installed on most computers. Most student software will export data to spreadsheets. PASCO Scientific (Science Workshop), National Instruments (LabVIEW and Measure), and Vernier Software (Multi-Purpose Laboratory Interface for Windows, Data Logger) have built-in analysis tools, but exporting the data to Excel gives the student and instructor more analysis power. Excel can not only acquire data and automate experiments, but it can generate signals and control experiments locally and worldwide, if desired, over the Internet.

Some of the software mentioned above have the Fast Fourier Transform (FFT) as part of their programs, but importing the raw data to Excel gives the student more flexibility, a feeling of being in control, and more of an appreciation for the process. In addition, spreadsheet graphs of publication quality and consistent format are easily included in laboratory reports composed on a word processor. This helps to develop personal communication skills.

Internet connections

The Internet is a great resource for engineers and scientists. Appendix 2 and the Bibliography make it easy for you to connect to useful information on the Internet. Just insert the CD that came with this book, open one of the HTML files and click on any web site of interest.

EXCEL 2002 is intimately connected to the Internet, and it is easy to import data from Internet sites. You can also routinely collect data from remote experiments in laboratories, manufacturing facilities, and even spacecraft and other planets. If you need to replace the data often to keep it current the refreshable Web queries now available in EXCEL 2002 make that task easy.

If you are connected to the Internet, just click on http://www.microsoft.com. This web site has free downloads from Microsoft.

How to use this book

EXCEL versions

The latest version of Excel (in Microsoft Office XP) is required for full functionality of the workbooks on the CD. However, this book and its workbooks can be used effectively with previous versions of Excel. The oldest version that I recommend using is Excel 97.

EXCEL 2002 can import workbooks composed using earlier versions of EXCEL and other spreadsheets such as Lotus 1-2-3 and Quattro.

Turn on your computer and insert the CD that comes with this book. Start EXCEL and load a file of your choice. You'll find the most effective use of this book is when you work with it at your computer, and follow the discussion by exploring worksheets on your monitor as you read about them.

This book is designed for a short course or as supplementary material for a longer course. Most of this book is for beginners and it does not cover every feature in Excel. A few sections and exercises, and the last two chapters, may appeal to more advanced students; these are marked with the symbol ✪.

Chapter 1 Getting Started
Chapter 2 Exploring EXCEL
Chapter 3 EXCEL's Graphics
Chapter 4 Quick-Start Math

> The first four chapters are essential.

Chapter 5 Differentiation and Integration

> Sections 5.1–5.2 cover basic numerical differentiation and integration. The remaining sections cover two special tools in EXCEL (Moving Average and Exponential Smoothing) and other filtering techniques.

Chapter 6 EXCEL's Engineering Functions

> This chapter is a survey of all operations in EXCEL's *Engineering Functions* category, and matrix methods.

Chapter 7 Differential Equations

> This could be omitted in a short course. There are two interactive finite-element workbooks for Laplace's equation, in addition to methods for ordinary differential equations.

Chapter 8 Analysis ToolPak

> This is a survey of some of the most-used analysis tools in EXCEL.

Chapter 9 EXCEL in the Lab

This chapter is about applications of EXCEL in the student lab with two popular educational data acquisition packages and one industrial-strength EXCEL software add-in from National Instruments.

Chapter 10 Complex Math

This could be omitted for beginning students, but Chapters 11 and 12 depend on Chapter 10. This chapter is on the CD.

Chapter 11 Analysis ToolPak: Fast Fourier Transform ✪

This shows how to use the most powerful tool in EXCEL, the FFT (Fast Fourier Transform). Some student lab software packages have the FFT, but you can do more and get better results using EXCEL. Workbooks for FFT tutorial, windowing, aliasing, frequency scaling, and power spectral density are included. This chapter is on the CD in an Adobe Acrobat PDF file. The Acrobat Reader is included on the CD.

Chapter 12 Analysis ToolPak: FFT Applications ✪

This chapter shows applications of the FFT, including convolution, deconvolution, cross-correlation function, system identification, coherence function and SNR function. Chapter 12 is on the CD in an Acrobat PDF file. The latest version of Acrobat Reader can be downloaded free at www.adobe.com.

More exercises for each chapter are in folders on the CD. When you finish this book you will have a set of skills that will probably last you throughout your career, because future versions of EXCEL will build on these basics.

Advanced mathematics programs also work with EXCEL. For example, MATLAB (www.mathworks.com) has EXCEL LINK and EXCEL BUILDER for creating MATLAB-based add-ins for EXCEL. MATHEMATICA (www.wolfram.com) has MATHEMATICA LINK FOR EXCEL, and MATHCAD (www.mathsoft.com) has a component for data I/O with EXCEL. Waterloo MAPLE (www.maplesoft.com) has an EXCEL add-in.

Acknowledgments

It is a pleasure to acknowledge the assistance, guidance, and patience of the people at John Wiley & Sons. In alphabetical order, my thanks go to Mary Beth Bohman, Monique Calello, Jack Drucker, editor Joseph P. Hayton, Katherine Hepburn, Mary Moran, Kenneth Santor, Eric Shivak, and Lisa Van Horn.

For the First Edition I am also pleased to acknowledge the assistance of Professors William Beckwith (Clemson University), Melanie Bengtson (North Dakota State University), Daniel A. Gulino (Ohio University) and Georg F. Mauer (University of Nevada, Las Vegas) in reviewing the manuscript.

For the Second Edition I would like to thank Dr. Roy Fitzgerald López Carrera, Professor Darrell G. Fontane (Colorado State University), Dr. Calvin Johnson, Professor Patrick J. Jordan (University of Canterbury, New Zealand), Professor J. C. Simonis (University of Texas-San Antonio), Professor Garry W. Warren (University of Alabama), and at John Wiley & Sons, Simon Durkin, Bonnie Kubat and Angie Vennerstrom. Again, special thanks go to editor Joseph P. Hayton.

I am very grateful for the suggestions, comments, and encouragement from Dr. Lawrence Edward Bloch, Dr. Robert Dressler, Professor Donald T. Haynie (Louisiana Tech University), Curt Lorenc, and Janis Walters. Thanks also go to Dr. Daniel H. Fylstra of Frontline Systems (www.solver.com) for permission to include the Solver tutorials on the CD, National Instruments (www.ni.com), PASCO Scientific (www.pasco.com), and Vernier Software (www.vernier.com).

Contacts and Updates

For information on this title and related books, go to the web sites:
http://www.wiley.com/college/bloch and http://www.wiley.com
For technical support concerning the CD go to the web site:
http://www.wiley.com/techsupport
or e-mail techhelp@wiley.com
For updates and new downloads for this book, go to the web site:
http://sylvanbloch.hypermart.net/

If you have suggestions or find a correction that is not listed, please send it to the e-mail address in the Contact section at the web site.

Excel!

Sylvan Charles Bloch
Tampa, Florida

Contents

Chapter 10 is on the CD.

10. Complex Math 10-1

✪ *Chapter 11 is on the CD.*

11. Analysis ToolPak: Fourier Analysis 11-1

Note: Additional exercises for Chapters are on the CD.

The science of calculation also is indispensable as far as the extraction of the square and cube roots; algebra as far as the quadratic equations; and the use of logarithms are often of value in ordinary cases; but all beyond these is but a luxury; a delicious luxury indeed; but not to be indulged in by one who is to have a profession to follow for his sustenance.

Thomas Jefferson
1743 – 1826

Mathematics may be compared to a mill of exquisite workmanship which grinds you stuff of any degree of fineness; but, nevertheless, what you get out depends upon what you put in . . .

Thomas Henry Huxley
1869

. . . when you can measure what you are speaking about and express it in numbers, you know something about it; but when you cannot measure it, when you cannot express it in numbers, your knowledge is of a meager and unsatisfactory kind . . .

Lord Kelvin
in a lecture to the Institution of Civil Engineers, May 3, 1883

If engineers would read the manual, the world would be a better place.

Andrew S. Grove
CEO, Intel Corporation, 1999

Chapter 1
Getting Started

The spreadsheet originated as a computerized accountant's grid, designed to do mathematical and statistical calculations and sort lists of information. It quickly evolved into a powerful mathematical program that caught the attention of engineers and scientists; EXCEL, in particular, became their favorite computation tool. In addition to calculation, spreadsheets are handy for creating quick charts of publication quality, and performing database operations. The chart (or graph) feature is extremely important for visualization of numerical relationships. It is remarkable how much a simple graph can aid in understanding relationships; EXCEL excels at this.

In this chapter we'll discuss the basics so you can get up and running quickly. Later, we'll go into more advanced topics.

You are in control of your spreadsheet, from the numbers that go in it to how it looks on the screen. To understand the spreadsheet, you don't need to be an expert. You just need to understand cells and formulas.

1.1 Cells, worksheets, workbooks

A *worksheet* is made up of *cells*. A cell is the intersection of a row and a column. The cell that resides at the intersection of column C and row 2 is called cell C2. (See Fig. 1-1.) The symbols C2 are the *cell address*. A cell address is like a mail box. Later you'll see that cell addresses come in two flavors, relative and absolute, but don't worry about this now. The EXCEL worksheet shown in Fig. 1-1 is one of three sheets in this workbook. A *workbook* is a group of worksheets.

Tip
Enter cell addresses or formulas instead of numerical data whenever possible, so the spreadsheet can recalculate automatically when you revise input data.

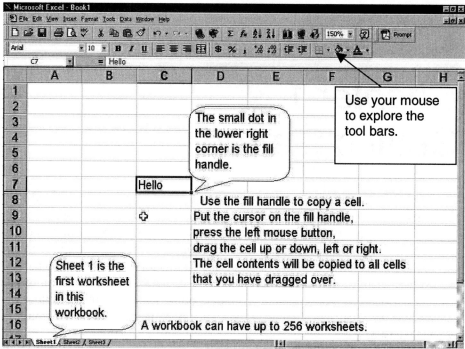

Figure 1-1. The EXCEL window. Cell C7 is selected but the mouse pointer is over cell C9. The mouse pointer has the shape of a cross. The cross changes to a small + symbol when you put it on the fill handle. Try this on your computer.

Open a new workbook and explore the tool bars at the top of the worksheet. Cell C7 is selected in Fig. 1-1. Notice that the content of cell C7 is shown in the cell editing box just above the column labels (column labels are A, B, C, and so on).

Notice the three tabs at the bottom left. These select the worksheets in this workbook. You can add more worksheets to a maximum of 256, or you can delete worksheets. You can also click on the tabs to rename them.

The slide bars at the right and bottom let you move quickly to other parts of the worksheet. Each sheet has 256 columns and 65,536 rows. Press the Home key to return to column A; press Ctrl+Home to go to cell A1, the upper left corner of the worksheet. Ctrl+Home means press both keys together.

Select an empty cell anywhere in the open worksheet and use a right mouse click. This activates a pop-up menu shown in Fig. 1-2. The pop-up menu has ten common operations that are grouped for easy use. You should experiment with the Cut, Copy and Paste operations because you will use them often. Click on the others to see what they do; we'll discuss them later.

Figure 1-3 shows the EXCEL window and MYWORKBOOK that you will compose. Start EXCEL and open a new workbook. Press Enter.↵ after you type the following information in each cell:

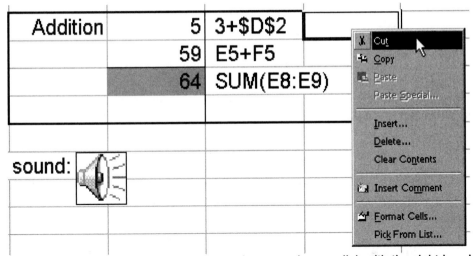

Figure 1-2. The pop-up menu appears when you do one click with the right-hand mouse button. The mouse pointer selects Cut when you click with the left button.

Type `MyWorkbook` in cell A1.

Type `Press Function Key F9 to recalculate` in cell E1. Press the **Align Right** button located above the cell editing box. See Fig. 1-3.

Type `2` in cell D2. Use the Borders icon and its menu arrow to place a box around cell D2.

Type `Enter a number` in cell C2. Press the **Align Right** button located above the cell editing box. The mouse pointer is the arrow in Fig. 1-3. (In later chapters we'll discuss inserting sound, photos, and video in a worksheet.)

	B10	▾	=	=ROUNDUP(22.959,0)			
	A	B	C	D	E	F	G	H
1	**MyWorkbook**			Press Function Key F9 to recalculate			
2	Chapter 1		Enter a number	2			
3							
4	Lottery Winning Numbers:						
5	79	85	44	86	51	8	
6							
7	Rounding:	22.959					
8	Integer	22		Addition	5	3+$D$2	
9	Rounddown	22			59	E5+F5	
10	Roundup	23			64	SUM(E8:E9)	
11	Round	23					
12							
13		Double-Click here for sound:					
14							

Figure 1-3. Your completed worksheet should look like this, except for the sound.

Type `Lottery Winning Numbers` in cell A4.

Type `=INT(RAND()*46*$D$2)` in cell A5. Let's examine this formula. INT is a worksheet function that rounds a number down to the nearest integer. RAND( ) is a worksheet function that returns an evenly distributed random number greater than or equal to 0 and less than 1. Don't forget to include the empty parentheses symbols ( ). A new random number is returned every time the worksheet is calculated. For more information, look up INT and RAND() in Help. $D$2 is an absolute cell address that always refers to cell D2, even when you copy it to another cell. *Don't put any spaces between symbols in a formula.*

Place your mouse pointer on the fill handle of cell A5 and drag it along row 5. Stop on cell F5. This copies the formula in cell A5 to all cells through cell F5. You should see something like Fig. 1-3, but the numbers in row 5 will be different. Press Function Key F9 and you will see the numbers change.

Type `Rounding` in cell A7 and click on the **Align Right** icon. Type `22.959` in cell B7.

Now let's look at some other useful operations. Look in Help for more information about the differences among these rounding functions and how they are used:

Type `=INT(22.959)` in cell B8. (This returns the nearest lower integer.)

Type `=ROUNDDOWN(22.959,0)` in cell B9. (See Help for properties.)

Type `=ROUNDUP(22.959,0)` in cell B10. (0 selects zero decimal places.)

Type `=ROUND(22.959,0)` in cell B11. (See Help for properties.)

Now we'll write three more formulas and see how to add a range of numbers.

Type `Addition` in cell D8. Click on the **Align Right** icon.

Type `=3+$D$2` in cell E8. This adds 3 and the contents of cell D2.

Type `=E5+F5` in cell E9. This adds the contents of cells E5 and F5.

Type `=SUM(E8:E9)` in cell E10. This adds the range of cells E8 through E9 and puts the total in cell E10. Go to Help for more information how to use SUM, and how SUM treats non-numeric values. It is more powerful than simple addition.

Type `3+$D$2` in cell F8. Notice that this appears in Cell F8 exactly as you typed it because it is not a formula without the equality symbol =.

Type `E5+F5` in cell F9.

Type `SUM(E8:E9)` in cell F10.

Move your mouse pointer over the tab named **Sheet 1** at the lower left corner of your worksheet. The cross will change to an arrow.

Do a right click with your mouse and a little menu will pop up. There are six items on the menu. Do a left click on Rename and use the Delete or BackSpace key to remove Sheet 1. Type in `Main` and click on any cell in the worksheet. Click on the tab and drag it to another location among the other tabs.

Go to the **File** menu and click on **Save As**. Choose a location and name for your workbook. Congratulations! You have just created an interactive workbook.

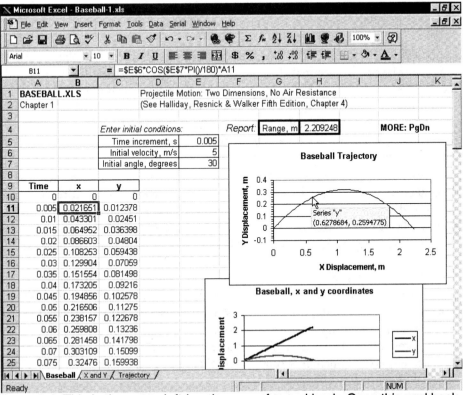

Figure 1-4. This is the upper left-hand corner of a workbook. Open this workbook in your computer and place the mouse pointer on each icon to learn what it does. Note that the box is on cell B11 and its formula is displayed in the cell editing box, below the tool bars. The mouse pointer is on the graph, where it reads out an *x,y* value. Note tabs at bottom left; they correspond to named worksheets in this workbook.

Now let's look at a more elaborate workbook that we'll examine in detail later. Open the worksheet named BASEBALL and you should see Fig. 1-4.

You can type numbers, text or formulas in a cell. Position your cursor (which looks like a box in the spreadsheet) on a cell by moving the arrow keys or using the mouse. Put the pointer (which looks like a cross) over the cell, then click the left button once. All of EXCEL's operators and functions can be accessed by clicking on the f_x icon named **Paste Function** (see Section 2.6, Chapter 2).

If you ever need to know where your cursor is, look in the cell reference in the upper left corner, just above where the column letters and row numbers meet (see Fig. 1-4, which says B11). Notice the small black dot at the lower right-hand corner of the box on cell B11. This is the *fill handle* that we mentioned earlier.

1.2 Cell information

You can enter three basic types of information in a spreadsheet cell:

Numbers are the essential input to a worksheet. You can set the number of digits displayed, in decimal format (like 3.14159) or scientific format (like 6.02E23 or 6.02*10^23). These in-line numbers are equivalent to 6.02 x 10^{23}.

Formulas compute results based on numbers or cell references in the formulas. When you enter a formula, it displays the result. In order for EXCEL to recognize a formula, the formula must begin with an equal sign (like =2+3 or =A3+B7/10).

Text information can be used to identify data series, attach notes, and general communication. It's a good idea to use text to document what you're doing and why you did it. A workbook without documentation can be a mystery, even to the person who wrote it. Comments can also be attached to a cell (see Figs. 2-7 and 2-8). See the paper by K. R. Morison and P. J. Jordan in References, page 20.

Enter text, numbers or formulas by putting the cursor on the cell you want, then typing the information. You'll see the symbols go in the cell, but you're actually working in the cell editing line above the column letters. To put the information in the cell, do one of the following: press Enter↵, press Tab, or move out of the cell by pressing an arrow key. If you make a mistake and want to start over, select the cell, press Function Key F2, then click the "*X*" button on the cell editing line. It will cancel any changes.

1.3 Formulas

Formulas are mathematical or statistical equations entered into a cell to perform a calculation. The elementary algebraic operations in formulas are
    2+2 (add)
    2–2 (subtract)
    2*2 (multiply)
    2/2 (divide)
    2^2 (exponentiate).
Formulas always start with the = symbol and are nested in parentheses. If you forget the = symbol, the formula will appear as text and EXCEL will not calculate anything based on this cell.

When you write formulas, you can use numbers and cell references. For example, the formula to calculate a percentage is: a particular data point divided by the sum of all data, times 100. If B9 is a particular data point and B10 is the sum of all data, then this formula could be =(B9/B10)*100.

EXCEL has functions to calculate things like averages, medians, and sums. To use a function you type the = symbol, the name of the function and, in parentheses, the cell range separated by a colon. For example, to find the average of data in cells B5 through B8, the formula would be =AVERAGE(B5:B8).

1.4 COPY operation

This operation can save you a lot of time and typing. Instead of typing formulas into each cell, the COPY operation enables you to type a few formulas one time, and then copy these formulas to all of the cells that you need.

1. Select the cell that contains the formula you want to move or copy.
2. Point to the border of the selected cell.
3. To move the cell, drag the selection to the upper-left cell of the paste area. EXCEL replaces any existing data in the paste area.

To copy the cell, hold down CTRL as you drag your mouse. You can also copy formulas into adjacent cells by using the *fill handle* we mentioned earlier. (The fill handle is the little black dot at the lower right corner.) Select the cell containing the formula, then drag the fill handle over the range you want to fill.

(Click on Help for more information about special copying operations, and absolute and relative cell references.)

1.5 Cell references

A reference identifies a cell or a range of cells in a worksheet and tells EXCEL where to look for the data you want to use in a formula. With references, you can use data contained in different parts of a worksheet in one formula or use the value from one cell in several formulas. You can also refer to cells in other sheets in the same workbook, to other workbooks, and to data in other programs. References to cells in other workbooks are *external* references. References to data in other programs are *remote* references.

Tip
When you *move* a formula with Cut and Paste, the cell references within the formula will *not* change.
When you *copy* a formula, *absolute* cell references will *not* change.
When you *copy* a formula, *relative* cell references *will* change in the copy.

By default, EXCEL uses the A1 reference style, which labels columns with letters (A through IV, for a total of 256 columns) and labels rows with numbers (1 through 65536). To refer to a cell, enter the column letter followed by the row number. For example, C61 refers to the cell at the intersection of column C and row 61. To refer to a range of cells, enter the reference for the cell in the upper-left corner of the range, a colon (:), and then the reference to the cell in the lower-right corner of the range. The following are examples of references.

To refer to:	Use
The cell in column A and row 10	A10
The range of cells in column A and rows 10 through 20	A10:A20
The range of cells in row 15 and columns B through E	B15:E15
All cells in row 4	4:4
All cells in rows 4 through 11	4:11
All cells in column C	C:C
All cells in columns D through K	D:K

✪ You can also use another reference style where both the rows and the columns on the worksheet are numbered. R1C1 style is useful for computing row and column positions in macros and can be useful for showing relative cell references. In R1C1 style, EXCEL indicates the location of a cell with an "R" followed by a row number and a "C" followed by a column number. For more information about R1C1 references, see online Help or your instruction manual.

Tip
Depending on the task you want to perform, you can use either *relative* cell references or *absolute* references. Relative references are references to cells *relative to the cell of the formula*. For example, C12 is a relative cell reference. If you Copy and Paste this to another cell position, it will change to the new cell. Absolute references always refer to cells in a specific location. For example, $C$12 will remain the same if you copy it to another cell.

You can also use mixed references. For example, $C12 will always refer to column C, but the row number will change if you copy this to another position. Also, C$12 will always refer to row 12, but the column will change when this is copied to another cell.

That's all you need to know to start working with spreadsheets. You can make your spreadsheet as big or as complicated as you like. Later we'll see how to use some sophisticated statistical analysis to dig out more information.

1.6 Example workbook: baseball trajectory

Every student in engineering and the sciences works the problem of the trajectory of an object under constant gravitational acceleration, and without air resistance. The first problem you work involves a mass falling straight down. Next you do a two-dimensional example, like a baseball, soccer ball, or cannonball (Fig. 1-5).

When you do problems with a calculator, you get a single answer like the time of flight, the maximum height, or the range. You can get a lot more information using a spreadsheet. For example, you can follow the trajectory in vertical and horizontal components, and in space and time. A simple graph on a spreadsheet lets you check your analytical calculations.

Before you start your spreadsheet, you need to know a few things about formulas. When you use a function, the argument of the function must be enclosed in parentheses. For example, the natural log of 10 must be written as $=\ln(10)$.

Trigonometric functions use *radians* as their argument, not degrees. Because there are 2π radians in 360 degrees, you can convert degrees to radians by multiplying degrees by $\pi/180$. For example, the formula for the sine of 30 degrees should be written as $=\sin(30*PI()/180)$. Always write π as PI(). Don't forget the parentheses with nothing between them!

Let's examine the physical situation shown in Fig. 1-5, and write the equations for the horizontal and vertical displacements as functions of time t, initial positions x_o and y_o, initial speed v_o, and initial angle θ_o.

$$x(t) = x_o + v_o \cos(\theta_o)t \qquad (1\text{-}1)$$

Equation (1-1) says that the horizontal displacement at any time is the initial displacement from $x = 0$, plus the displacement due to the constant horizontal component of the initial velocity, multiplied by t.

$$y(t) = y_o + v_o \sin(\theta_o)t - 0.5gt^2 \qquad (1\text{-}2)$$

Equation (1-2) says that the vertical displacement is the initial displacement from $y = 0$, plus the displacement due to the vertical component of the initial velocity times t, minus the displacement due to the acceleration of gravity, g m/s^2.

You can enter the equations directly in EXCEL. Time appears as a parameter in Eq. (1-1) and (1-2), so you can eliminate time between these equations to obtain the horizontal range R as a function of the initial speed and launch angle,

$$R = \frac{2v_o^2}{g}\sin(\theta_o)\cos(\theta_o). \qquad (1\text{-}3)$$

The range can be expressed even more simply using the trigonometric identity for the double angle, $\sin(2\theta) = 2\sin(\theta)\cos(\theta)$. Equation (1-3) becomes

$$R = \frac{v_o^2}{g}\sin(2\theta_o). \qquad (1\text{-}4)$$

Worksheet Construction

Now let's build the worksheet based on this information. We will use cell references to enter initial data. This is a great convenience and time-saver, because you can enter new data and the entire worksheet will recalculate. You do not need to enter new data in each cell, or do any copying operation.

Refer to Figs. 1-4 and 1-6. Cell E5 contains the input time increment. This is used in column A in the following way: Cell A10 has the initial time, which is 0 in this example. Cell A11 has the formula =A10+$E$5, shown in Fig. 1-6. Cell A11 is copied to the desired range in column A.

Cells in column B contain Eq. (1-1), the formula for the x coordinate at any time. A typical formula, for cell B10, is shown in Fig. 1-7.

Finally we come to column C, which contains the y coordinate formula, corresponding to Eq. (1-2). The formula in cell C10 is shown in Fig. 1-8. (When you type formulas, don't leave any spaces.)

Look back at Fig. 1-4. Cell H4 reports the range, corresponding to Eq. (1-4). When you build a worksheet, you'll often find it convenient to report computed values (like mean value, r.m.s., standard deviation, variance, and so on) in a box located in a prominent position. Figure 1-9 shows details of the range report.

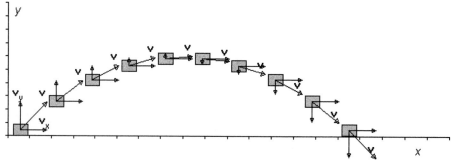

Fig. 1-5. Trajectory without air resistance. The initial speed is v_o, and the initial angle is θ_o measured counterclockwise from the x-axis. The object is launched from the origin (0, 0). Notice that the horizontal component of velocity is constant as the vertical component changes.

A11	▼		=	=A10+$E$5	
	A	B	C	D	E
1	**BASEBALL.XLS**			Projectile Motion: Two	
2	Chapter 1			(See Halliday, Resnick	
3					
4				*Enter initial conditions:*	
5				Time increment, s	0.005
6				Initial velocity, m/s	5
7				Initial angle, degrees	30
8					
9	**Time**	**x**	**y**		
10	0	0	0		
11	0.005	0.025	0.012378		

Fig. 1-6. Typical formula to establish a time base. Cell A11 uses the starting value in cell A10 and the increment in cell E5. Note use of both relative and absolute cell references in one formula.

B10	▼	=	=$E$6*COS($E$7*PI()/180)*A10		
	A	B	C	D	E	F

	A	B	C	D	E	F
1	**BASEBALL.XLS**			Projectile Motion: Two Dimensioı		
2	Chapter 1			(See Halliday, Resnick & Walkeɪ		
3						
4				*Enter initial conditions:*		*Report:*
5				Time increment, s	0.005	
6				Initial velocity, m/s	5	
7				Initial angle, degrees	30	
8						
9	**Time**	**x**	**y**			
10	0	0	0	⊕		

Fig. 1-7 The formula for the x coordinate at time $t = 0$ is shown in cell B10. Note use of absolute cell references to initial velocity and initial angle, and relative cell reference to the time in cell A10. Also, note the conversion of degrees ($E$7) to radians which is required by the cosine in Excel.

C10	▼	=	=$E$6*SIN($E$7*PI()/180)*A10-0.5*9.8*A10^2			

	A	B	C	D	E	F	G
1	**BASEBALL.XLS**			Projectile Motion: Two Dimensions, No A			
2	Chapter 1			(See Halliday, Resnick & Walker Fifth Eɪ			
3							
4				*Enter initial conditions:*			
5				Time increment, s	0.005		
6				Initial velocity, m/s	5		
7				Initial angle, degrees	30		
8							Bɑ
9	**Time**	**x**	**y**				
10	0	0	0	⊕			3

Fig. 1-8. The formula for the y coordinate at time $t = 0$ is shown in cell C10. The factor 9.8 is g, the acceleration of gravity in m/s^2. This formula is the spreadsheet version of Eq. (1-2), for initial coordinates of (0, 0).

H4	▼	=	=($E$6^2/9.8)*SIN(2*$E$7*PI()/180)				

	A	B	C	D	E	F	G	H
1	**BASEBALL.XLS**			Projectile Motion: Two Dimensions, No Air Resistance				
2	Chapter 1			(See Halliday, Resnick & Walker Fifth Edition, Chapter 4)				
3								
4				*Enter initial conditions:*			*Report:* Range, m	2.209248
5				Time increment, s	0.005			
6				Initial velocity, m/s	5			Baseball, x and y ⊕
7				Initial angle, degrees	30			

Fig. 1-9. The pointer arrow is on cell H4, which reports the range according to Eq. (1-4).

1.7 Is your Analysis ToolPak installed?

Now is a good time to see if the Analysis ToolPak is installed in EXCEL. The
ToolPak is like the key to the front door of a gold mine.

Click on the Tools menu to see Data Analysis, as shown in Fig. 1-10, then
click again to see Fig. 1-11. If Data Analysis does not appear, then follow the
directions below Fig. 1-12.

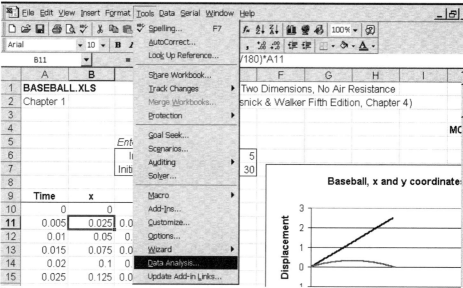

Fig. 1-10. Tools menu with Data Analysis installed. Click on Data Analysis to
bring up the Analysis ToolPak.

The Data Analysis selection box is shown in Fig. 1-11. Use the scroll bar on
the right hand side of the list to view the rest of the items.

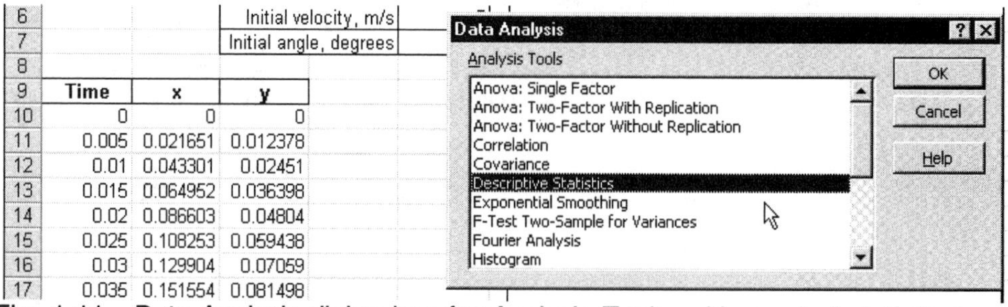

Fig. 1-11. Data Analysis dialog box for Analysis Tools, with a set of statistical
tools and Fourier Analysis (see Chapters 9 and 11).

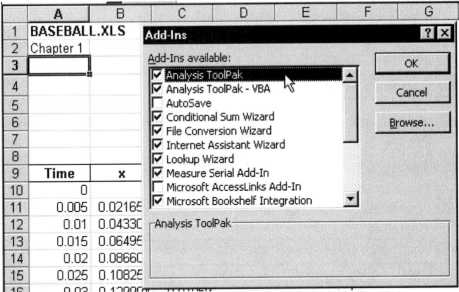

Fig. 1-12. The Add-Ins dialog box. In addition to the Analysis ToolPak, you may want to use Analysis ToolPak–VBA. (VBA refers to the Visual Basic for Applications Add-In; it is needed to record macros. See Chapter 9.)

Figure 1-11 shows only part of the Data Analysis menu. If you have a few hours of free time, use the scroll bar to explore these tools. I think you'll be delighted. If Data Analysis does not show up on your Tools menu, click on Add-Ins on the Tools menu (see Fig. 1-10). You can select Add-Ins from the dialog box shown in Fig. 1-12. The Analysis ToolPak is the one we will be most interested in. The Measure Serial Add-In probably will not appear on your menu. This refers to a program named MEASURE for data acquisition into EXCEL; see Chapter 9. (MEASURE is a product of National Instruments, http://www.ni.com.)

1.8 Navigation tips for EXCEL

Usually, there is more than one way to move around in EXCEL, and more than one way to perform operations. As you become familiar with the spreadsheet you will develop your own habits of working with toolbars and hot keys for your most-used procedures. When you become a power-user you can customize toolbars and keys according to your personal preferences.

Press the Home key. It takes your cursor to column A of the row where you are now located. To go to the first filled cell on the left, press End and then press the left arrow ←.

Press Ctrl and Home to return to the upper left-hand corner, cell A1.

Press Home to go to the left-hand column of the worksheet.

To go to the last entry in a column, press End, then press the down arrow ↓.

To go to the last entry in a row, press End and then press the right arrow →.

Press End and then press the up arrow ↑ to go to the first entry at the top of a column.

1.9 Function Keys

As you begin using your spreadsheet, you will probably find that the most-used Function Keys are F1 and F2. Function Key F1 brings up online Help, and Function Key F2 lets you edit the cell outlined by the cursor box. Table 1-1 shows a few shortcuts; many more are available in Help under the Function Key category. All twelve Function Keys have assigned operations.

Table 1-1. Frequently-used Function Key shortcuts.				
	Function Key	Shift	Alt	Alt + Shift
F1	Display Help or the Office Assistant	Answers the question, What's this?	Insert a new chart sheet	Insert a new worksheet
F2	Edit the active cell	Edit a cell comment	Save As command	Save command

Examples:

To display Help, press F1.

To edit a cell comment, hold down Shift and press Function Key F2.

To insert a new worksheet, hold down Alt and Shift and press Function Key F1.

1.10 The right mouse button

Your index finger will get a lot of exercise using EXCEL, because it controls the left mouse button and that is most used. However, the right mouse button contains some handy operations, shown in Fig. 1-2. The right mouse button provides a quick, alternate way to select these items, which also could be selected from the drop-down menu bar or some icons at the top of EXCEL.

Let's look at the pop-up menu in a little more detail (see Fig. 1-13). You already know how to use Cut, Copy, and Paste. Look at the Paste Special command. This is very powerful and a little too complicated to discuss at this point. Look in Help for an explanation about how to use Paste Special with embedded and linked objects in EXCEL.

The Insert command lets you insert rows or columns, and shift cells right or down. The Delete command lets you delete rows or columns and shift cells left or up. Clear Contents empties all selected cells.

Figure 1-13. The pop-up menu appears when you do a right mouse click. The Insert Comment command will be discussed in Section 2.3; when you insert a comment three new commands appear. Click on Format Cells and explore the possibilities! You can even adjust the angle of a line of text.

1.11 Using CONVERT

One of the most annoying tasks faced by students involves changing units between metric (SI) and British engineering units. It can be discouraging to work a problem correctly, but get the wrong answer because of an error in units. EXCEL can be a great help, because it contains a worksheet function named CONVERT that will change almost any number from one measurement system to another.

For example, CONVERT can translate a table of distances in miles to a table of distances in kilometers, or inches, or almost any length unit. This function also converts mass and weight, time, power, liquid measure, temperature, energy, and force. See Section 6.4 for complete details and examples of this function.

If the CONVERT function is not available, run the Setup program to install the Analysis ToolPak (see Section 1.7).

1.12 The save-a-screen trick

This trick will work in any Windows application. It enables you to copy whatever you see on your monitor and place it in other Windows applications as a picture. Or, you can save the screen as a file that you can edit (crop, rotate, change colors, and so on).

To capture a screen, press the Print Scrn key. This will place the screen on the Windows clipboard. To put the screen in another application, just go to that application (Microsoft WORD, for example) and click on the Paste icon or go to the Edit menu and click on Paste. The screen shot will appear in the document and you can re-size it using the mouse.

If you want to save the screen shot as a file for later use, click on [Start][Programs][Accessories][Paint] and then click on the Paste icon. Now you can edit the screen shot and save it as a file using [File][Save As]. Of course, you can also use other graphics programs, such as *Corel* or *Adobe PhotoShop*.

1.13 Customizing EXCEL

Click on [Tools] on the top menu bar. In the lower part of the drop-down menu, click on [Customize]. This produces a dialog box that enables you to customize Toolbars, Commands, and Options.

Do it your way
There is usually more than one way to accomplish an operation in EXCEL. For example, you can use your mouse to click on a menu item or command, you can use a Function Key, or you can use a *keyboard shortcut*. As you progress you will develop habits that you find most natural.

Vision-impaired users
Click on the Options tab and you can select Large Icons for the toolbar. For additional ideas, click on Help, select Contents and Index, and type in *accessibility* or *vision*. You can find even more information on the Internet at: http://www.microsoft.com/

1.14 Tips on worksheet composition

When you start EXCEL and you see a blank worksheet, think of yourself as an artist. You are going to compose a masterpiece (*one* of your masterpieces) and you want other people to appreciate it and understand it. Also, when you return to it some time in the future you will want to understand it. Let's consider a few tips on worksheet composition here; you can see these as you explore the BASEBALL worksheet, Fig. 1-4. As we proceed in later chapters you will see more ideas.

- Use comments in cells so you will remember what you did.
  You can add comments by clicking on [Insert][Comment].
  Also, see Fig. 1-13. Your comments can be hidden until you
  put the cursor on the cell, or you can let a comment be con-
  tinuously visible. (See Figs. 2-7 and 2-8.) Hiding comments
  reduces worksheet clutter. Describe your work!

- Wherever possible, enter cell references instead of numerical
  values. This lets you copy cell formulas to rows, columns, or
  single cells, and it makes the worksheet recalculate quickly.
  Also, this lets you enter data easily (see next tip).

- Use absolute and relative cell references appropriately to
  make the Copy operation effective. See how this is done in
  the BASEBALL worksheet.

- Put input data, such as mass, initial temperature, and initial
  velocity, in boxed cells at the top of the worksheet. Then use

absolute cell references to include these data in formulas in the body of the worksheet. See *Initial Conditions* boxes in the BASEBALL worksheet.

- Collect and report important results (such as input variance, output variance, peak value, average value, time delay) in boxed cells at the top of the worksheet so any user can find them. When results appear embedded in the worksheet, copy the results, using absolute cell references, to the boxed cells at the top. See *Range Report* in the BASEBALL worksheet.

- Include descriptive titles in rows and columns of data! Titles remove some of the mystery from worksheets.

- You can use a chart embedded in Sheet 1 of the worksheet, but don't clutter the sheet with a lot of them. Instead, save charts on other sheets in the workbook and access them by clicking on their Tabs at the bottom of the worksheet.

- Put descriptive names on the Tabs for different sheets. Right-click on a Tab and then select Rename. See Fig. 1-4.

- Avoid clutter in a worksheet. Do auxiliary calculations on other sheets and swap data between sheets. In other words, use a 3-D workbook. See Section 2.7.

- The worksheet can be set to recalculate automatically or manually. In either mode, press Function Key F9 to recalculate immediately. To see which mode you're in, type `=INFO("recalc")` and press Enter⏎ . To set the mode, click on [Tools][Options][Calculation].

- Adjust column widths for optimum data display. You don't need to be restricted to equal spacing. Adjust font size.

- Use colors for fonts and cells to call attention to important items. Use colors in charts to enhance clarity.

- A collection of tips on various aspects of EXCEL can be found at http://www.j-walk.com/ss/excel/usertips/index.htm. Many of these tips are for advanced users.

1.15 Using OFFICE BINDER as digital duct tape

If you installed EXCEL as part of Microsoft OFFICE, you can use the OFFICE BINDER as duct tape or a binder clip to keep related files together so you can produce a professional-looking document. (This is in the Top Ten List of Ways to Impress Your Instructor.) For example, if you have a Microsoft WORD document, an EXCEL workbook, and POWERPOINT slides that make up a single report, put them in a binder to work on them together. When your files are in a binder you can

- check spelling,

- apply a consistent style,

- add page numbers consecutively across all the files (Note: files are called *sections* in the binder.),

- print the sections,

- work on the sections individually,

- preview or print an individual section in a binder, selected sections in a binder, or the entire binder,

- print the same header and footer for all sections in the binder, or create a different header and footer for each section.

To start a new binder, click New Binder on the File menu in OFFICE BINDER, or just open OFFICE BINDER. When you're working in the OFFICE BINDER window, the left pane shows the sections that make up the binder you're working on, and the right pane shows the active section. The files you add to the binder can be new, blank files or existing files. To add an existing file to a binder, drag the file from WINDOWS EXPLORER to the left pane of the OFFICE BINDER window, or click Add from File on the Section menu in OFFICE BINDER.

To start OFFICE BINDER, click the WINDOWS Start button, point to Programs, and then click MICROSOFT BINDER. (It has an icon that looks like a metal clip.) To start OFFICE BINDER under WINDOWS NT, consult your User's Manual or Help. If the Microsoft BINDER command or the BINDER icon is not available, run Office Setup again to install OFFICE BINDER.

FAQ

Q. *Where can I find* OFFICE BINDER *in* OFFICE XP*?*

A. You can't find it because OFFICE XP does not have it. However, you can insert EXCEL worksheets and POWERPOINT slides in a WORD document to achieve similar results. (See Chapter 9.)

1.16 What's new in EXCEL 2002

EXCEL 2002 and OFFICE XP have several new features that you will find convenient, including Task Pane, Ask a Question, and Refreshable Web Query.

Task Pane
Task panes provide a single location for common operations, thereby saving you

from scrolling through lists of options in menus. Copying and pasting, adding graphics, creating presentations, applying styles to documents, and many other everyday tasks can now be accomplished with a single click of a mouse. See Figure 1-14. Go to the Office Assistance Center to learn more:
http://office.microsoft.com/assistance/2002/articles/oTaskPanes.aspx

Ask A Question
This new feature is an alternative to using the Help menu. Type a question in the Ask A Question box and you will get Help topics that match your question.

Using EXCEL 2002 on the Internet
EXCEL can be used for remote data collection on the Internet. Web pages often contain information that is easy to analyze in EXCEL. For example, you can use EXCEL to analyze stock prices copied from a Web page and data transmitted from remote instruments. You can update the information often to keep it current by using the *refreshable Web queries* available in EXCEL 2002.

To create a new, refreshable Web query:

1. In your browser, go to the Web page from which you want to query data. For example, go to http://moneycentral.msn.com/home.asp.

2. Copy the data and paste it into an EXCEL worksheet. A Paste Options button will appear just below your pasted data.

3. Click the arrow on the right side of the Paste Options button, and click Create Refreshable Web Query.

4. In the New Web Query dialog box, click the yellow arrow next to table of data you want in your Web query.

5. Click Import.
For more tips go to: http://www.microsoft.com/office/using/tips/winners.htm

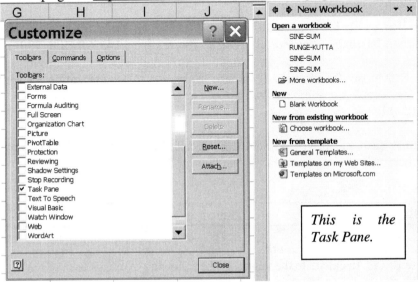

Figure 1-14. Use the Customize box to activate the Task Pane in EXCEL 2002.

Go to http://www.ni.com for information on using EXCEL on the Internet for remote control of experiments, data collection, and distance learning. National Instruments has an add-in for EXCEL named MEASURE that enables EXCEL to collect data from a variety of instruments. See Chapter 9.

What's next?

Now that you know some of the ways to use EXCEL, it's time to dig a little more deeply. We'll explore more spreadsheet features in Chapter 2, introduce you to graphing techniques in Chapter 3, and develop skills with math in Chapter 4.

References

Robert K. Adair, *The Physics of Baseball*, (HarperCollins, New York, 1991). Bart Giamatti appointed Professor Adair to the coveted post of Physicist to the National League, 1987–1989.

Robert K. Adair, "The physics of baseball," *Physics Today* **48** (5), 26–31 (1995).

A. R. Penner, "The physics of golf", *American Journal of Physics* **69** (10) 1073–1081 (2001). Golf balls are more complicated than you may imagine.

D. Halliday, R. Resnick, and J. Walker, *Fundamentals of Physics*, Sixth Edition, (John Wiley & Sons, Inc., New York, 2001), Chapter 4.

S. P. Hendee, R. M. Greenwald, and J. J. Crisco, "Static and dynamic properties of various baseballs," *Journal of Applied Biomechanics* **14**, 390–400 (1998).

Ken. R. Morison and Patrick J. Jordan, "Spreadsheet documentation for students and engineers," *International Journal of Engineering Education* **16**, No. 6, 509–515 (2000).

Kyle Forniash and Raymond Wisman, "Simple Internet data collection for physics laboratories," *American Journal of Physics* **70** (4), 458–461 (2002).

Test your skills

Note: More exercises are on the CD.
1. Use EXCEL to calculate the values of the following expressions:
=3+11−6

=2+4/5
=(2+4)/5 (Note the difference in how EXCEL calculates using the / sign.)
=2²+4/5 (Note: This must be entered as =2^2+4/5)
=(2²+4)/5
=log(10)   (Note: this is the common log, base 10.)
=ln(10)   (This is the natural log, base e.)
=exp(5)
=ln(exp(11))   (Note the use of nested parentheses.)
=sin(2)   (This is the sine function. The default angle is in radians.)
=sin(radians(2))   (Use this method to enter an angle as degrees.)
=sin(0.001)/0.001
=sin(0)/0   (What value should this actually be? See Section 4.2.)
=sin(exp(0.2))

2. ✪ Bungee jumpers beware. Bungee jumping, the triumph of Optimism over Intelligence, is a popular sport in Great Falls, Montana. A static cord of fixed length D is attached to an elastic cord of unstretched length L and force constant k. The static cord is attached to the ankles of the jumper who dives head-first from a distance H above concrete, water, or dirt. It could be a fatal error to assume that the static cord would simply add a length D to the total extension of the stretched elastic cord at the bottom. For a jumper of mass m, conservation of energy gives the value of the maximum length of the stretched bungee system,

$$y_{max} = L + D + \frac{mg}{k} + \frac{1}{k}\sqrt{2m^2 g^2 + 2kmg(L+D)},$$

where g is the acceleration of gravity. Assume that g is 9.8 m/s² and D includes the height of the jumper.

Compose a worksheet to compute y_{max} for m = 70 kg, k = 10 N/m, and L = 10 m, for D = 1.5 to 10 m in steps of 0.5 m. Your spreadsheet could save your life! This relates to the National Science Education Standard *conservation of energy*.

3. Suppose you have a 200 kg object on a frictionless horizontal plane. When you push on the object with a constant horizontal force of 11.7 N the object accelerates. The object starts from rest at x = 0. Compose a worksheet to compute the acceleration, velocity, and displacement of the object as a function of time, for $0 \le t \le 30$ seconds. Hint: use Newton's second law $F = ma$. For constant acceleration, $v = v_0 + at$ and $x = x_0 + vt + 0.5at^2$. Arrange your data in columns, with time in column A, acceleration in column B, velocity in column C and displacement in column D. Enter the mass and force in cells at the top of the worksheet and reference these cells in your formulas. (Use *absolute cell references*.) By using absolute references to data entry cells you can change the mass and/or the force without having to rewrite the worksheet. This exercise relates to the National Science Education Standard *position and motion of objects – motions*

and forces.

4. Baseball on other planets and the moon: Make a copy of the BASEBALL workbook and rename it. Modify the worksheet to include input data for *g*, the acceleration of gravity. Compare baseball trajectories on Earth with Earth's moon and other planets. Note: *g* is measured at the equator of the planets in the following Table.

Object	Acceleration of gravity, m/s^2
Earth's moon	1.67
Mercury	3.78
Earth	9.78
Venus	8.60
Mars	3.72
Jupiter	22.9
Saturn	9.05
Uranus	7.77
Neptune	11.00
Pluto	0.50

Shimizu Construction Corporation has been studying plans for lunar tennis courts and golf courses, and Nishimatsu Construction Corporation has proposed building a high-rise resort on the moon. http://www.shimz.co.jp/english/index.html

Chapter 2
Exploring EXCEL

What this chapter is about

EXCEL is a powerful application with many functions and presentation options. You may never need some of them, but if you aren't aware of them, how will you know if you don't need them? We're not going to go deeply into most of them here; we'll only discuss the basics that you'll need to get started. Later, we'll go into some of the more sophisticated operations.

There are nine pull-down menus at the top of the EXCEL worksheet: File, Edit, View, Insert, Format, Tools, Data, Window and Help. If you knew all of the sub-menus and dialog boxes available here, you would be qualified to be a Power User. Don't worry about all of the details now, but you should open a blank worksheet and explore the menus as you read this chapter.

2.1 The Office Assistant

First, let's look at the Office Assistant, which is a common element in all MICROSOFT OFFICE programs. Click on the box with the question mark (?) at the upper right on the top icon menu bar and you'll see a cute little creature asking what you would like to do. You can change the creature by clicking on Options. The one named Genius is shown in Fig. 2-1. Genius is replaced by Merlin the Magician in EXCEL 2002 and associated programs.

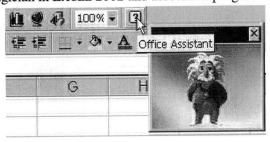

Figure 2-1. The Office Assistant is just a left mouse click away. Click on the bar at the top of the assistant (to the left of the [x]) to see Figure 2-2. In EXCEL 2002 you can use the Task Pane instead of the Office Assistant. See page 19.

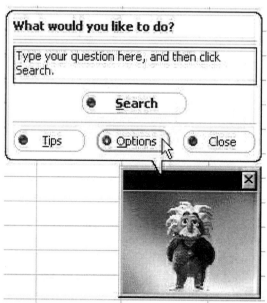

Figure 2-2. Type your question in the Dialog Box and click Search. Click on Options and you will see Figure 2-3.

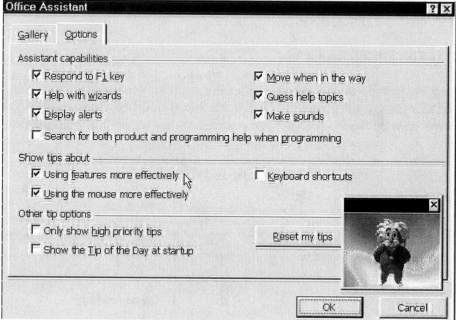

Figure 2-3. Customize your assistant with the Options Dialog Box. Function Key F1 is a shortcut key that brings up Help. To see Figure 2-4, click on the Gallery tab. You can also click on Help on the top right of the menu bar.

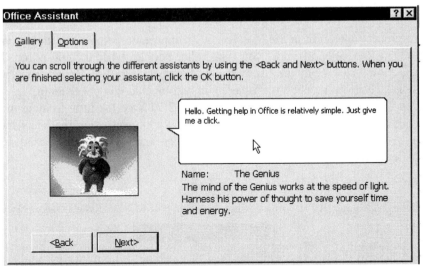

Figure 2-4. Choose your assistant here. Assistants include a perky paper clip, a robot, William Shakespeare, a Power Pup, and a cat, among others.

2.2 File, Edit, and View menus

Figure 2-5 shows the selections in these menus. Use your mouse to explore them.

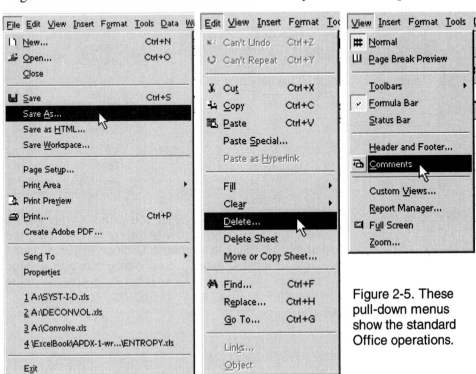

Figure 2-5. These pull-down menus show the standard Office operations.

2.3. Insert, Format and Tools menus

The Comments operation in the View menu is important, because it lets you view notes added to a cell to remind you (and other people) what the cell is for. The comment is inserted from the Insert menu shown in Fig. 2-6. Be generous with comments; when you revisit a worksheet you will be glad you put them in.

A typical commented cell is shown in Fig. 2-7. Note the little triangle in the upper right-hand corner. You can view a hidden comment using the View menu shown in Fig. 2-5. Modify the comment appearance using the [Tools] [Options][View][Comments] menu.

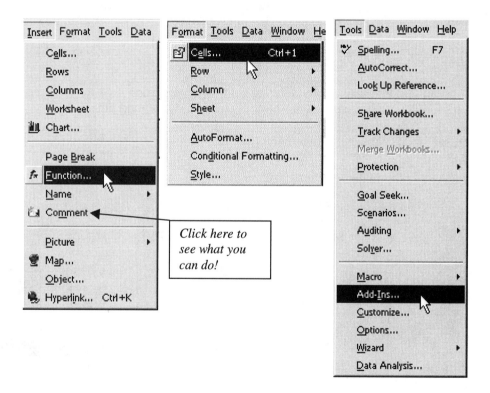

Figure 2-6. Insert, Format, and Tools menus. When you insert a comment, a small marker appears at the upper right-hand corner of the commented cell; see Fig. 2-7. Use your mouse to explore these menu items. Click on Picture to insert a photo or graphic file. Click on Object to bring up a dialog box with a large selection of insertable items. We'll discuss Hyperlinks later. Data Analysis in the Tools menu will be used extensively in Chapters 9, 11 and 12.

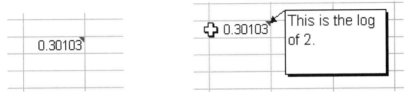

Figure 2-7. *Left*: A commented cell. Note marker. *Right:* You can view a commented cell by placing the cursor on it. Do *not* click on the cell.

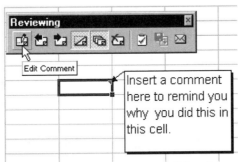

Figure 2-8. The Reviewing Box becomes visible when you click on Comments in the View menu (see Figure 2-5).

There are nine icons in the Reviewing Box at the right in Fig. 2-8. This is a very powerful little box. From left to right, the icons are Edit Comment, Previous Comment, Next Comment, Hide Comment, Hide All Comments, Delete Comment, Create Microsoft Outlook Task, Update File and Send To Mail Recipient.

Use your mouse to investigate these icons. Notice that you can use this box to work with other people on an intranet or on the Internet.

2.4 Data, Window and Help menus

The Help menu is self-explanatory, but let's look at the Window menu, Fig. 2-9.

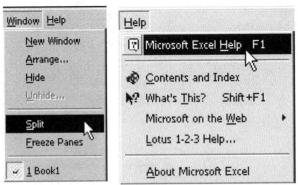

Figure 2-9. The Window and Help dropdown menus. The top three options in Window are obvious. **Split** lets you view widely separated parts of a worksheet on the same screen. **Freeze Panes** lets you view part of a worksheet at all times, as you move around. This is handy for viewing column or row titles far away from Home screen.

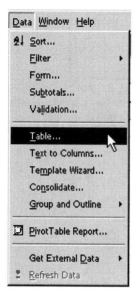

Figure 2-10. The Data pull-down menu.

The Data menu in Fig. 2-10 has advanced features that will be treated in other chapters. Don't worry about it now. (You're not forbidden to explore it.)

2.5 Where's the chart menu?

The Chart menu is invisible until you click on the *Chart Wizard* icon and let it guide through the steps to create a chart. After you finish the Chart Wizard you'll see the Chart menu in place of the Data menu on the Tool Bar. The Chart Wizard is at the upper right on the top menu bar. See Chapter 3 for more on the Wizard.

Fig. 2-11. The Chart menu contains many sub-menus with powerful options. These will be discussed in detail in Chapter 3. The Chart Menu appears on the Tool Bar only when you complete a chart or click on an existing chart.

2.6 Paste Function

The little icon, $\boxed{f_x}$ for Paste Function, is located on the top menu bar, three positions to the left of the Chart Wizard. It opens all of the functions in EXCEL, in sub-menus and categories. This is like the key to the front door of the bank. Figure 2-12 shows where the icon is located to the right of the AutoSum icon, $\boxed{\Sigma}$.

The right-hand side of Figure 2-12 shows the Paste Function dialog box with Engineering Functions selected. At the top of the categories, above category All, is "Most Recently Used", but this is not shown in Figure 2-13. Open your spreadsheet and explore this dialog box. A very brief description of each function is given, but you can find out complete information in Help. Click OK to see Figure 2-14.

Use your mouse to click on each Function category and explore the Functions. We will be most interested in Math & Trig, Statistical, and Engineering, but Logical also contains some very useful functions. Don't be overwhelmed by all of these functions; as you become familiar with them you will probably find a small group that you use most of the time. Nevertheless, you should know what is available so you can use functions when the need arises. Remember, Help is only a mouse-click away.

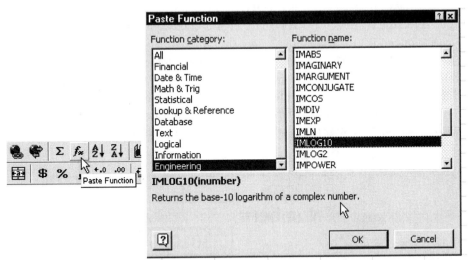

Figure 2-12. *Left:* Click on the Paste Function icon and enter the wonderful world of EXCEL's functions. *Right:* The Paste Function dialog box. The Engineering Function category is selected with Function name IMLOG10. This category and its functions will be discussed in Chapters 6 and 10. Chapter 4 is devoted to the Math & Trig category.

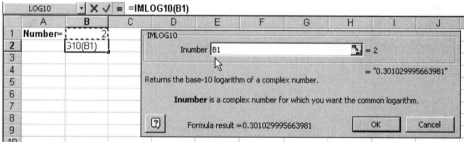

Figure 2-13. This is what you get when you click on OK for the Category and Function shown in Fig. 2-13. Type in the cell address for **Inumber**. (Note: Because 2 is a real number, IMLOG10 gives the same result as LOG10 in the Math & Trig Category.) Now click OK and you will see Fig. 2-14.

2.7 3-D worksheet references

A worksheet has 256 columns and 65536 rows. You may think this is rather large, but there is more. You can use up to 256 worksheets in a workbook, and any cell in any worksheet can link to any other cell in any other worksheet. This is a huge three-dimensional array of cells; see Fig. 2-15. What can you do with a three-dimensional workbook? Just use your imagination!

It's easy to cross-reference cells in three dimensions. Try this example in your spreadsheet: In cell D7 (or any cell you choose) in Sheet 1, type Hello. In Sheet 2 in cell B9 (or any cell you choose) type =Sheet1!D7 and press Enter↵. (Be sure to include the ! sign.) You should see the greeting Hello appear in cell B9 of Sheet 2. Now, anything in cell D7 of Sheet 1 will appear in cell B9 of Sheet 2. Similarly, you can reference a cell in any sheet from any other sheet. You will receive a *circular reference* warning if you happen to reference a cell to itself. This happens sometimes when you're linking several sheets.

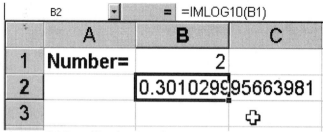

Figure 2-14. This is the final result of using Paste Function for the Category and Function in Fig. 2-13. Cell B2 contains the base-10 logarithm of cell B1. The IMLOG10 function will also work with complex numbers (see Chapter 10.) For purely real numbers you can use LOG10.

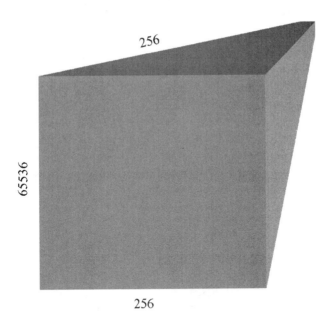

256

65536

256

Figure 2-15. The workbook is a huge 3-D array of cells, and all of them can be cross-referenced. You have 256 columns, 256 sheets, and 65536 rows. You can also cross-reference to other workbooks, so you are only limited by the size of your hard disk and memory.

Hyperlinks

A *hyperlink* is like a super worksheet reference. You can insert a hyperlink using the Insert menu (see Fig. 2-6, at the bottom). Alternatively, you can click on the hyperlink icon which is located to the left of the Web toolbar icon on the top menu. A hyperlink can access another file in a spreadsheet, word processor, or a URL on the Internet. Hyperlink use is shown in the ENSEMBLE worksheet.

What's next?

Even if you don't know everything that you can do with the menus we have discussed, you now know enough to perform many useful tasks. As you go forward, you will pick up more skills. In Chapter 3 we will take up elementary graphing.

Why are we discussing graphing so early? EXCEL has powerful tools for visualization, and these tools can help you by providing an overview of a vast array of numbers that otherwise might not make much sense. Graphing is an effective way of summarizing and compressing information. Also, examining a graph can often help you to check for errors in the data. After you learn basic graph techniques we will take up the essentials of spreadsheet math in Chapter 4.

Test your skills

An electric battery is like a checking account in which you are charged a bank fee for every withdrawal but you do not earn any interest. The first four exercises relate to the National Science Education Standard *electricity and magnetism*.

1. *Automobile battery.* You use a high-resistance voltmeter to measure the terminal voltage of a battery with its cables disconnected. Your voltmeter reads 12.0 volts. This is the open-circuit voltage V_o, or *emf* of the battery. The FET voltmeter has a high resistance (about $10^{12}\ \Omega$) so the current drain is practically zero. Now, connect the battery to a resistor. You measure a current $I = 10$ amps and the terminal voltage V_T drops to 11 volts. What is the internal resistance r of the battery? (Hint: By Kirchoff's law, the sum of the voltages around a closed loop is zero. $V_o - V_T - Ir = 0.$) Use your spreadsheet to make a Table of the terminal voltage as a function of the current, as I goes from 0 to 120 amps in steps of 2 amps.

2. What is the power loss in the internal resistance for each current step in Question 1? (Hint: Power loss is $I^2 r$.)

3. What is the power generated by the battery for each current step in Question 1? (Hint: Power generated is $V_o I$.)

4. What is the percent efficiency of the battery for each current step in Question 1? (Hint: Percent efficiency is $100 \times$ (Power Out)/(Power Generated.)

5. ✪ The power transmission coefficient is the ratio of transmitted power to incident power. For acoustics, this coefficient is conveniently defined in terms of the characteristic impedance R measured in *rayls* (in honor of Lord Rayleigh). This impedance is the product of the volume density (kg/m^3) times the speed of sound in the medium (m/s). At an interface between two media, this coefficient is $4r/(1+r)^2$, where $r = R_1/R_2$ is the ratio of the characteristic impedance on the incident side to the transmitted side of the interface. Compose a worksheet to compute the power transmission coefficient for $0 \le r \le 5$ in steps of 0.1. This exercise relates to the National Science Education Standard *transfer of energy*.

6. In Question 5, for what value of r is the power transmission coefficient a maximum? (This is the reason that impedance-matching transformers are used in electrical circuits. Automobile gears are mechanical transformers, and human and animal ears are acoustic transformers.)

7. *Catenary.* A uniform chain 30 m long has a linear density of 0.5 kg/m and a total weight of 15 x 9.8 N. (Use $g = 9.8$ m/s^2.) The chain is suspended between two vertical posts. The special shape of a chain hanging under its own weight is called a *catenary*, $y(x) = a\cosh(x/a)$. (See Section 4.5 for hyperbolic functions like cosh.) Compose a worksheet to compute the tension in the chain for 9 equally-spaced points, including the ends. Let the distance between the posts go from 15 m to 25 m in steps of 1 m.

Chapter 3
Excel's Graphics

What this chapter is about

Start EXCEL now and use it as you read this chapter. EXCEL has a powerful set of graphing tools (14 standard charts, 20 custom charts) that enable you to visualize data and present data so you and other people can understand it. We are going into graphing early because it will help you to see what you're doing. A graph gives you a quick overview of data that you can't visualize using the numerical worksheet by itself.

In EXCEL and other Microsoft programs, graphs are called *charts* for unknown reasons, and polar graphs are called *radar charts*. In this chapter you will learn the basics of constructing:

- *xy* (scatter) charts, including two *y*-axes, log, and dB,
- column and bar charts,
- radar and polar charts.

EXCEL's charts also include a little statistical analysis. In later chapters you will learn techniques involving more advanced data presentation, but the three chart types above will get you started and will take care of your basic needs.

3.1 Chart Wizard: making a simple *xy* chart

Making a chart is easy; EXCEL has a *Chart Wizard* to help you. The Chart Wizard icon is in the upper right hand corner of the icon tool bar, between Sort Descending and Map icons. The Wizard icon looks like a column chart (Fig. 3-2).

The *xy* (or *scatter*) chart is the most commonly used presentation in engineering and science, because it uses data in pairs. This is the way data are often recorded in real life. For example, you may measure temperature at various times, which may not be at evenly spaced intervals. EXCEL contains five standard *xy* charts and several related custom charts. These Standard Types appear on the left tab of the dialog box (see Fig. 3-3) as soon as you start to graph data by clicking on the Chart Wizard icon, and the Custom Types appear when you click on that tab.

The *xy* chart looks like the *line* chart, but the line chart is less useful because it requires evenly-spaced data. The *xy* chart works with *data pairs*.

Open the workbook named XY-EXAMPLE and let's examine the details. It is always easier to learn by editing a worksheet than by being confronted with a blank array of cells. You should see Fig. 3-1 on your monitor. This worksheet contains two convenient tricks to let you change the *x*-increment almost instantly, without having to go through the [Edit][Fill] routine (Chapter 2).

Cell D3 contains a value that you enter to set the *x*-increment. (You could fill this column by using the [Edit][Fill][Series] routine, but if you wanted to change the increment you would have to go through this again.) This worksheet uses cell D3 with a formula in column A to do this automatically. Cell A6 contains the initial value of *x* and cell A7 has the formula =A6+$D$3, shown in the cell editing box. Notice the use of the *absolute cell address*, designated by the $ signs, which locks in column D at cell 3. When you use the fill handle to copy cell A7 to the rest of column A, all cells will refer to your choice of increment in cell D3.

Cell B6 contains the formula =2*A6 , and this is copied to the other cells in column B. This makes data set *y1* equal to two times the value of data set *x*. The chart in Fig. 3-1 shows these data sets. What is the formula in cell C6?

Place the cursor on cell A5 and hold down the left mouse button. Move the cursor to column B and then move down both columns to the end of the data sets. This selects the data you want in the first chart. Now click on the Chart Wizard.

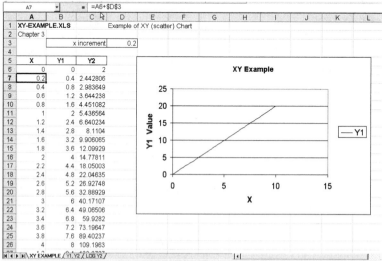

Figure 3-1. Home screen of XY-EXAMPLE. Note formula in cell A7, which sets the *x*-increment using the value in cell D3.

Figure 3-2. Click on the Chart Wizard to start your graph operation.

The Dialog Box (Step 1) is shown in Fig. 3-3 with the *xy* type selected, and a specific *xy* chart is shown by the mouse pointer. The selected type is "scatter with data points connected by smooth lines without markers." Click on the bar at the bottom of the box ("press and hold to see sample") to see a thumbnail preview of the chart. If this looks OK, click on Next and you will see Fig. 3-4.

Tip

Graphing sets of data in adjacent columns is easy, but trying to graph sets of data in *separated* rows or columns can be annoying. Here are two tricks that can make it easy. As usual in EXCEL there is more than one way of doing things.

First method
- Use the left mouse button to select the first range.
- Hold down the Ctrl key and select the second range using click and drag with the left mouse button.

Second method
- In the Edit menu select Go To.
- In the Reference box type the two ranges, separated by a comma.
- Click the OK button. (Also, see Fig. 3-5 for another way.)

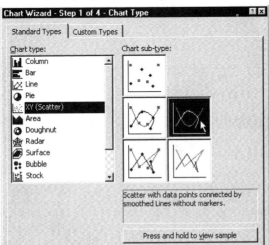

Figure 3-3. Step 1 of 4 of the Chart Wizard. An XY (Scatter) sub-type is selected.

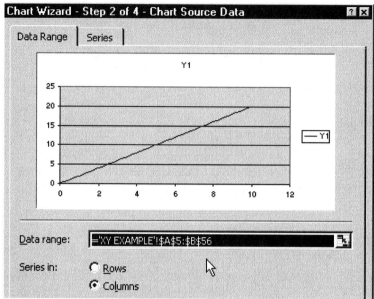

Figure 3-4. Step 2 of the Chart Wizard, showing the source data range.

Click on the Series tab of this Box to examine the series content. If these selections are not correct, you can make changes in this Box, shown in Fig. 3-5.

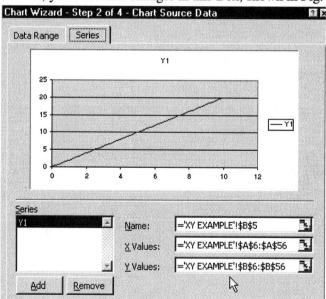

Figure 3-5. Add, remove, or make changes in the data series using this part of Step 2. You can use this for data sets that are not in adjacent columns. You can add and remove series in this dialog box. This is a third way of graphing data that are not in adjacent columns. See Tip on page 35.

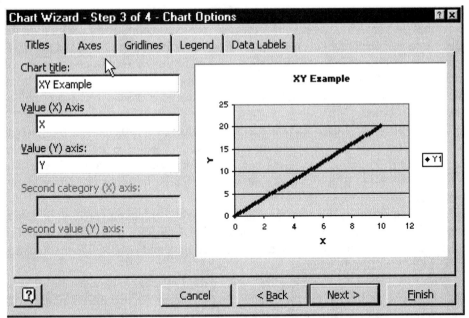

Figure 3-6. Step 3 of the Chart Wizard. The titles have been entered by the keyboard. Click on the other four tabs at the top to see what options they provide.

Step 3 is shown in Fig. 3-6. This step gives you considerable control over the chart appearance. For example, you can click on the Legend tab to remove the legend or change its location.

Step 4 is shown in Fig. 3-7. This is the final step in creating the chart. Here you can place the chart in a new sheet or as an insert in an existing sheet (see Fig. 3-1). Notice the mouse pointer on the Question button. When you click on this button the Office Assistant comes to your aid. This is available in all Dialog Boxes and on the upper right hand end of the Tool Bar in EXCEL.

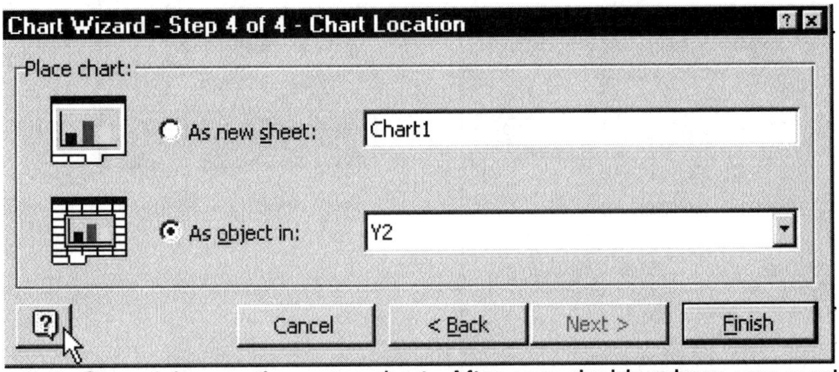

Figure 3-7. Step 4 in creating your chart. After you decide where you want it placed, click on Finish. The mouse pointer is on the Office Assistant button.

Modifying your chart

Now that you have a basic *xy* chart created, you can modify it by clicking on the chart area and selecting various objects. For example, in Fig. 3-1 the chart shading has been removed. In the worksheet, place the cursor on the *chart area* (the outer portion of the chart) and click the right-hand mouse button. This will bring up the controls shown on the left in Fig. 3-8. Use your mouse to explore the options on this menu.

Click on the *plot area* (where the graph is located) with the left mouse button, then click once with the right mouse button. You will see the controls shown on the right in Fig. 3-8. Again, explore the options with your mouse. These controls can make you a power user, but you don't need to know everything about these right now.

You can instantly change the chart type by clicking on, obviously, **Chart Type**. You can view or modify the source data by clicking on **Source Data**. Try this; you can add, remove, or change all source data and ranges. Want to change a title? Click on **Chart Options**.

Now let's see how to customize your chart. Left-click on the *x*-axis of your chart and you will bring up the Dialog Box shown in Figure 3-9. This lets you format this axis in a variety of ways. Explore the tabs with your mouse. When you click on the *y*-axis, a similar Dialog Box will pop up.

Figure 3-10 appears when you click on the Scale tab. Experiment with the options here, and click on the other tabs to see what you can do.

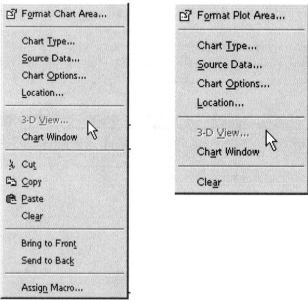

Figure 3-8. *Left:* Format Chart Area options, just a right mouse click away. *Right:* Format Plot Area options. Some selections appear on both menus.

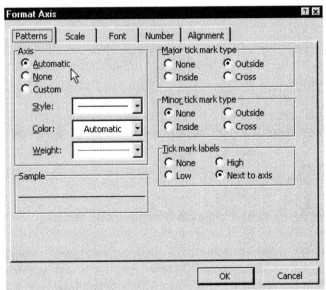

Figure 3-9. This Dialog Box lets you format the *x*-axis. A similar Box lets you format the *y*-axis.

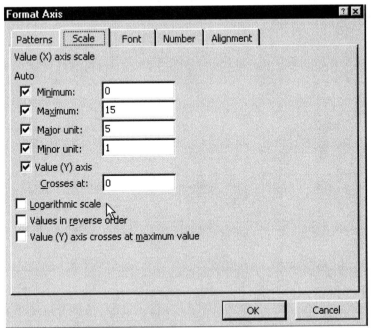

Figure 3-10. This tab is very important because it lets you set the scales. Note the Logarithmic scale box. We will discuss this in Section 3.3.

3.2 Two *y*-axes

When you have two sets of data that have a considerable difference in their range of values, it is useful to plot one set on the left-hand *y* axis and the other on the right-hand *y* axis.

Let's see how to do this. Open the TWO-Y worksheet. Save it as MyChart-1. We are going to create a new chart and add another *y*-axis on the right hand side for data set Z, and later we'll use this to experiment with logarithmic scales.

Hold the left mouse button down. Select the data marked X, Y, and Z in columns A, B, and C.

Click on the Chart Wizard icon and select *xy* (scatter).

Continue with the Chart Wizard through Finish.

While viewing your chart, right-click on the Z data series.

Left-click on Format Data Series in the pop-up dialog box.

Left-click on the Patterns tab.

Under the column Line (on the left) select Automatic and Smoothed Line

Left-click on the Axis tab in the Format Data Series box.

Select Secondary Axis in "Plot Series On".

(Now you should see a chart like the one shown in Fig. 3-12.)

Right-click on the Value (x) Axis and select Format Axis.

Click on the Scale tab. Enter –0.6 in the box "Value (y) Axis Crosses At."

(This moves the left *y*-axis to –0.6 or the first data point greater than –0.6.)

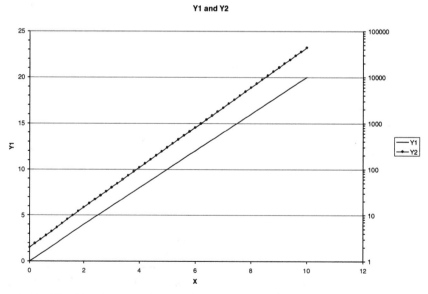

Figure 3-11. The Y1 data set (no markers) is plotted on the left axis and the Y2 data set (markers) is plotted on the right axis. The *x*-axis is common to both sets.

3.3 Logarithmic and dB axes

In engineering and scientific applications we often deal with data that cover a large range of values, millions or billions or more, too large to plot using a linear scale on a paper of reasonable size. If you used a linear scale you wouldn't be able to see small values in the presence of large values. This problem can be solved using logarithmic graph scales, or converting data to a decibel (dB) format. *Caution:* negative values cannot be graphed on a log scale! You'll get a nasty warning if you try to graph, or even enter, the log of a negative number.

Nature has addressed this problem in the context of human survival. Humans developed the ability to hear on a logarithmic scale (see Decibels, below) so they could hear a tiger creeping up on them during a thunderstorm. Humans without this ability became tiger food and helped the tigers to survive.

A very common requirement involves charting data representing magnitude and phase response of systems. The magnitude and frequency ranges can be very large, covering many decades, but the phase only goes from zero to 360 degrees. The standard way of graphing data of this type is the *Bode plot* (invented by Hendrik Bode for use in electronics) which has a logarithmic scale for frequency on the x-axis, a logarithmic or dB scale for magnitude on the left-hand y-axis and a linear scale for phase on the right-hand y-axis. (By the way, Bode is pronounced *Bo-dee*.) This type of chart is used often in electrical and mechanical engineering to characterize the frequency response of systems.

Decibels and dB scales

Why do we use a decibel scale? Like a log scale, a dB scale is useful for compressing data that has a large range of values, but a dB scale looks like a linear scale so it is somewhat easier to interpret. Nevertheless, a dB scale is basically logarithmic.

Decibels are particularly useful with audio data because humans do not perceive changes in sound intensity as $I_1 - I_2$. Sound is perceived approximately as $\log(I_1) - \log(I_2)$. By the rules of logarithms, this can be written as,

$$\log\left(\frac{I_1}{I_2}\right). \tag{3-1}$$

Equation (3-1) is the definition of the Bel, but it is not used much because people can detect a change of about 1/10 of a Bel. So, the *decibel* is defined as,

$$10\log\left(\frac{I_1}{I_2}\right). \tag{3-2}$$

Because intensity is proportional to power, we often measure decibels as,

$$10 \log \left(\frac{P_1}{P_2} \right).$$

(3-3)

Finally, power is proportional to the square of voltage or amplitude, so

$$10 \log \left(\frac{V_1}{V_2} \right)^2 = 20 \log \left(\frac{V_1}{V_2} \right)$$

(3-4)

because $\log(x^n) = n \log(x)$, by the rules of logarithms.

You are always safe when you measure power, but be careful when you use voltage. Volts must be the r.m.s. (root-mean-square) voltage. Also, both voltages must be measured across the same impedance. For example, if V_2 is the input or *reference* and V_1 is the output, then Eq. (3-4) gives the *gain* of the device under test.

The limitation of log and dB scales is that you cannot use them to graph negative values. Never try to find the log of a negative number!

What does zero dB mean? Zero dB simply means that the output (or measured value) is equal to the reference value, because $\log(1) = 0$.

What does a negative dB mean? A negative decibel means that the output (or measured value) is less than the reference value because the log of a number less than 1 is negative.

Some people say that decibels are used when you don't know what you are measuring. That's not a correct statement, but it contains a partial truth. Because the decibel is a ratio, the units cancel. It doesn't make any difference what units you use, as long as you are consistent in using the same units.

The Neper

The decibel is defined in terms of the common log (log base 10), but natural logs (log base e) appear frequently in natural processes. So it seems natural to define some unit based on natural logs, similar to the decibel, and this has been done. The *neper* is used in some European countries as a telecommunications transmission unit, and it is defined as,

$$N_p = 0.5 \ln \left(\frac{P_o}{P_r} \right) = \ln \left(\frac{V_o}{V_r} \right)$$

(3-5)

where P_o and P_r are the output and reference powers, and V_o and V_r are the output and reference voltages (measured across the same impedance).

To convert dB to nepers, multiply dB by 0.1151. To convert nepers to dB, multiply nepers by 8.686. These units are often used to describe attenuation per unit length in coaxial cable, fiber optic cable, and waveguide, as well as bulk material. For example, fused silica optical fiber may have attenuation of about 0.2 dB/km, but plastic optical fiber has attenuation in the range 15 dB/km to 100 dB/km. Erbium-doped optical fiber can be used as a distributed amplifier, so it will have a *negative* attenuation (or positive gain) if it's working properly.

Examples

If the reference is 1 mV and the output is 50 mV (or 0.050 V), express this in dB.

$$20 \log\left(\frac{50}{1}\right) = 20\,(1.301) = 26.02 \text{ dB}$$

The output power is half of the input power. Express this in dB.

$$10 \log\left(\frac{0.5}{1}\right) = -3.01 \text{ dB}$$

In other words, the half-power point is the –3 dB point.

Open the worksheet TWO-Y, place the mouse pointer on a cell in column B, left-click on the Insert menu and click on Columns. In cell B4, type dB. In cell B5 type =20*log(C5) and press Enter⏎. Now, use the mouse to drag the fill handle on cell B5 to copy it to cells B6:B25.

Use the mouse pointer to select cells A4:B25, that is, columns A and B from cell 4 through cell 25. Next, click on the Chart Wizard and make an *xy* chart with a dB scale using your data. Your finished chart should look like Fig. 3-12.

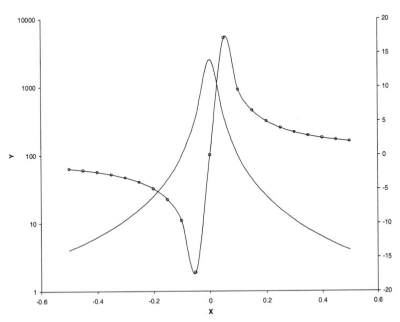

Figure 3-12. The left axis is scaled logarithmically. You can see details of the small values as well as the large values on the curve with no markers. Right axis is the scale for the curve with markers. Data associated with the right-hand axis have positive and negative values with a relatively small range.

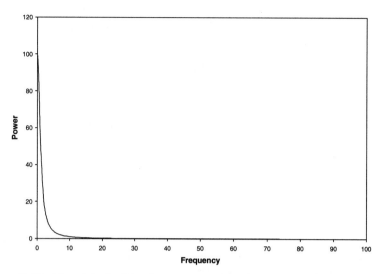

Figure 3-13. The data in this chart extend to a frequency of 100, but the range of power is so large that small values at high frequencies cannot be seen.

The worksheet TWO-XY has two charts that illustrate the usefulness of logarithmic scales. Figure 3-13 is the chart named Lin-Lin in this worksheet; it is linear on both axes. Figure 3-14 shows the chart named dB-Log. The data are the same in both charts, but the log scales enhance representation of the data.

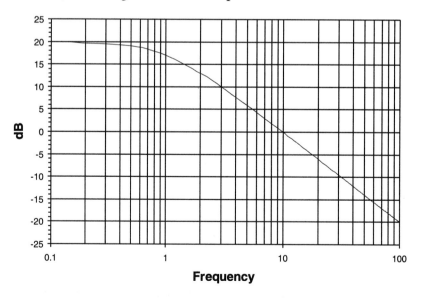

Figure 3-14. This chart has the same data as Figure 3-13, but here the data are represented in a dB-log format (Bode plot) that improves understanding.

3.4 Column and bar charts

Column (vertical) and bar (horizontal) charts are appropriate for discrete data sets in which you know that there are no data points between the ones recorded in your worksheet. For example, a time sequence in which the data exist for each month or each year is conveniently presented in a column chart. A column chart also clearly compares several variables side-by-side in the same time frame.

Turn on your computer. Select the column chart in Step 1 of the Chart Wizard (see Fig. 3-3). EXCEL contains several varieties of these charts.

Standard column types

Clustered column: compares values across categories (*x* axis).

Stacked column: compares the contribution of each value to a total across categories.

100% stacked column: compares the percentage each value contributes to a total across categories.

Clustered column with 3-D visual effect.

Stacked column with 3-D visual effect.

100% stacked column with 3-D visual effect.

3-D column: compares values across categories and across series.

Custom column types

EXCEL has 20 custom charts (see Chart Wizard) that will probably satisfy all of your needs. The built-in charts can give you ideas so you can customize any chart to meet special needs. (See the THIN-LENS workbook.)

Avoid fancy charts; keep the data presentation simple so someone else can understand it easily. We will only list three of the most useful custom column charts.

Area blocks: a colorful (or shades of gray) 3-D area chart, useful for comparing series.

Line-column: Line series and column series are plotted on the same axis.

Line-column on 2 axes: combination chart. Columns are plotted on the primary (left) axis, and lines are plotted on the secondary (right) axis.

Now let's make a column chart with a *visible data table*, using our dB data in Fig. 3-12. As before, select data in the range A4:B25 and click on the Chart Wizard. To get a little fancy, click on the Custom tab and select B&W Column. This is a 3-D column chart in shades of gray with a data table. The result is shown in Fig. 3-15. This column chart emphasizes that data are taken at discrete points, in this case at discrete frequencies away from the resonant frequency. When you are using EXCEL you can examine the values of the *x,y* data points using the mouse, but when you print a chart the data must be measured on the chart. It is convenient to provide a data table with the chart if the data are of reasonable size.

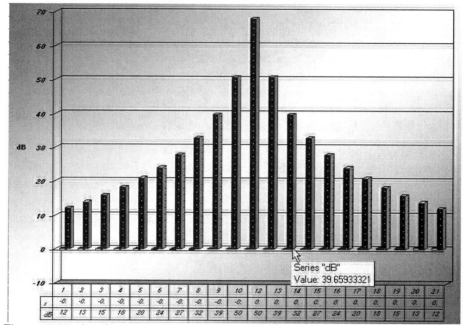

Figure 3-15. A column chart emphasizes the discrete nature of the data in the resonance curve. These are the same data shown in Fig. 3-12, left *y*-axis.

On the top menu bar, click on [Chart][3D-View] to bring up the dialog box shown in Fig. 3-16. This box gives you full control over the 3D properties of your chart. You can rotate the chart around the vertical and horizontal axes, move the chart up and down, and adjust scaling and right-angle axes.

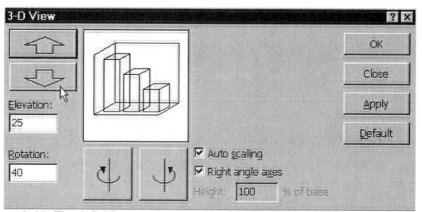

Figure 3-16. The 3-D View dialog box. The mouse pointer is on the control to rotate the figure toward you, around a horizontal axis.

3.5 Radar and polar charts

Radar and polar charts can bring a new perspective to data. Often you can gain new insights by viewing data in more than one way. (In Chapter 11 we will see how to view the spectrum of data, that is, data in the frequency domain.) One of the Standard Types in EXCEL is the radar chart, and it comes in three sub-types:

- Radar chart that displays changes in values relative to a center point.
- Radar chart with markers at each data point.
- Filled radar, with the area covered by the data series filled with a color.

These chart types from the POLAR workbook are shown in Fig. 3-17. A radar chart is a type of polar chart, but it is not a pure polar chart because you cannot choose r, θ as independent data pairs. However, you can make a pure polar chart using the xy scatter chart.

Make your own polar chart
A polar chart is an excellent alternative method of displaying magnitude and phase, with magnitude on the radius and phase in the angle coordinate. The radius can be scaled logarithmically or in dB.

Here's how to make a true polar chart. (Open the workbook named POLAR to follow the instructions in the examples below.)

Example: Original data in *x,y* format.
This is easy. Just use the mouse to select the x and y data. The x data should be in a column to the left of the y data. Click on the Chart Wizard, select XY (Scatter) in the Standard Types, and go through the usual steps. See Fig. 3-17 for results.

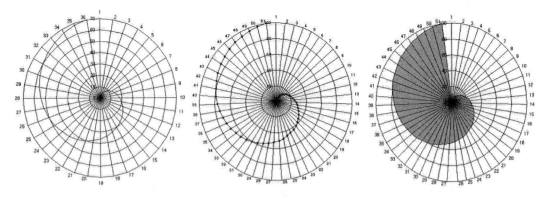

Figure 3-17. Three standard radar charts in EXCEL's Chart Wizard. *Left:* radar chart. *Center:* radar chart with markers. *Right:* Filled radar chart.

Open a new worksheet and use [Edit][Fill][Series][Column] to make a time axis in steps of 1 from 0 to 100 in column A. This is the time axis.

In cell B1 enter the formula =COS(A1/3)*exp(–0.02*A1) and copy this to cells B2:B100. This is $x(t)$.

In cell C1 enter the formula =SIN(A1/3)*exp(–0.02*A1) and copy this to cells C2:C100. This is $y(t)$.

Use your mouse to select cells A1:C100 and click on the Chart Wizard. Choose XY (Scatter) and complete the chart. You should see something like Fig. 3-18. Next, make a graph of $y(t)$ versus $x(t)$ and you will see Fig. 3-19.

Example: original data in r, θ format.

Data in r, θ format, such as magnitude and phase, cannot be graphed directly in a scatter chart, but it is easy to convert them to x, y format using the standard polar-to-rectangular transformation:

$$x = r \cos \theta \qquad y = r \sin \theta . \qquad (3\text{-}6)$$

If you have the r, θ data in columns, make two more columns for x and y and write these formulas in the new columns. Remember, be consistent using radians and degrees!

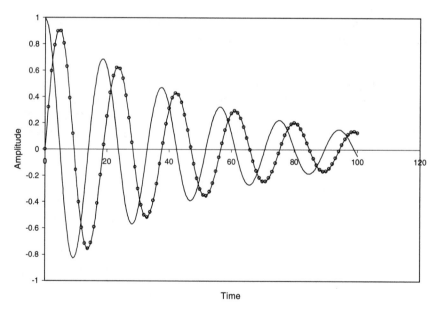

Time

Figure 3-18. This is the *xy* chart showing the two functions of time. These waveforms are an exponentially decaying sine (with markers) and an exponentially decaying cosine (no markers). In Figure 3-19 we will use the cosine waveform as the *x*-function and the sine waveform as the *y*-function, and plot *y* versus *x* to obtain a polar chart. (This chart is in the POLAR workbook.)

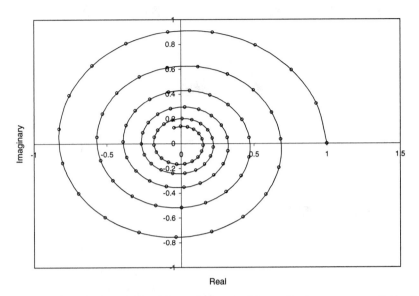

Real

Figure 3-19. This is the polar chart constructed from the two exponentially decaying waveforms shown in Fig. 3-18. You can think of this as a view from the left side of Fig. 3-18, looking forward into the time axis. From this perspective, the two waveforms can be thought of as the components of a vector rotating counterclockwise.

In Chapter 10 we will see more applications of polar charts. In Chapter 11 we will see how to use polar charts with the spectrum of waveforms, using the Fast Fourier Transform (FFT) in EXCEL.

3.6 Chart statistics

EXCEL provides a convenient tool in charts for applying elementary statistical analysis to your data. Open the workbook named OLYMPIC and click on a tab to bring a chart on your monitor. Right-click on a curve in the chart and you will see a pop-up menu shown in Fig. 3-20. Now click on Add Trendline to see Fig. 3-21. In the dialog box, click on Options to see Fig. 3-22.

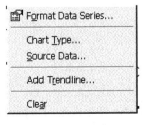

Figure 3-20. Pop-up menu in a chart. You can also access **Add Trendline** on the Chart Menu on the top of the tool bar. See Appendix 3 for trendline equations and options.

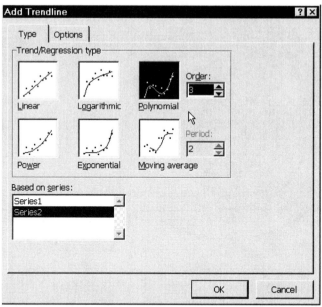

Figure 3-21. Choose the Trend/Regression type here. For a polynomial fit, you can choose the order of the polynomial. For the moving average, you can choose the period (number of data points). Experiment with Type for best fit.

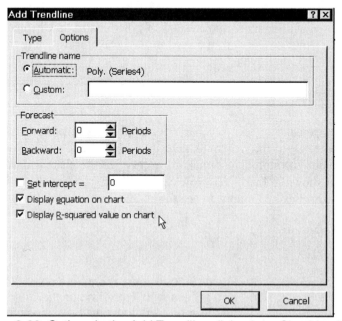

Figure 3-22. Options in the Add Trendline dialog box. Checking "Display equation on chart" and "Display R-squared value on chart" gives Fig. 3-23.

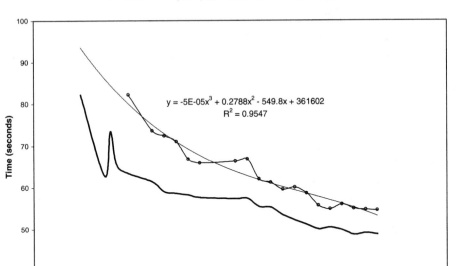

100 meter Free-style Olympic Gold Medal Swimming Records

$$y = -5\text{E-05}x^3 + 0.2788x^2 - 549.8x + 361602$$
$$R^2 = 0.9547$$

Figure 3-23. *Thin line with markers:* women. *Thin line:* Polynomial trendline. *Thick line:* men. The equation for the women's trendline is shown with the R^2 value, which is a measure of how well the trendline fits the data (see Help and Appendix 3). Men's records begin in 1896; women's records begin in 1912.

In Fig. 3-22 you can see a box named "Set intercept" which you can check to anchor the trendline to a selected point on the *y*-axis. This is useful for noisy data because it will improve the fit of the trendline. For example, if you know that the data begin at 0,0 but the first measured data point is not zero, then set the intercept at 0. Experiment with this feature with different intercepts and see how it affects the R^2 value (goodness of fit, based on least squares). Press Function Key F9 repeatedly and watch the R^2 value change. See Appendix 3 for more.

3.7 Rocket science: Tsiolkovskii's equation

Konstatin Tsiolkovskii (sometimes spelled Tsiolkovskiy) was a schoolteacher in a small Russian town. He was far ahead of time, and in 1895 he published a paper that proposed launching a satellite around Earth. Earlier, Sir Isaac Newton had calculated various orbits of an Earth satellite, based on his law of universal gravitation. Tsiolkovskii also patented a rocket engine using liquid oxygen and hydrogen, and he applied Newton's laws of motion to rocket flight.

Tsiolkovskii's most famous result is the basis of multi-stage rockets, which are more efficient than a single stage with the same amount of fuel. The "Ley de Tsiolkovskii" is shown on a postage stamp in Figure 3-24. This "law" is shown in clearer notation in Eq. (3-7), where v_f is the final velocity of the rocket, v_i is the initial velocity of the rocket, v_{rel} is the velocity of the rocket motor exhaust gas *relative to the rocket*, m_i is the initial mass of the rocket, and m_f is the final mass of the rocket. This equation is applied sequentially to each rocket stage.

$$v_f - v_i = v_{rel}\, \ln\left(\frac{m_i}{m_f}\right) \tag{3-7}$$

Notice that this "law" is completely general because it is a consequence of Newton's laws of motion. Long ago some people thought rockets worked by "pushing on the air" but they actually work better in outer space where there is no air.

The instantaneous acceleration of the rocket is also of interest. This is also a consequence of Newton's second law applied to the system consisting of the rocket and its exhaust:

$$Ma = Bv_{rel}\,. \tag{3-8}$$

In Eq. (3-8) M is the instantaneous mass of the rocket (kg), a is the acceleration (m/s^2) of the rocket relative to an inertial reference frame (like the fixed stars), B is the rate of fuel burning (kg/s), and as before v_{rel} is the velocity of the exhaust gas relative to the rocket.

These equations make more sense when you can view them in graphical form and you can change the quantities. Figure 3-25 shows the Home screen of the ROCKET SCIENCE workbook.

Figure 3-24. The Law of Tsiolkovskii (Ley de Tsiolkovskii) is one of the ten formulas that changed the face of the world.

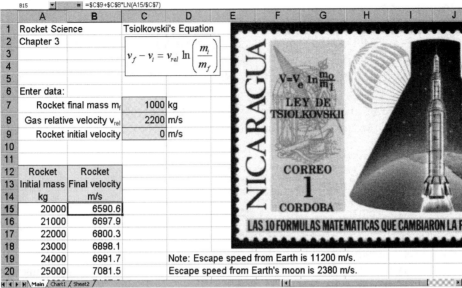

Figure 3-25. Home screen of the ROCKET SCIENCE workbook for stage 1 ($v = 0$).

Equation (3-7) is applied sequentially to each stage of the rocket. The Internet has many web sites devoted to rockets. Here are two of them:

Single stage rocket equations

http://www.execpc.com/~culp/rockets/rckt_eqn.html

Multistage rocket equations

http://www.execpc.com/~culp/rockets/multistg.html

Expert opinion on graphics

In his famous book *The Visual Display of Quantitative Information* Edward R. Tufte wrote, "At their best, graphics are instruments for reasoning about quantitative information." Good graphics reveal data patterns that clearly demonstrate, or show the limitations of, our summary statistics.

For engineers and scientists, graphics are an essential tool for representing and communicating complicated ideas. Through a combination of lines, points, symbols, coordinate systems, shades and color, graphics can reveal the story contained in complicated data. Graphics encourage our eyes to compare, contrast and condense information coming from single or multiple sources.

What's next?

Now that you know how to view data in several graphic forms, let's go to Chapter 4 and learn how to manipulate data with basic math operations. In Section 7.6 we will use 3-D charts for two-dimensional data.

References

E. R. Tufte, *The Visual Display of Quantitative Information*, (Graphics Press, Cheshire, CT, 1983).

W. S. Cleveland, *The Elements of Graphing Data*, (Wadsworth, Monterey, CA, 1985).

If you need even more specialized graphs, try ORIGIN which works seamlessly with EXCEL. Download a free demo at http://www.microcal.com .

Test your skills

1. Graph the function $y(x) = \dfrac{1}{x^2 + 0.05^2}$ for $-0.5 \le x \le +0.5$. Use an increment of 0.05 for x, and linear scales on both axes.

On the right-hand axis of the chart in Exercise 1, graph the function $y(x) = \dfrac{x}{x^2 + 0.05^2}$ for $-0.5 \le x \le +0.5$. Use the same increment of x, and linear scales on all axes.

2. Semi-log (log-lin) chart. Using the chart you made in Exercise 2, change the left y-axis to a log scale.

3. Log-Log chart. Graph the function $y(x) = \dfrac{1}{x^2 + 1}$ for $.01 \le x \le 1000$. Use log scales on both axes. (This is a frequency response curve for a single-pole low-pass filter. It is used to reduce harmonics and high-frequency noise.)

4. Decibel chart. Graph the same function in Exercise 4, but convert the y-values to dB. Graph dB on a linear scale and x on a log scale. (The -3 dB point is called the *cut-off frequency* or half-power frequency of the filter. Output power drops to half of the maximum value at the cut-off frequency.)

Observe the linearity of the response above the cut-off frequency (the frequency corresponding to the -3 dB point on the Bode plot). Measure the slope (dB/decade) on the high-frequency side of the cut-off frequency.

5. Swimming record times. Use the Olympic data on the next page to create an XY chart, and apply a Polynomial trend line to each data set. Use three different orders of polynomials. On another chart using these data, apply an Exponential trend line. With another chart, apply a Power trendline. Compare the R^2 values for each trendline. Experiment with the Moving Average (we'll see more of this in Chapter 5).

100 meter Free-style Olympic Gold Medal Swimming Records (seconds)		
Year	Men	Women
1896	82.2	
1904	62.8	
1906	73.4	
1908	65.6	
1912	63.4	82.2
1920	61.4	73.6
1924	59.0	72.4
1928	58.6	71.0
1932	58.2	66.8
1936	57.6	65.9
1948	57.3	66.3
1952	57.4	66.8
1956	55.4	62.0
1960	55.2	61.2
1964	53.4	59.5
1968	52.2	60.0
1972	51.11	58.59
1976	49.99	55.65
1980	50.4	54.79
1984	49.8	55.92
1988	48.63	54.93
1992	49.02	54.64
1996	48.74	54.50
2000	48.30	53.83
2004		
2008		

(Go to http://www.usswim.org/history/index.html for the latest data.)

6. Refer to Section 3.3. Use your spreadsheet to fill in this Table:

Table 3-1. Power, dB, and Nepers			
Power Ratio	Voltage ratio	dB	Neper
0.01	0.1		
1.0233	1.0116		
1.2589	1.1220		
1.9953	1.4142		
10	3.16228		
100	10	20 (example)	2.30 (example)
1000	31.6228		
10000	100		

7. Refer to Questions 1 and 2 in Chapter 2. Graph the terminal voltage and power loss as functions of current.

8. Refer to Questions 3 and 4 in Chapter 2. Graph the power generated and efficiency as functions of current.

9. Refer to Questions 3 and 4 in Chapter 2. Graph the efficiency as a function of power generated.

10. EXCEL "radar" chart. Graph $r = \log(x)$ for $1 \le x \le 100$ in steps of 5.

11. Graph the function $y(x) = \dfrac{x}{1+x^2}$ for $.01 \le x \le 1000$. Use a log scale on the x-axis (frequency) and dB on the y-axis. (This is a frequency response curve for a high-pass filter. It is used to reduce low-frequency power in a system.)

12. Baseball game on a merry-go-round (Coriolis "force"). The pitcher is at the center; the batter is on the circumference at 0. Use EXCEL to make a polar chart and a "radar" chart of the ball's trajectory as seen by the pitcher.

	Pitcher to Ball	
Time	Range	Angle
0	0	0°
1	2	90
2	4	180
3	6	270
4	8	360
5	10	90
6	12	180
7	14	270
8	16	360

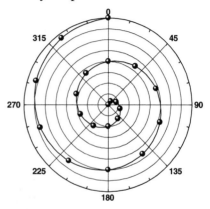

13. Isothermal compression and expansion. An ideal gas is described by the equation $PV = nRT$, where P is the pressure (N/m²), V is the volume (m³), n is the number of moles, R is the universal gas constant (8.31 J/mol K), and T is the absolute temperature (K). Make a chart of expansion and compression of an ideal gas at constant temperature. For input data, use number of moles, initial volume, volume increment, and temperature. Suggested values: $n = 0.1$, initial $V = 0.05$, V increment $= 0.005$, $T = 273$. Put input data in data entry boxes and use absolute cell references to put the data in the ideal gas law. Plot pressure as a function of volume. Use at least 20 values of volume. Volume increments can be positive or negative. Isothermal compression and expansion are half of the Carnot cycle for the ideal heat engine. Hint: your graph should look something

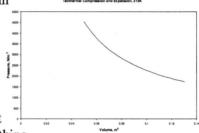

like this. Also, see the PV-GAS data file on the CD. (This exercise relates to the National Science Education Standards *heat* and *transfer of energy*.)

Chapter 4
Quick-Start Math

What this chapter is about

In this chapter we are going to review the elementary operations of addition, subtraction, multiplication, division, exponentiation, trigonometric functions and logarithmic functions. This sounds simple, but it is different than paper and pencil operations. We are going to show how you can do things with addition, subtraction, multiplication and division that may at first look complicated, but are really easy. We will also demonstrate some of EXCEL's trigonometric functions. In Chapter 5 you will learn some numerical techniques based on these simple operations that are useful in handling real-world data. Here we will introduce:

- EXCEL's operators and their order of precedence,

- how to use EXCEL's calculation and comparison operators in formulas,

- how to use EXCEL's text and reference operators in formulas,

- EXCEL's ten trigonometric functions.

We will go into detail in two simple applications using trig functions,

- inclined plane with friction,

- Fourier series.

4.1 Operator basics

Operators specify the type of calculation that you want to perform on the elements of a formula. EXCEL includes four different types of calculation operators: *arithmetic, comparison, text,* and *reference*. EXCEL performs operations in formulas in a specific order. If you combine several operators in a single formula, the operations are done in the order shown in Table 4-1.

If a formula contains operators with the same precedence (for example, if a formula contains both a multiplication and division operator) EXCEL evaluates the operators from left to right (Table 4-1). To change the order of evaluation, enclose the part of the formula to be calculated first in parentheses. For more information about calculation operators, consult Help.

Arithmetic, comparison, text, and reference operators are explained in detail in Tables 4-2, 4-3, and 4-4.

Table 4-1. Order of Precedence for Operators	
Operator	*Description*
: (colon) , (comma) (single space)	Reference operators
–	Negation (as in –1)
%	Percent
^	Exponentiation
* and /	Multiplication and division
+ and –	Addition and subtraction
&	Connects two strings of text (concatenation)
= < > <= >= <>	Comparison

Arithmetic (calculation) operators perform basic mathematical operations such as addition, subtraction, or multiplication; combine numbers; and produce numeric results.

Table 4-2. Calculation Operators in Formulas		
Arithmetic operator	*Meaning*	*Example*
+ (plus sign)	Addition	22+63
– (minus sign)	Subtraction (Negation)	36–22 – 11
* (asterisk)	Multiplication	3*4
/ (forward slash)	Division	3/4
% (percent sign)	Percent	22%
^ (caret)	Exponentiation	3^4 (same as 3*3*3*3)

Comparison operators (see Table 4-3) compare two values and then produce the logical value TRUE or FALSE. (These are useful with the IF function.)

Table 4-3. Comparison Operators in Formulas		
Comparison operator	*Meaning*	*Example*
= (equal sign)	Equal to	A1=B1
> (greater than sign)	Greater than	A1>B1
< (less than sign)	Less than	A1<B1
>= (greater than or equal to sign)	Greater than or equal to	A1>=B1
<= (less than or equal to sign)	Less than or equal to	A1<=B1
<> (not equal to sign)	Not equal to	A1<>B1

The text operator "&" (Table 4-4) combines one or more text values to produce a single piece of text.

Table 4-4. Text Operator in Formulas		
Text operator	*Meaning*	*Example*
& (ampersand)	Connects, or concatenates, two values to produce one continuous text value	"North" & "wind" produce "Northwind"

Reference operators (Table 4-5) combine ranges of cells for calculations.

Table 4-5. Reference Operators in Formulas		
Reference operator	*Meaning*	*Example*
: (colon)	Range operator, which produces one reference to all the cells between two references, including the two references	C5:C22
, (comma)	Union operator, which combines multiple references into one reference	SUM(B5:B15,D5:D15)
(single space)	Intersection operator, which produces one reference to cells common to two references	SUM(B3:B22 A3:D11) In this example, cell B7 is common to both ranges. (Try it).

4.2 Trigonometric functions

EXCEL contains a collection of 10 of the most useful trigonometric circular functions, shown in Table 4-6. These are explained in detail below. The hyperbolic functions are shown in Table 4-7.

Table 4-6. Basic Trigonometric Functions				
ACOS	ASIN	ATAN	ATAN2	COS
DEGREES	PI()	RADIANS	SIN	TAN

ACOS(number) returns the arccosine of a number. The arccosine is the angle whose cosine is number. The returned angle is given in radians in the range 0 (zero) to π.
Syntax
ACOS(number)
number is the cosine of the angle you want and must be from –1 to 1.
If you want to convert the result from radians to degrees, multiply it by 180/PI().
Examples
ACOS(–0.5) equals 2.094395 (this is $2\pi/3$ radians)
ACOS(–0.5)*180/PI() equals 120 (degrees)

ASIN(number) returns the arcsine of a number. The arcsine is the angle whose sine is number. The returned angle is given in radians in the range $-\pi/2$ to $\pi/2$.
Syntax
ASIN(number)
number is the sine of the angle you want and must be from –1 to 1.
To express the arcsine in degrees, multiply the result by 180/PI().
Examples
ASIN(–0.5) equals –0.5236 (this is $-\pi/6$ radians)
ASIN(–0.5)*180/PI() equals –3 0 (degrees)

ATAN(number) returns the arctangent of a number. The arctangent is the angle whose tangent is number. The returned angle is given in radians in the range $-\pi/2$ to $\pi/2$. In other words, this is *two-quadrant* arctangent.
Syntax
ATAN(number)
number is the tangent of the angle you want.
To express the arctangent in degrees, multiply the result by 180/PI().
Examples
ATAN(1) equals 0.785398 (this is $\pi/4$ radians)
ATAN(1)*180/PI() equals 45 (degrees)

ATAN2(number) returns the arctangent of the specified x and y coordinates. The arctangent is the angle from the x-axis to a line containing the origin (0, 0) and a point with coordinates (x_num, y_num). The angle is in radians between $-\pi$ and π, excluding $-\pi$. (This is a *four-quadrant* arctangent. Compare ATAN.)

Syntax

ATAN2(x_num,y_num)

X_num is the x-coordinate of the point.

Y_num is the y-coordinate of the point.

A positive result represents a counterclockwise angle from the x-axis; a negative result represents a clockwise angle.

ATAN2(a,b) equals ATAN(b/a), except that a can equal 0 in ATAN2.

If both x_num and y_num are 0, ATAN2 returns the #DIV/0! error value.

To express the arctangent in degrees, multiply the result by 180/PI().

Examples

ATAN2(1, 1) equals 0.785398 (this is $\pi/4$ radians)

ATAN2(−1, −1) equals −2 .35619 (this is $-3\pi/4$ radians)

ATAN2(−1, −1)*180/PI() equals −135 (degrees)

COS(number) Returns the cosine of the given angle.

Syntax

COS(number)

number is the angle in radians for which you want the cosine. If the angle is in degrees, multiply it by PI()/180 to convert it to radians.

Examples

COS(1.047) equals 0.500171

COS(60*PI()/180) equals 0.5, the cosine of 60 degrees

DEGREES(angle) converts radians into degrees.

Syntax

DEGREES(angle)

where angle is the angle in radians that you want to convert.

Example

DEGREES(PI()) equals 180

PI() returns the number 3.14159265358979, the mathematical constant π, accurate to 15 digits.

Syntax

PI()

Examples

PI()/2 equals 1.57079...

SIN(PI()/2) equals 1

If the radius of a circle is stored in a cell named Radius, the following formula calculates the area of the circle: PI()*(Radius^2)

RADIANS(angle) converts degrees to radians.
Syntax
RADIANS(angle)
angle is an angle in degrees that you want to convert.
Example
RADIANS(270) equals 4.712389 (this is $3\pi/2$ radians).

SIN(number) returns the sine of the given angle.
Syntax
SIN(number)
number is the angle in radians for which you want the sine. If your argument is
in degrees, multiply it by PI()/180 to convert it to radians.
Examples
SIN(PI()) equals 1.22E-16, which is approximately zero. The sine of π is zero.
SIN(PI()/2) equals 1
SIN(30*PI()/180) equals 0.5, the sine of 30 degrees

TAN(number) returns the tangent of the given angle.
Syntax
TAN(number)
number is the angle in radians for which you want the tangent. If your argument
is in degrees, multiply it by PI()/180 to convert it to radians.
Examples
TAN(0.785) equals 0.99920
TAN(45*PI()/180) equals 1

Using arctangent in EXCEL

Be careful using the arctangent function. It comes in two flavors listed above,
ATAN and ATAN2. Both of them return the value of an angle in radians, but the
function ATAN uses a single number as an input, and ATAN2 uses two numbers
as input. Figure 4-1 shows some examples of the two arctangent functions.

	A	B	C	D	E	F	G	H	I
1	ATAN & ATAN2.XLS								
2									
3		=ATAN2(62,62)		=ATAN2(-62,62)		=ATAN2(62,-62)		=ATAN2(-62,-62)	
4		0.785398		2.356194		-0.7854		-2.35619	
5									
6									
7		=ATAN(62/62)		=ATAN(-62/62)		=ATAN(62/-62)		=ATAN(-62/-62)	
8		0.785398		-0.7854		-0.7854		0.785398	
9									

Figure 4-1. Comparison of ATAN and ATAN2 functions.

A positive result represents a counterclockwise angle from the *x*-axis; a negative result represents a clockwise angle. (Draw a sketch to see why.)

ATAN2(*a,b*) equals ATAN(*b/a*) when *a* and *b* are positive, except that *a* can equal 0 in ATAN2. If both *x*_num and *y*_num are 0, ATAN2 returns the #DIV/0! error value.

Radians to degrees: You can use DEGREES(ATAN2(*x*_num,*y*_num)) or DEGREES(ATAN(*n*)). Or, you can multiply the radian result by 180/PI().

TIP

The $(\sin x)/x$ function is something that engineers and scientists often encounter, because it is related to a rectangular pulse by the Fourier transform (see Chapter 11). This is so common that a slightly modified form is given a special name; the *sinc* function is $(\sin \pi x)/(\pi x)$. The sinc function is also called the *interpolating function*. It has some interesting properties. You have to be careful at $x = 0$ because spreadsheets will not evaluate it correctly. From calculus, you know that (sin 0)/0 = 1 but the spreadsheet gives a nasty message: #DIV/0!. You can take care of this error by adding a small value to *x*, like $x + 10^{-16}$.

4.3 Inclined plane workbook

Let's explore the use of trig functions in a specific application. Open the INCLINE workbook. This workbook is an example of the use of trig functions and *xy* charts in the context of a problem that confronts all beginning students in engineering and science. This workbook analyzes an object on an inclined plane with friction, shown in Fig. 4-2.

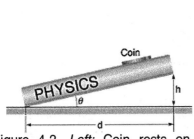
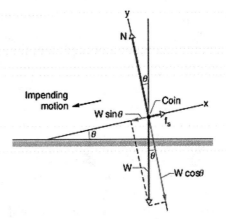

Figure 4-2. *Left:* Coin rests on inclined book. *Right:* Weight and friction forces are decomposed into components normal to the inclined plane and parallel to the inclined plane. Static friction force is always opposite to impending motion. (From *CD Physics*, Version 3.0, Wiley.)

An inclined plane is related to the method that the ancient Egyptians probably used to build the pyramids, because it effectively dilutes the force of gravity. Using an inclined plane you can raise an object by exerting a smaller force through a greater distance to reach the same height that would be achieved by exerting a larger force through a smaller distance in the vertical direction.

The usual (and easiest) way of analyzing the inclined plane is to decompose the weight and the friction force into components parallel to, and perpendicular to, the inclined plane. We will make a worksheet that produces a Table of these forces as a function of angle. When the component of weight down the plane becomes greater than the maximum friction force, the object begins to move.

The weight can be decomposed into the force $W \sin \theta$ down the plane and the force $W \cos \theta$ perpendicular to the plane. This makes sense because the force down the plane is zero when the angle is zero, and the normal force is equal to the weight when the angle is zero.

The maximum friction force is μN, where μ is the coefficient of static friction and N is the normal force. The component of the maximum friction force up the plane is $\mu W \cos \theta$. Motion is impending when the force down the plane is equal to the maximum static friction force, $W \sin \theta = \mu W \cos \theta$.

This system is easy to analyze in a spreadsheet. As usual, we are going to include some convenient features. Cells D3:D6 contain the input data used by the formulas in columns A, C, E, and H. (Including the acceleration of gravity as an input makes the worksheet more general; it could be used on other planets or their moons.) The Home page is shown in Fig. 4-3. Examine the cells in row 9:

Cell A9 contains the value 0, to start the angle axis at 0. Cell A10 contains the formula =A9+$D$6 which generates the angle axis by adding the increment in cell D6 to the value in the previous cell. This formula is copied to the end of the desired range.

Cell C9 contains the formula =$D$3*$D$4*COS(RADIANS(A9)) which is the spreadsheet version of the formula $mg \cos \theta$ for the normal force on the plane (the component of weight perpendicular to the plane). Note use of RADIANS to convert degrees to radians.

Cell E9 contains the formula =$D$3*$D$4*SIN(RADIANS(A9)) which is the spreadsheet version of the formula $mg \sin \theta$ or $W \sin \theta$ for the component of weight down the plane.

Cell H9 contains the formula =$D$5*C9 which is the maximum friction force at this angle, that is, the coefficient of static friction times the normal force.

The chart in Fig. 4-4 shows the results. Note where the graph of the force down the plane crosses the maximum force of friction. Motion begins when the force down the plane exceeds the force of static friction. After motion begins, these graphs are no longer valid because the coefficient of static friction becomes the coefficient of kinetic friction (usually smaller). It is common experience that it is harder to start an object moving than to keep the object moving.

	C10	▼	=	=$D$3*$D$4*COS(RADIANS(A10))						
	A	B	C	D	E	F	G	H	I	J
1	INCLINE.XLS		Inclined Plane							
2	Chapter 4									
3			Mass	10	kg					
4		Acceleration of gravity		9.8	m/s²					
5		Coefficient of static friction		0.5						
6			Angle increment	1	degree					
7										
8	ANGLE (degrees)		Normal Force		Force Down the Plane			Friction Force		
9	0		98		0			49		
10	1		97.98507		1.710336			48.99254		
11	2		97.9403		3.420151			48.97015		
12	3		97.86569		5.128924			48.93285		
13	4		97.76128		6.836134			48.88064		
14	5		97.62708		8.541263			48.81354		
15	6		97.46315		10.24379			48.73157		
16	7		97.26952		11.9432			48.63476		
17	8		97.04627		13.63896			48.52314		
18	9		96.79346		15.33058			48.39673		
19	10		96.51116		17.01752			48.25558		
20	11		96.19946		18.69928			48.09973		
21	12		95.85846		20.37535			47.92923		
22	13		95.48827		22.0452			47.74413		
23	14		95.08898		23.70835			47.54449		

Figure 4-3. Home screen of INCLINE. The formula in cell C10 is shown in the formula editing box.

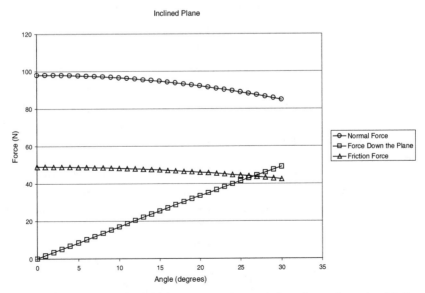

Fig. 4-4. Forces for the inclined plane system as a function of angle. Motion starts when force down the plane exceeds the maximum force of static friction.

4.4 Fourier series workbook

Next, let's see what we can do by merely adding sines and cosines. While study-ing heat transfer, Count Jean Baptiste Joseph Fourier discovered that almost every periodic function can be represented by a series of sines and cosines. The Fourier series, and the Fourier transform, must certainly be among the most im-portant discoveries of the nineteenth century. This simple, but extraordinary, dis-covery opened a rich field of mathematics and applications in engineering and science that is still the subject of intense research.

An unusually large number of applications came after the development of digital computers and the Fast Fourier Transform (FFT) algorithm in the twenti-eth century. (EXCEL has the FFT in the Analysis ToolPak, see Chapter 11.) Fou-rier wrote in his diary, "Yesterday was my twenty-first birthday, at that age New-ton and Pascal had already acquired many claims to immortality." Fourier at-tained immortality, and his name will be remembered forever in connection with his series and transform.

Adding Fourier components (or *harmonics*) to make a periodic function is called *Fourier synthesis*; dissecting a function into its components is called *Fou-rier analysis*. A convenient form of the series is given by,

$$f(t) = \frac{A_o}{2} + \sum_{n=1}^{\infty} \left[A_n \cos\left(\frac{2\pi nt}{T}\right) + B_n \sin\left(\frac{2\pi nt}{T}\right) \right] \tag{4-1}$$

where $f(t)$ is the function that you want to represent as a series,

A_o is a constant, which may be zero (it's the "dc" value of the function),

A_n are the Fourier coefficients of the even parts of the series (cosines),

B_n are the Fourier coefficients of the odd parts of the series (sines),

T is the period of the periodic function $f(t)$.

The series is easy to implement in a spreadsheet. To keep it simple, we will only do an example of Fourier synthesis. Open the workbook FOURIER and you will see nine Fourier coefficients used to synthesize an approximation to a square wave (see Fig. 4-5). More coefficients will make the approximation better. Count the bumps on the square wave; there are five, indicating that five non-zero har-monics are present. For convenience, the period and time increment are entered in cells F6 and G6. Experiment by changing the period and time increment.

Move your mouse around the worksheet and examine the cell contents. You will see that the columns simply add up nine terms in the series of Eq. (4-1). The Fourier series for the square wave shown in Fig. 4-5 is given by,

$$f(t) = \frac{1}{1}\sin\left(\frac{2\pi \times 1t}{9.375}\right) + \frac{1}{3}\sin\left(\frac{2\pi \times 3t}{9.375}\right) + \frac{1}{5}\sin\left(\frac{2\pi \times 5t}{9.375}\right) + \cdots$$

and all higher *odd* harmonics, representing a square wave of amplitude $\pi/4$.

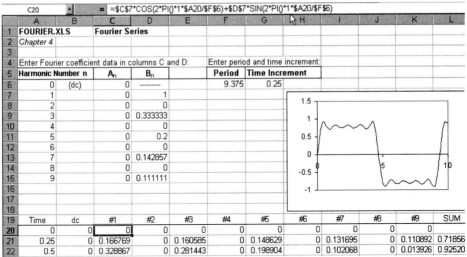

| C20 | | = | =$C$7*COS(2*PI()*1*$A20/$F$6)+$D$7*SIN(2*PI()*1*$A20/$F$6) | | | | | | | | |

Fig. 4-5. Home screen of the Fourier series workbook. The coefficients C6:D15 are used to synthesize a square wave using nine components, of which four are zero. The choice of these coefficients produces a square wave that starts at the up-going zero-crossing and has no dc component. (That is, the square wave is symmetrical about the time axis.) Note that the amplitude of the square wave with these coefficients is $\pi/4$, not 1. The amplitude of the *fundamental frequency* is 1.

The Fourier series is not restricted to continuous functions; the series has the remarkable ability to represent a *discontinuous* periodic function. At points of discontinuity, the series converges to the average value of points before and after the break. The Fourier series is the optimum series representation, in the sense that no other series has a smaller least-mean-square error in representing a given periodic function.

Figure 4-6 shows the Fourier components of the square wave, and Fig. 4-7 shows the spectrum of the square wave, that is, the amplitudes of the Fourier components. A square wave is used as a common test signal. Note that a pure square wave does not have any even harmonics. So, if you use a square wave as the test input to a system and you see any even harmonics at the output, you know the system has *harmonic distortion*. (This is common in amplifiers at high output.) If the ratio of harmonic amplitudes in the output is not the same as the input, you know the system has *frequency distortion*. A long-period square wave can approximate a *step function*, which can be used to get the complete frequency response (amplitude and phase) of a linear system (see Chapter 11).

Try the FOURIER workbook exercises at the end of this chapter. You will see how to synthesize other common periodic waveforms. Experiment with different harmonics and coefficients. (This is how music synthesizers work.)

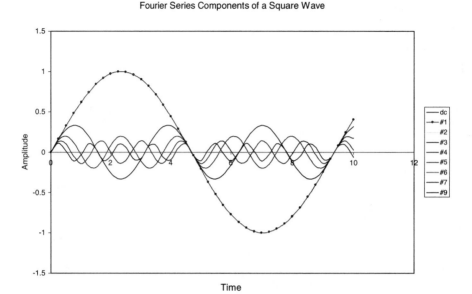

Figure 4-6. Components of the square wave in Fig. 4-4. This chart is easier to interpret in color on your monitor. (The chart is in the FOURIER workbook.)

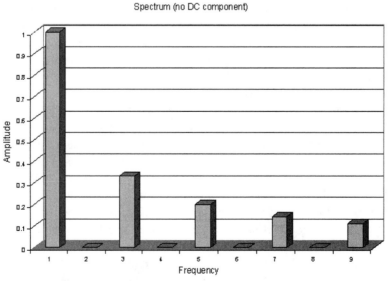

Figure 4-7. Spectrum of the square wave in Fig. 4-5. Note that only odd harmonics (1, 3, 5, . . .) are present, which is one indicator of a pure square wave.

TIP

All of EXCEL's math functions can be accessed quickly by clicking on the f_x icon. This is called the Paste Function icon, and it is located on the top row of the menu bar, between the Auto Sum (Σ) and Sort Ascending icons.

4.5 Hyperbolic functions

The hyperbolic functions involve real exponentials. They are real time-savers in many problems. (See Exercise 7, Chapter 2.)

Table 4-6. Hyperbolic Functions in EXCEL		
ACOSH	ASINH	ATANH
COSH	SINH	TANH

ACOSH returns the inverse hyperbolic cosine of a number.
Number must be greater than or equal to 1. The inverse hyperbolic cosine is the value whose hyperbolic cosine is number, so ACOSH(COSH(number)) equals number.
Syntax
ACOSH(number)
Number   is any real number equal to or greater than 1.
Examples
ACOSH(1) equals 0
ACOSH(10) equals 2.993223

ASINH returns the inverse hyperbolic sine of a number. The inverse hyperbolic sine is the value whose hyperbolic sine is number, so ASINH(SINH(number)) equals number.
Syntax
ASINH(number)
Number   is any real number.
Examples
ASINH(−2.5) equals −1.64723
ASINH(10) equals 2.998223

COSH returns the hyperbolic cosine of a number.
Syntax
COSH(number)

The formula for the hyperbolic cosine is: $\cosh(z) = \dfrac{e^{+z} + e^{-z}}{2}$

Examples
COSH(4) equals 27.30823
COSH(EXP(1)) equals 7.610125, where EXP(1) is e, the base of the natural logarithm.

SINH returns the hyperbolic sine of a number.
Syntax
SINH(number)
Number   is any real number.

The formula for the hyperbolic sine is: $\sinh(z) = \dfrac{e^{+z} - e^{-z}}{2}$

Examples
SINH(1) equals 1.175201194
SINH(−1) equals −1.175201194
You can use the hyperbolic sine function to approximate a cumulative probability distribution. Suppose a laboratory test value varies between 0 and 10 seconds. An empirical analysis of the collected history of experiments shows that the probability of obtaining a result, x, of less than t seconds is approximated by the following equation:

$$P(x < t) = 2.868 * SINH(0.0342 * t), \text{ where } 0 < t < 10$$

To calculate the probability of obtaining a result of less than 1.03 seconds, substitute 1.03 for t:
2.868*SINH(0.0342*1.03) equals 0.101049063
You can expect this result to occur about 101 times for every 1000 experiments.

TANH returns the hyperbolic tangent of a number.
Syntax
TANH(number)
Number   is any real number

The formula for the hyperbolic tangent is: $\tanh(z) = \dfrac{\sinh(z)}{\cosh(z)}$

Examples
TANH(−2) equals −0.96403
TANH(0) equals 0 (zero)
TANH(0.5) equals 0.462117

What's next?

In Chapter 5 we'll explore some techniques of numerical differentiation and integration. Integration leads naturally to the Moving Average and Exponential

Smoothing tools in EXCEL. We'll also see how easy it is to implement some useful integration operations with simple arithmetic. Integration helps when data are noisy or you need to extract information from corrupted data.

References

N. Morrison, *Introduction to Fourier Analysis* (John Wiley & Sons, Inc., New York, 1994). This shows how to compute Fourier coefficients of the series, which is beyond the scope of this chapter.

R. G. Wilson, *Fourier Series and Optical Transform Techniques in Contemporary Optics* (John Wiley & Sons, Inc., New York, 1995).

S. C. Bloch, "Fourier Perspective," Chapter 6 in *Introduction to Classical and Quantum Harmonic Oscillators* (John Wiley & Sons, Inc., New York, 1997). This has examples of how to compute Fourier coefficients for a square wave and a triangular wave.

Test your skills

Use your spreadsheet to do the following calculations:
1. =ATAN2(15,30)
2. =ATAN2(15,−30)
3. =ATAN2(−15,30)
4. =ATAN2(−15,−30)
5. =DEGREES(ATAN2(36,36))
6. =DEGREES(ATAN2(−36,36))
7. =ATAN(30/15)
8. =ATAN(−30/15)
9. =ATAN(30/−15)
10. =ATAN(−30/−15)
11. Compose a worksheet for an object being pushed up an inclined plane with friction. This is somewhat similar to Figs. 4-2 and 4-3, but now the friction force and the component of weight down the plane are in the same direction because impending motion is up the plane. The force applied to move the object up the plane must be greater than the sum of the forces down the plane. What is the minimum force required to move the object, as a function of angle? Show data in an XY chart. (This exercise is related to the National Science Education Standard *position and motion of objects – motions and forces.*)
12. A concrete block is resting on a wood board. When the board is inclined at an angle of 60 degrees the block starts to slide. What is the coefficient of

static friction? (This is a standard method of measuring the coefficient of static friction between two surfaces, like rubber and asphalt. Note that the coefficient is independent of weight and interface area.)

13. Express the amplitudes of harmonic components 3, 5, 7, and 9 of a square wave in dB, relative to harmonic 1 (the fundamental frequency).

14. Use the FOURIER workbook to synthesize a sawtooth wave. All harmonics are present. The amplitudes of the harmonics are: 1/1, 1/2, 1/3, 1/4, 1/5, 1/6, and so on. You see this often; the sawtooth wave is used as the horizontal sweep on computer monitors, oscilloscopes and TV screens.

15. Synthesize the Fourier series for a triangular wave. Use the FOURIER workbook to synthesize a triangular wave. Here, all even harmonics are zero. The odd harmonic amplitudes are: $1/1^2$, $1/3^2$, $1/5^2$, $1/7^2$, $1/9^2$, and so on.

16. ✪ Banking a highway curve. In Section 4.3 we discussed the inclined plane with friction. When a vehicle goes around a curve on a highway you cannot expect that friction will prevent you from sliding because of water and oil on the road, and changing road conditions. Highways are inclined (or "banked") on a curve to prevent slipping. This is a dynamic problem but it can be reduced to a static problem similar to the inclined plane. We want to bank the road to tilt the normal force toward the center of curvature of the road to provide a centripetal force. There is no acceleration perpendicular to the road so $N_y = N \cos\theta = W = mg$. In the radial direction the component of N is

$$N_r = N \sin\theta = \frac{mv^2}{R}$$

where R is the radius of the curve and v is the speed of the vehicle. Divide N_r by N_y to find the tangent of the angle, $\tan\theta = v^2/(gR)$. Notice that the angle is independent of the mass of the vehicle. This is important, because the banked curve should have the same effect on all vehicles with the same speed. Compose a worksheet that will calculate the required angle for maximum speeds of 20, 30, 40, and 50 m/s and R of 50, 75, 100, and 125 m. This exercise relates to the National Science Education Standard *position and motion of objects – motions and forces*.

17. Hector the vector collector. The workbook named VECTORS shows how you can add, subtract, and multiply vectors. Vector multiplication comes in two forms, scalar (or dot) and vector (or cross). Explore the formulas in the cells to see how easily this is done. Let $A = 3\mathbf{i} + 4\mathbf{j} – 5\mathbf{k}$ and $B = 2\mathbf{i} + 11\mathbf{j} – 3\mathbf{k}$. Enter these in the worksheet to find A+B, A–B, |A+B|, |A–B|, |A|, |B|, A×B, B×A, A•B and the smallest angle between A and B. Confirm your answers by hand calculation. What is A×A ? What is A•A ? Why?

Chapter 5
Differentiation and Integration

What this chapter is about

The basic calculus operations of differentiation and integration can be approximated in numerical form in EXCEL. We will explore several methods of both operations, and look at their good and their bad features. Integration is related to smoothing and we'll see how to use two tools in EXCEL (Moving Average and Exponential Smoothing) that do special types of integration.

We will show how to use Savitsky-Golay functions, which combine differentiation and integration for least-mean-square estimation of noisy data. These functions originated in chemistry, but they are universally useful and you should know about them. Finally, you will see how to use the TrendLine tool in EXCEL with noisy data, and you will compute centers of mass and moments of inertia.

An integrator is available on the Internet. You can type in a function and immediately get the integral produced by MATHEMATICA. Go to the web site http://integrals.wolfram.com/index.en.cgi . See Figure 5-8 for an example.

When do you need numerical differentiation and integration? Experimental data often do not involve known functions, so numerical methods are essential.

5.1 Differentiation

Taking the derivative of a function is a fundamental analytical skill that you learn in calculus. The derivative answers the question, what is the rate of change of a function? The derivative emphasizes changes in a function or a data set. This is the opposite of integration, which de-emphasizes (or smoothes) changes.

We are often interested in the time rate of change, but the derivative is not limited to time. For example, we may need to know the rate of change in space, like a gradient, if we are working with temperature, pressure, or electric potential. The geometric interpretation of the first derivative is the *slope* of the function at a point. The second derivative is the rate of change of the slope. Second derivatives appear in Newton's laws of motion and identification of maxima and minima.

This interpretation is OK for continuous functions and infinitesimal increments, but with discrete data we must be concerned about intervals between data points. For example, the average speed is given by,

$$\bar{v} = \frac{\Delta s}{\Delta t} \tag{5-1}$$

where Δs is the space interval associated with the time interval Δt. The bar above v indicates "average value" over the time interval. We need to decide what we are going to do about the ends of the increments in space and time. This will become clear when you use the DERIVATIVE workbook. There are three ways to do these increments with discrete data sequences:

- forward derivative,
- backward derivative,
- central derivative.

Let's look at a point with coordinates x_0, y_0. The coordinates of the previous point are x_{-1}, y_{-1} and the coordinates of the point after the present point x_0, y_0 are x_{+1}, y_{+1}. (Draw a curve on a piece of paper and label three points like this. I could show you a picture but you'll learn more if you do it yourself.) In your calculus course you learned that the first derivative of a function is given by,

$$\frac{dy}{dx} = \frac{y_2 - y_1}{h} \tag{5-2}$$

in the limit as h goes to zero, where h is the increment in x. Before h goes to zero, there is an error in the estimation of the derivative, of order h, abbreviated as $O(h)$.

So, it appears that a small increment is desirable, but we also need to examine the effect of round-off error and precision with discrete data, so we have to be careful about making general statements here. Table 5-1 summarizes the three types of first derivatives at the point x_0, y_0.

Table 5-1 appears to say that you should always use the central derivative, but this derivative requires the same number of data points on both sides of the point in question. At the ends of a data sequence you will have to use forward or backward derivatives to avoid serious errors. Also, forward and backward derivatives produce better results in data that have large changes. Use a backward derivative before a large change, and a forward derivative after the change.

Table 5-1. Estimation of First Derivative for Discrete Data		
Type of derivative	Formula	Order of error
Forward. (See worksheet for formula.)	$\dfrac{\Delta y}{\Delta x} = \dfrac{y_{+1} - y_0}{h}$	h
Backward. (See worksheet for formula.)	$\dfrac{\Delta y}{\Delta x} = \dfrac{y_0 - y_{-1}}{h}$	h
Central. (See Fig. 5-2, cell F105 for formula.)	$\dfrac{\Delta y}{\Delta x} = \dfrac{y_{+1} - y_{-1}}{2h}$	h^2

Because the first derivative is analogous to speed (or velocity, if it's a vector), the second derivative is analogous to acceleration. In other words, the second derivative is the derivative of the first derivative. Table 5-2 shows the formulas and error orders of the second derivative types.

Table 5-2. Estimation of Second Derivative for Discrete Data		
Type	Formula	Order of error
Forward. (See worksheet for formula.)	$\dfrac{\Delta^2 y}{\Delta x^2} = \dfrac{y_{+2} - 2y_1 + y_0}{h^2}$	h
Backward.(See worksheet for formula.)	$\dfrac{\Delta^2 y}{\Delta x^2} = \dfrac{y_0 - 2y_{-1} + y_{-2}}{h^2}$	h
Central. (See Fig. 5-1, cell J12 for formula.)	$\dfrac{\Delta^2 y}{\Delta x^2} = \dfrac{y_1 - 2y_0 + y_{-1}}{h^2}$	h^2

Of course, to get higher derivatives you can use repeated applications of the first derivative instead of using special formulas.

Let's implement these derivatives in a workbook, and compare the results with a continuous function $y(t) = 6t^2$ that we can differentiate analytically to find $dy/dt = 12t$. [In 1676 Leibniz proved $d(x^n) = n\,x^{n-1}dx$.] Open the workbook named DERIVATIVE and you should see Figures 5-1 and 5-2.

At the increment of 1, Forward and Backward first derivatives have constant errors of +6 and –6, respectively. Clearly, the increment of 1 is too large to give acceptable results for the rate of change of this data set.

Next, let's reduce the increment from 1 to 0.1. Figures 5-3 and 5-4 show the reduction in constant error for Forward and Backward first derivatives as the increment decreases. Nevertheless, the end errors are always present.

Observe the errors of Forward, Backward, and Central derivatives at both ends of the data. Now you can understand why it is often desirable to shift from Forward to Central to Backward so you can include all data points, even though the ends will still have more errors than the rest of the data.

Even though numerical differentiation is not perfect, it still lets you do things that you cannot do with analytical calculus. Data from real-world experiments always have random noise, and it is often impossible to represent data in terms of known functions. In the real world, we need numerical operations.

J12 = =(B13-2*B12+B11)/$D$3^2

	A	B	C	D	E	F	G	H	I	J
1	DERIVATIVE.XLS					First and Second Derivative				
2	Chapter 5									
3			Increment	1		$y(t) = 6t^2$				
4										
5			Analytical	Forward	Backward	Central	Analytical	Forward	Backward	Central
6	Time	y(t)	dy/dt	Δy/Δt	Δy/Δt	Δy/Δt	d^2y/dt^2	$\Delta^2y/\Delta t^2$	$\Delta^2y/\Delta t^2$	$\Delta^2y/\Delta t^2$
7	0	0	0	6	#VALUE!	#VALUE!	12	12	#VALUE!	#VALUE!
8	1	6	12	18	6	12	12	12	#VALUE!	12
9	2	24	24	30	18	24	12	12	12	12
10	3	54	36	42	30	36	12	12	12	12
11	4	96	48	54	42	48	12	12	12	12
12	5	150	60	66	54	60	12	12	12	12
13	6	216	72	78	66	72	12	12	12	12
14	7	294	84	90	78	84	12	12	12	12
15	8	384	96	102	90	96	12	12	12	12

Figure 5-1. Home screen of DERIVATIVE. Note that Backward and Central have errors at the beginning of the data, but Forward is OK. At other points Central agrees with Analytical. The Forward first derivative has a constant error of +6. The Backward first derivative has a constant error of –6. Note the points of agreement for the second derivatives.

F105 = =(B106-B104)/(2*$D$3)

	A	B	C	D	E	F	G	H	I	J
1	DERIVATIVE.XLS					First and Second Derivative				
2	Chapter 5									
3			Increment	1		$y(t) = 6t^2$				
4										
5			Analytical	Forward	Backward	Central	Analytical	Forward	Backward	Central
6	Time	y(t)	dy/dt	Δy/Δt	Δy/Δt	Δy/Δt	d^2y/dt^2	$\Delta^2y/\Delta t^2$	$\Delta^2y/\Delta t^2$	$\Delta^2y/\Delta t^2$
102	95	54150	1140	1146	1134	1140	12	12	12	12
103	96	55296	1152	1158	1146	1152	12	12	12	12
104	97	56454	1164	1170	1158	1164	12	12	12	12
105	98	57624	1176	1182	1170	1176	12	12	12	12
106	99	58806	1188	1194	1182	1188	12	-61194	12	12
107	100	60000	1200	-60000	1194	-29403	12	60000	12	-61194
108										

Figure 5-2. At the end of the data sequence, for this increment, the Forward and Central derivatives have large errors but the Backward derivatives may be acceptable. Compare with Fig. 5-1. Except at the ends, Central agrees with Analytical. (This worksheet uses the Freeze Panes option in the Window menu.)

| I12 | | ▼ | ■ | =(B12-2*B11+B10)/$D$3^2 | | | | | |

	A	B	C	D	E	F	G	H	I	J
1	DERIVATIVE.XLS					First and Second Derivative				
2	Chapter 5									
3			Increment	0.1		$y(t) = 6t^2$				
4										
5			Analytical	Forward	Backward	Central	Analytical	Forward	Backward	Central
6	Time	y(t)	dy/dt	$\Delta y/\Delta t$	$\Delta y/\Delta t$	$\Delta y/\Delta t$	d^2y/dt^2	$\Delta^2 y/\Delta t^2$	$\Delta^2 y/\Delta t^2$	$\Delta^2 y/\Delta t^2$
7	0	0	0	0.6	#VALUE!	#VALUE!	12	12	#VALUE!	#VALUE!
8	0.1	0.06	1.2	1.8	0.6	1.2	12	12	#VALUE!	12
9	0.2	0.24	2.4	3	1.8	2.4	12	12	12	12
10	0.3	0.54	3.6	4.2	3	3.6	12	12	12	12
11	0.4	0.96	4.8	5.4	4.2	4.8	12	12	12	12
12	0.5	1.5	6	6.6	5.4	6	12	12	12	12
13	0.6	2.16	7.2	7.8	6.6	7.2	12	12	12	12
14	0.7	2.94	8.4	9	7.8	8.4	12	12	12	12

Figure 5-3. The same data $y(t)$ in Figs. 5-1 and 5-2 are differentiated here with an increment of 0.1. The Central derivatives are in perfect agreement with the analytical derivatives, except at the ends. The Forward and Backward first derivatives have errors of +0.6 and –0.6, respectively, with this increment. As expected, these errors are ten times less than with the increment of 1.

Figures 5-2 and 5-4 have the worksheet pane locked vertically so you can see the column headings (rows 5 and 6) at all times. To freeze the pane, select a cell, go to the Window menu, and click on Freeze Panes. Figure 5-5 shows an example of the forward derivative applied to a function composed of a pulse and sine segment.

| F102 | | ▼ | ■ | =(B103-B101)/(2*$D$3) | | | | | |

	A	B	C	D	E	F	G	H	I	J
1	DERIVATIVE.XLS					First and Second Derivative				
2	Chapter 5									
3			Increment	0.1		$y(t) = 6t^2$				
4										
5			Analytical	Forward	Backward	Central	Analytical	Forward	Backward	Central
6	Time	y(t)	dy/dt	$\Delta y/\Delta t$	$\Delta y/\Delta t$	$\Delta y/\Delta t$	d^2y/dt^2	$\Delta^2 y/\Delta t^2$	$\Delta^2 y/\Delta t^2$	$\Delta^2 y/\Delta t^2$
100	9.3	518.94	111.6	112.2	111	111.6	12	12	12	12
101	9.4	530.16	112.8	113.4	112.2	112.8	12	12	12	12
102	9.5	541.5	114	114.6	113.4	114	12	12	12	12
103	9.6	552.96	115.2	115.8	114.6	115.2	12	12	12	12
104	9.7	564.54	116.4	117	115.8	116.4	12	12	12	12
105	9.8	576.24	117.6	118.2	117	117.6	12	12	12	12
106	9.9	588.06	118.8	119.4	118.2	118.8	12	-61194	12	12
107	10	600	120	-6000	119.4	-2940.3	12	60000	12	-61194
108										

Figure 5-4. This is the bottom of the DERIVATIVE screen, showing errors at the ends of the derivatives. Compare with Fig. 5-2. (Frozen pane shows rows 1–6.)

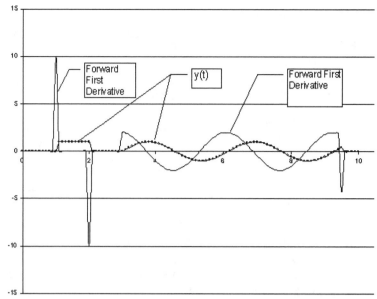

Figure 5-5. The forward first derivatives of a rectangular pulse and a segment of a sine. The original function *y(t)* is identified by markers at data points. The derivative of the pulse (no markers) emphasizes the start and stop of the pulse (like an *edge detector*). The first derivative of the sine is a cosine, as you would expect. Note the derivative at the abrupt end of the sine segment.

FAQ

Q. *Is there a simple explanation of what derivatives and integrals are?*
A. Yes. Consider a graph of a function. The first derivative can be visualized geometrically as the slope of a function. When the first derivative is evaluated at a point it has the value of the slope of the line that is tangent to a function's curve at that point. If the first derivative is zero, this indicates that a function is either a constant, or the derivative is evaluated at a maximum or a minimum.

The second derivative is "the slope of the slope," or the rate of change of the slope. When the second derivative is positive the graph of a function is cup-shaped. A negative second derivative indicates that a function is like a cup upside down. So, a zero first derivative with a positive second derivative identifies a minimum of a function. A zero first derivative with a negative second derivative identifies a maximum of a function. Note that functions may have more than one minimum or maximum.

The geometric interpretation of an integral is the area under a curve. An integral can be interpreted as the limit of a sum of elemental areas that add up to the total area. This enables us to approximate integrals numerically by a finite number of terms. The great engineer and mathematician Archimedes (287 B.C.–212 B.C.) had some of the basic ideas of calculus, but the ancient ones did not have a fully developed concept of an infinite series with a finite value.

FAQ

Q. *What are higher derivatives used for?*
A. Most of the time all you need are the first and second derivatives. In mechanics the third time derivative is the rate of change of acceleration. The third time derivative also appears in radiation reaction. The fourth space derivative is required to analyze mechanical bending of beams. Higher derivatives are used in Taylor's series to achieve better approximations to functions.

5.2 Integration

Modern calculus was invented by Sir Isaac Newton (1642–1727) when he needed it for his development of mechanics. Almost simultaneously calculus was invented by Gottfried Wilhelm von Leibniz (1646–1716), a lawyer and mathematician. Today we use the convenient notation of Leibniz. Following their work, calculus was put on a firmer foundation by the efforts of many mathematicians. Figure 5-7 shows a French stamp honoring the contributions of Augustin Cauchy. The graph on the lower left side of the stamp shows the approximation of the integral of the parabola $y(x) = x^2$ by a series of vertical rectangular strips. Later Riemann firmly established this method as the Riemann integral.

Analytical evaluation of integrals is a skill you learned in calculus, but experimental data are seldom in the form of known functions with known integrals. Numerical integration was recognized as the solution to this problem, and many analog methods of integration were developed before digital computers were available. For example, ball-disc integrators were widely used in mechanical analog computers. Mechanical and electronic planimeters are used for graphical integration. The mechanical planimeter was invented by Jacob Amsler (1835–1912). The first large electronic digital computer, built with vacuum tubes in the 1940s, was named ENIAC (Electronic Numerical Integrator and Computer).

Figure 5-7. Vertical strips approximate the area under the curve $y = x^2$.

Rusty razor method

To get an intuitive feeling for methods of practical integration, consider the problem faced by early steam engine designers. They wanted to maximize the efficiency of their engines, so they had to measure the energy input and the work output. The engineers found that they could do this on a graph of pressure P versus volume V, because the product PV is work. Recall, pressure is N/m^2, volume is m^3, so pressure times volume is $N/m^2 \times m^3 = N{\cdot}m$ or Joule, the unit of work and energy.

By attaching an ink pen to a pressure gauge on the engine cylinder and also to the connecting rod of the piston, the pen was forced to move in two perpendicular directions on a sheet of paper, thus drawing the PV curve. However, it was necessary to find the area enclosed in the curve as the engine went through its cycle.

The area could be approximated by counting squares on the paper, but this lacked precision. The area could be found more precisely by using a razor blade to cut out, and then weigh, the paper under the top of the curve on the PV diagram (the energy input). Next, the paper enclosed in the cycle (the work output) could be cut out and weighed. Figure 5-9 shows a typical example. The ratio of the work output to the energy input equals the efficiency.

Let's put away the rusty razor and look at some standard methods of numerical integration. We will assume that all data are in discrete form. In other words, even if the original data were continuous, we will treat it as sampled data.

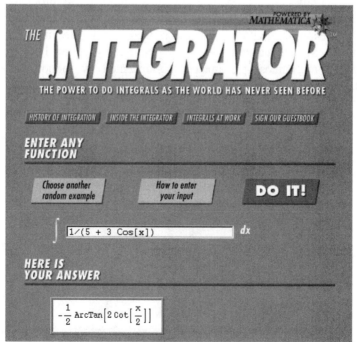

Figure 5-8. Integrate your functions at http://integrals.wolfram.com/index.en.cgi.

Sampled data result in discrete sequences. Open the workbook named INTEGRATION-101 and explore the formulas as you read on.

Rectangular method

The simplest method estimates the integral I as the sum of the areas of rectangular strips $y \Delta x$ as in Figure 5-7,

$$I \approx \sum_{i=1}^{n} y_i \, \Delta x_i \, . \tag{5-3}$$

If the increment Δx is constant, then it can be factored out of the sum. As a simple example using an increment of 0.1, consider the sum

$$I \approx 0.1 \sum_{n=1}^{5} y_i \approx 0.1(0.22 + 0.36 + 0.46 + 0.65 - 0.66) \, . \tag{5-4}$$

If the data sequence has rapid changes then you can use a smaller Δx. When the changes are slow you can use a larger Δx. This is called *adaptive step size*. Of course, if Δx varies then it cannot be factored out of the sum and you must use Equation (5-3). When experimental data are collected at regular intervals you can decrease the step size by interpolating between data points.

Figure 5-10 shows the Home screen of the INTEGRATION-101 workbook. This workbook contains three methods of numerical integration and compares them with the exact result of analytical calculation.

As you might guess, the accuracy improves as n increases and Δx decreases, but finite rectangles cannot match a curve very closely unless their width is much less than the corresponding changes in the curve. See Figs. 5-12 and 5-13.

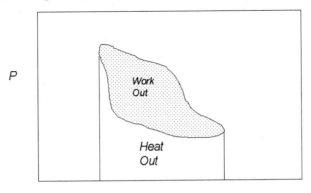

Figure 5-9. *PV* diagram of an engine cycle. Work Out + Heat Out = Energy Input, by first law of thermodynamics. Efficiency is (Work Out)/(Energy Input). The area under the curves can be determined by numerical or analog integration methods.

This workbook also shows a problem that arises with the rectangular method. You need to decide whether to choose the rectangular strips as left-rectangular or right-rectangular. See Figures. 5-11 and 5-12.

Trapezoidal method

This simple method of numerical integration is usually more accurate than the rectangular method but less accurate than Simpson's rules.

The trapezoidal method estimates the integral I as the sum of the areas of trapezoidal strips. In other words, the vertical strips are formed by joining adjacent y_i values with a straight line. The trapezoidal rule can be expressed as,

$$I \approx \frac{1}{2}\sum_{i=1}^{n-1}(y_i + y_{i+1})(x_{i+1} - x_i) \qquad (5\text{-}5)$$

where the increment is $x_{i+1} - x_i = \Delta x_i$. If data points are evenly spaced, then the increment is constant and it can be taken outside of the sum, as before. Observe how Eq. (5-5) is implemented in the workbook INTEGRATION-101, Fig. 5-10.

Note the great simplification in the trapezoidal method for evenly spaced data. With the same data that we used for the rectangular method we have,

$$I \approx \frac{1}{2} \times 0.1\big[(0.22 + 0.36) + (0.36 + 0.46) + (0.46 + 0.65) + (0.65 - 0.66)\big].$$

This reduces to

$$I \approx 0.1\left[\frac{1}{2}(0.22) + 0.36 + 0.46 + 0.65 - \frac{1}{2}(0.66)\right].$$

E18		=100*(E16-E17)/E17				
	A	B	C	D	E	F	G
1	INTEGRATION-101.XLS			Comparison of Numerical and Exact Integration			
2	Chapter 5			Rectangular and Trapezoidal Methods			
3	x	exp(-x)	Left Rect	Right Rect	Trapez		
4	0	1	0.1		0.05	See Equation (5-5)	
5	0.1	0.904837	0.090484	0.090484	0.090484		
6	0.2	0.818731	0.081873	0.081873	0.081873		
7	0.3	0.740818	0.074082	0.074082	0.074082		
8	0.4	0.670320	0.067032	0.067032	0.067032		
9	0.5	0.606531	0.060653	0.060653	0.060653		
10	0.6	0.548812	0.054881	0.054881	0.054881		
11	0.7	0.496585	0.049659	0.049659	0.049659		
12	0.8	0.449329	0.044933	0.044933	0.044933		
13	0.9	0.406570	0.040657	0.040657	0.040657		
14	1	0.367879		0.036788	0.018394		
15							
16		INTEGRAL	0.6642533	0.6010412	0.6326472		
17		EXACT	0.6321206	0.6321206	0.6321206		
18		% ERROR	5.0833194	-4.916681	0.0833194		
19			Left Rect	Right Rect	Trapez		

Figure 5-10. Left and right rectangular and trapezoidal numerical integration.

It may be surprising that the trapezoidal method looks like the rectangular method, except that you only use half of the first and last data points for the trapezoidal method. This simple modification can often produce a large increase in accuracy. Compare cells in row 18 of Fig. 5-10.

exp(-x), Left Rectangular

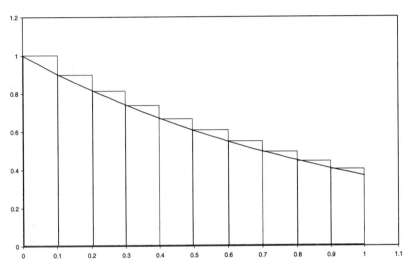

Figure 5-11. Left Rectangular integration overestimates the value of the integral for this function. Observe that the error decreases as the slope decreases.

exp(-x), Right Rectangular

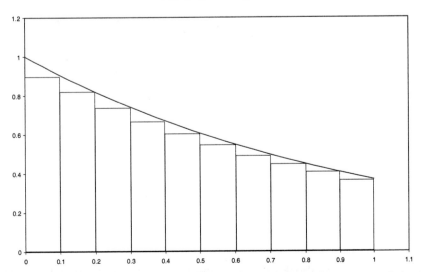

Figure 5-12. Right rectangular integration underestimates the value of the integral for the exponential decay function. Also see the parabola in Figure 5-7.

In this example of an exponential decay you can see that the left rectangles overestimate the integral and the right rectangles underestimate the integral. How would you get a better estimate?

If one method is over and the other method is under, you could try taking the average of the two results. Look at rows 17 and 18 in Fig. 5-10. You will find that the average of left and right rectangles gives the result of the trapezoidal method. If you give this a little thought, you will see that this is exactly what you would expect. This how the trapezoidal method works!

Simpson's 1/3 rule

Simpson's rules are simple and can be quite accurate. The 1/3 rule uses a second-order polynomial (quadratic or parabola) through three adjacent, equally spaced data points. The integral I can be approximated as,

$$ I \approx \frac{1}{3} \sum_{i=1,3,5,\cdots}^{n} (y_i + 4y_{i+1} + y_{i+2}) \Delta x . \tag{5-6} $$

The increments are constant, so Δx can be taken outside of the sum and used as a single multiplication after summation, as before. The number of strips is even; index i is an odd integer. Equation (5-6) can be put in a more convenient form for use in a spreadsheet. Observe how this is implemented in the workbook INTEGRATION.

$$ I \approx \frac{b-a}{3n} (y_0 + 4y_1 + 2y_2 + 4y_3 + 2y_4 + \ldots + 4y_{n-1} + y_n) . \tag{5-6a} $$

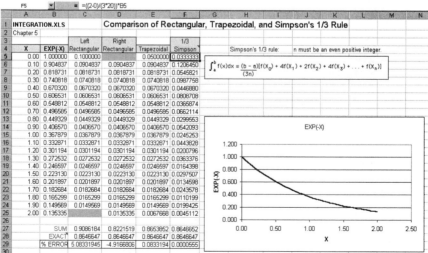

Figure 5-13. This workbook calculates the integral of the exponential decay by four methods and compares the results with the exact analytical calculation.

In Equation (5-6a) the constants a and b are, respectively, the start and stop limits and n is the number of strips.

Simpson's 3/8 rule

Simpson's 3/8 rule has the potential to yield even better results, but in some cases it is no better, or even worse, than the 1/3 rule. You may do better just by using a smaller increment in the 1/3 rule.

The 3/8 rule uses a third-order polynomial (cubic) through four adjacent, equally spaced data points. If the number of data points is n, then the integral I can be approximated as,

$$I \approx \frac{3}{8} \sum_{i=1,4,7,\cdots}^{n-3} (y_i + 3y_{i+1} + 3y_{i+2} + y_{i+3}) \Delta x \ . \tag{5-7}$$

This method is not shown in the workbook INTEGRATION. It is left for you to enjoy doing as a problem. You can learn a lot by tinkering with a workbook, just as you can learn by tinkering with an automobile engine.

Analytical example

Let's do an integral to remind you of the relation of approximate numerical methods to the analytical method of calculus. In the workbook INTEGRATION-101 you should see Figure 5-14, which shows the comparison of three numerical results with the exact result. The exact value of the integral is,

$$I = \int_0^1 \exp(-x) \, dx \ . \tag{5-8}$$

This is an elementary definite integral that we evaluate as,

$$I = \frac{1}{-1} \exp(-x) \, |_0^1 = \frac{1}{-1} \left[\exp(-1) - \exp(0) \right] \ . \tag{5-9}$$

$$I = \frac{1}{-1} [(\exp(-1) - 1)] = 1 - \exp(-1) \approx 0.6321206... \tag{5-10}$$

The value obtained in Eq. (5-10) is used in row 17 of the workbook INTEGRATION-101. This is also shown in Figure 5-10.

For row 28 in Figure 5-13 (workbook INTEGRATION) we only need to change the limits on the integral to get the result for $x = 0$ to $x = 2$:

$$I = \frac{1}{-1} \exp(-x) \, |_0^2 = \frac{1}{-1} \left[\exp(-2) - \exp(0) \right] \approx 0.8646647... \tag{5-11}$$

27		SUM	0.9086184	0.8221519	0.8653852	0.8646652
28		EXACT	0.8646647	0.8646647	0.8646647	0.8646647
29		% ERROR	5.08331945	-4.9166806	0.0833194	0.0000555
30			Left	Right	Trapezoidal	1/3
31			Rectangular	Rectangular		Simpson

Figure 5-14. Comparison of results of four numerical methods of integration with the exact result. Note use of Comments in "EXACT" and "Simpson" cells.

These analytical results are used in Figures 5-10, 5-13, and 5-14 for the "exact" value. The base of natural logarithms e is a transcendental number, so we cannot get perfectly *exact* results even when we use calculus. In the year 2002 the value of e was computed to more than 10^{10} decimal digits. This is usually adequate except for the most demanding users.

Our favorite transcendental number π has held a mystical fascination for people for thousands of years, and it has been computed to more decimal places than e. The award-winning science fiction movie *Pi*, written and directed by Darren Aronofsky, is available from www.Amazon.com.

5.3 Moving average

What is it?
A moving average is a form of integration of a data set over a part of the set, usually a few terms at a time. The standard form of integration has one number as the final result, but a moving average produces a new data set as the final result.

What does it do?
A moving average modifies the original data set, acting like a low-pass electronic filter, because it reduces high frequencies in the original data. In other words, a moving average is a smoothing process that minimizes rapid changes. The downside is that you might miss something important that gets smoothed out. Also, there is a time delay in the output, or a phase shift when processing periodic data. These things will become clear when you use the workbook.

The moving average in EXCEL is a special type that attempts to forecast the value of data points, based on the average over a few previous equally-weighted data points. (Beware of things that attempt to forecast the future.) Later, we'll discuss the usual moving average that does smoothing with adjustable weights with no forecasting.

Who needs it?
You may have noticed that the real world is a noisy, messy place and it produces noisy, messy data. Trying to make sense of noisy data is a science and an art. All engineers and scientists need help in extracting information from noisy data.

Other people use moving averages, too. On the Internet you can see moving averages in charts of stock market prices, coffee prices, and so on.

EXCEL's moving average analysis tool is located in the Analysis ToolPak. The moving average is a good example of a simple use of elementary arithmetic in EXCEL. Click on [Tools][Data Analysis] and you will see the Data Analysis dialog box shown in Fig. 5-15. It is easy to make a moving average tool for your own use, but EXCEL has included some features that are especially convenient.

As we said before, the moving average is based on the average value of the data over a specific number of preceding data points. A moving average provides trend information that a simple average of all historical data would wipe out, because a simple average is a single number.

You can use the moving average to reduce noise in data, forecast sales, inventory, or other trends. See Section 8.8 for the formula used by this tool. Click on the Moving Average in the Data Analysis dialog box and you will see something like Fig. 5-16.

About the Moving Average dialog box

Input Range

Enter the cell reference for the range of data you want to analyze. The range must consist of a single column that contains four or more cells of data.

Labels in First Row

Select if the first row of your input range contains labels. Clear the *check box* if your input range has no labels; EXCEL generates appropriate data labels for the output table.

Interval

Enter the number of values you want to include in the moving average. The default interval is 3.

Output Range

Enter the reference for the upper-left cell of the output table. If you select the Standard Errors check box, EXCEL generates a two-column output table with standard error values in the right column. If there are insufficient historical values to project a forecast or calculate a standard error, EXCEL returns the #N/A error value.

The output range must be on the same worksheet as the data used in the input range, so the New Worksheet Ply and New Workbook options are unavailable.

Chart Output

Select this to generate an embedded histogram chart with the output table.

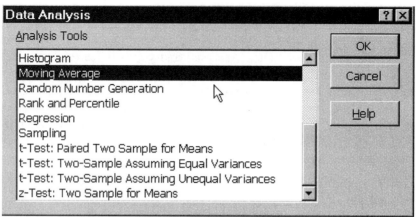

Figure 5-15. Data Analysis dialog box in the [Tools][Data Analysis] menu. Click OK to select Moving Average and see Fig. 5-16.

Standard Errors

Select this if you want to include a column that contains standard error values in the output table. Clear if you want a single-column output table without standard error values.

For more information about options in the Moving Average dialog box, go to Help.

Let's apply EXCEL's moving average to a signal consisting of a triangular pulse and a rectangular pulse. The triangular pulse changes less rapidly (it has less bandwidth) than the rectangular pulse. The result is shown in Fig. 5- for 2-point and 3-point processing. Note that distortions increase as smoothing increases.

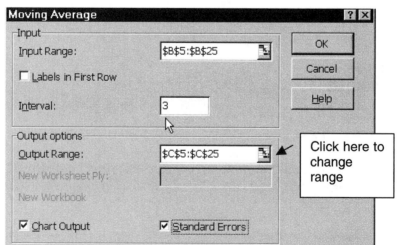

Fig. 5-16. Moving Average dialog box, with Chart Output and Standard Errors selected. Enter the range by typing in the box, or by clicking where indicated.

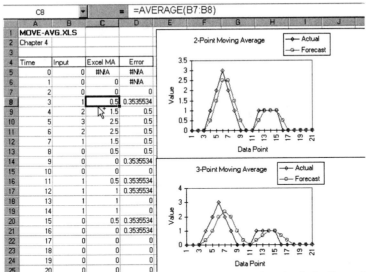

Fig. 5-17. Moving averages using 2-point and 3-point intervals in EXCEL's version of this tool. (This is a forecasting process.) Note Table of Errors in column D.

Next, let's apply this to a segment of a sine wave, shown in Fig. 5-18. The sine segment is a relatively narrow-band signal. Note the phase advance of the forecast data relative to the actual data, and the amplitude decrease.

Now let's see how the moving average looks with the same sine wave segment, but with added random noise. Figure 5-19 shows how the moving average decreases the randomness by reducing high frequencies.

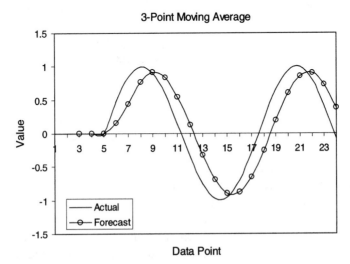

Figure 5-18. EXCEL's Moving Average tool applied to a noiseless sine test signal. Phase shift and amplitude distortion due to smoothing are evident.

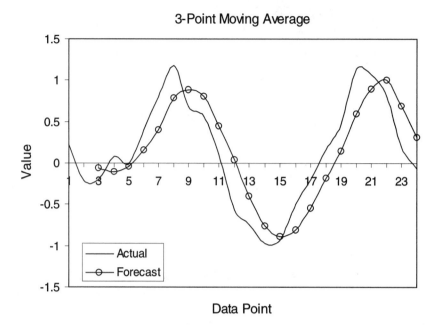

Figure 5-19. These are the same data used in Fig. 5-18, but random noise has been added here. Observe the smoothing action of the moving average, accompanied by the inevitable phase shift and amplitude distortion.

In Fig. 5-19, random noise has been added using RAND()–0.5. This produces a random number between –0 .5 and +0.5. As you view the worksheet with random noise, press Function Key F9. This recalculates the worksheet and produces a new set of random noise. Press F9 repeatedly and observe the action of the moving average. See Section 8.9 for more about the RAND() worksheet function.

✪ Weighted averaging

The moving average in EXCEL is a special case of a *weighted average* process, with equal weights. For equal weights, the moving average is sometimes called a *sliding window* because it is analogous to viewing a small part of a data sequence through a moving window. Equal weight assumes that all points are equally valid, but it often happens that the importance of previous data diminishes as you go back in time, or away from the data point of interest in two- or three-dimensional data.

The weighted average addresses this fact and adjusts the weights so that data close to the point in question have more influence than data that are far away. How should the weights be adjusted? Many people have worked on this, and their names (like Bartlett and Parzen) are attached to the weight set they invented. Weighted averaging is a special type of data filter known as *finite impulse response*, because a finite number of data points are used in computing the data point of interest. (We'll see more about *impulse response* in Chapter 12.) A generic weighted average is given by,

$$y_n = w_1 x_1 + w_2 x_2 + w_3 x_3 + \cdots \tag{5-12}$$

where y_n is the contemporary averaged output, the w_n are the weighting factors, and the x_n are the last n samples of data.

Let's look at some simple examples of Eq. (5-12) for two-point and five-point averaging in the workbook SMOOTH-2. The Home screen of this workbook is shown in Fig. 5-20. At the second data point the two-point equal-weight moving average is,

$$y_2 = 0.5x_1 + 0.5x_2 \; .$$

An example of a two-point weighted average, which gives the earlier value 1/3 of the importance of the contemporary value, is given by,

$$y_2 = 0.25x_1 + 0.75x_2 \; .$$

A five-point equal-weight moving average, at the fifth data point, is

$$y_5 = 0.2x_1 + 0.2x_2 + 0.2x_3 + 0.2x_4 + 0.2x_5 \; .$$

The sum of all weights must be equal to 1, to avoid changes in what can be thought of as "amplification." On the other hand, the sum of the squares of all weights does not need to be 1. The sum of the squares is related to the *variance*.

Variance is a measure of the smoothness of a data series. Variance is usually defined as the square of the *standard deviation* (see EXCEL Help).

The *variance ratio* $VR(n)$ is a measure of the smoothing produced by weighted averaging,

$$VR(n) = \sum_{i=1}^{n} w_i^2 \; . \tag{5-13}$$

The variance ratio is often expressed in decibels,

$$VR_{dB}(n) = 10 \log_{10}[VR(n)] \tag{5-14}$$

or

$$VR_{dB}(n) = 10 \log_{10}\left[\sum_{i=1}^{n} w_i^2\right] \; . \tag{5-14a}$$

	E17	▼		■	=($E$3*D17+$E$4*D16+$E$5*D15)/SUM($E$3:$E$5)				

	A	B	C	D	E	F	G	H	I
1	SMOOTH-2.XLS		Data Smoothing with Weighted Averagers						
2	Chapter 5				Weights	Noise	Noise Amplitude		
3					1	0.023905	0.5		
4					1				
5					1				
6					1				
7					1				
8									
9	VARIANCE	0.183533		0.184664	0.160208	0.153412 0.156655		0.166632	
10			(Press F9)	Signal +	3-Point	Normalization is automatic. See formula in cell E17.		Savitsky-	Savitsky-
11	Time	Signal	Noise	Noise	Moving Av.			Golay 5	Golay 7
12	-5	0	0.044437	0.044437					
13	-4	0	0.183376	0.183376					
14	-3	0	-0.03476	-0.03476					
15	-2	0	0.158693	0.158693					
16	-1	0	0.124971	0.124971					
17	0	0	-0.058	-0.058	0.075222	0.074856	0.028539	-0.00911	
18	1	0	0.018642	0.018642	0.028539	0.041909	0.051408	0.024832	
19	2	0	0.193578	0.193578	0.051408	0.087577	0.148536	0.166971	
20	3	0	0.233389	0.233389	0.148536	0.102517	0.213975	0.234159	
21	4	0	0.214958	0.214958	0.213975	0.120514	0.218153	0.252451	
22	5	0	0.206113	0.206113	0.218153	0.173336	0.086089	0.07856	
23	6	0	-0.1628	-0.1628	0.086089	0.137047	0.089936	0.048319	
24	7	0	0.226497	0.226497	0.089936	0.143631	0.031129	0.028692	
25	8	0	0.029692	0.029692	0.031129	0.102891	0.155358	0.18823	

◄ ◄ ► ►I \ **Main** / 3-BOX / 5-BOX / NonCausal-3 / SG-5 / SG-7 /

Fig. 5-20. Home screen of SMOOTH-2. This worksheet contains several convenient features described in the text. Note variances in row 9. Note Commented cells, indicated by marks in their upper right corners. Place your pointer over the marked cells to read comments.

Let's look at a simple example of the variance ratio for a two-point moving average. For the two-point equal-weight moving average, the variance ratio is

$$VR(2) = 0.5^2 + 0.5^2 = 0.5$$

or in decibels,

$$VR_{dB}(2) = 10 \log_{10}(0.5) = -3.01 \quad dB.$$

As we said before, the downside of using a moving average is that data become distorted, but this is the price you must pay to reduce random noise and interfering signals by this method. This is like a doctor treating a sick patient. The goal is to cure the disease without killing the patient. As you process data, remember the oath of Hippocrates (460 B.C.–377 B.C.): "First, do no harm."

Before we get into this workbook let's digress a moment to review the four types of variance worksheet functions.

TIP
EXCEL computes four types of variances: VAR, VARA, VARP, and VARPA.

VAR worksheet function. VAR estimates variance based on a sample.

Syntax: VAR(number1,number2,...)

number1,number2,...   are 1 to 30 number arguments corresponding to a sample of a population.

VAR assumes that its arguments are a sample of the population. If your data represent the entire population, then compute the variance using VARP.

Logical values such as TRUE and FALSE and text are ignored. If logical values and text must not be ignored, use the **VARA worksheet function**.

VAR uses the formula,

$$\frac{n\sum_i x_i^2 - \left(\sum_i x_i\right)^2}{n(n-1)} \tag{5-15}$$

VARP worksheet function. Based on the whole population, VARP uses the formula,

$$\frac{n\sum_i x_i^2 - \left(\sum_i x_i\right)^2}{n^2} \tag{5-16}$$

so VARP and VAR give almost the same result when $n \gg 1$.

VARPA worksheet function. This combines properties of VARP and VARA. VARPA represents the entire population. As in VARA, logical values such as TRUE and FALSE and text are included.

5.4 Exponential smoothing

EXCEL has an exponential smoothing analysis tool in the Analysis ToolPak. Exponential smoothing is different from the usual weighted average (which uses a finite number of data points) because exponential smoothing uses all of the earlier data, with an adjustable exponential decay time. Exponential smoothing is a special case of the *infinite impulse response* category. The Exponential Smoothing tool takes a little time to work properly, that is, the process has a "learning time." This will become clear as you use the EXP-SMOOTH workbook. The exponential smoothing tool in EXCEL uses the formula given in EXCEL's Help,

$$F_{t+1} = \frac{1}{N}\sum_{j=1}^{N} A_{t-j+1}$$ (5-17)

where F_{t+1} is the future predicted value, and A_t is the current predicted value. Notice that this tool predicts the value at a future point $t + 1$.

In the spreadsheet this formula is implemented as,

$$F_{t+1} = F_t + a(A_t - F_t)$$ (5-18)

where a is the damping factor, A_t is the actual present value, and F_t is the present predicted value. The magnitude of a determines how quickly the processed data respond to changes in the prior data.

Values of 0.2 to 0.3 for a are reasonable damping factors. (The default value is 0.3.) These values indicate that the predicted data point will be adjusted 20 to 30 percent for error in the prior data stream. A smaller constant yields a faster response, but it can produce erratic predictions. A larger constant can result in a long lag in response time and smoothed-out details.

Exponential smoothing is very sensitive to the damping factor. You should vary this parameter with a data set and observe the effects. As in Moving Average, Exponential Smoothing can produce a chart automatically.

Click on [Tools][Data Analysis][Exponential Smoothing] and you should see the dialog box shown in Fig. 5-21. Figure 5-22 is the Home screen of the EXP-SMOOTH workbook; Table 5-3 shows the structure of this workbook.

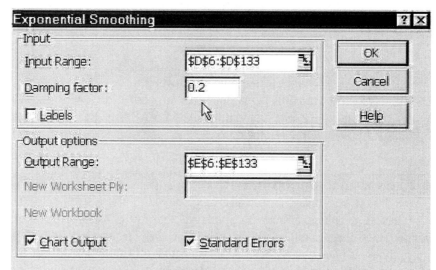

Figure 5-21. Exponential Smoothing dialog box with Chart Output and Standard Errors checked. The Input Range here is noisy data (see Fig. 5-14). Click on the icon by the Input Range and Output Range to select new ranges. Alternatively, type in the range cell address in the boxes, but don't forget the $ signs.

	C10	▾	= =$E$2*(RAND()*1-0.5)						
	A	B	C	D	E	F	G	H	I	J
1	EXP-SMOOTH.XLS			Exponential Smoothing Data Analysis Tool						
2	Chapter 5			Noise	0.5					
3			(Press Function Key F9 to change noise)							
4	VARIANCE:	0.281339		0.297514	0.270612		0.181617		0.184005	
5	Data Point	Data	Noise	Data + Noise	ExpAvg 0.2	Error	ExpAvg 0.7	Error	ExpAvg 0.7	Error
6	0	0	-0.18216	-0.18216	#N/A	#N/A	#N/A	#N/A	#N/A	#N/A
7	1	0	0.108483	0.108483	0	#N/A	0	#N/A	-0.18216	#N/A
8	2	0	0.013639	0.013639	0	#N/A	0	#N/A	-0.09497	#N/A
9	3	0	0.050289	0.050289	0	#N/A	0	#N/A	-0.06239	#N/A
10	4	0	-0.0047	Set noise amplitude in cell E2	0	0	0	0	-0.02858	0.190582
11	5	0	-0.03426		0	0	0	0	-0.02142	0.091399
12	6	0	0.095614	0.	0	0	0	0	-0.02527	0.066911
13	7	0	0.133112	0.133112	0	0	0	0	0.010994	0.071528
14	8	0.247404	-0.1032	0.144202	0	0	0	0	0.047629	0.099484
15	9	0.479426	0.057193	0.536619	0.197923	0.142839	0.074221	0.142839	0.076601	0.113802
16	10	0.681639	-0.20103	0.480613	0.423125	0.216373	0.195782	0.274104	0.214606	0.28039
17	11	0.841471	-0.16982	0.671649	0.629936	0.262857	0.341539	0.392197	0.294408	0.311824

Figure 5-22. Home screen of EXP-SMOOTH. This contains noiseless data in column B, noise in column C, and data + noise in column D. Two damping factors are used on noiseless and noisy data. Note variances in row 4, and formula for random noise in cell C10. Pressing Function Key F9 produces a new set of noise. The formula for noise generation using the RAND() function is shown in the formula editing box. The formula $E$2*(RAND()*1-0.5) generates noise sequences with an amplitude of 0.5 and a zero mean value. Remember to include the empty parentheses when using the RAND() function.

Table 5-3. Structure of the EXP-SMOOTH Workbook.		
Cell	Cell contents	Cell information
E2	Noise amplitude	Number. Typical: 1
B6	Noiseless data	Data supplied by user
C6	Random noise with zero mean value	=$E$2*(RAND()*1-0.5)
D6	Data + noise	=B6+C6
E4	Smoothed noiseless data, $a = 0.2$	Input data from column B
Column F	Standard error, $a = 0.2$	Generated automatically
Column G	Smoothed noiseless data, $a = 0.7$	Input data from column B
Column H	Standard error, $a = 0.7$	Generated automatically
Column I	Smoothed noisy data, $a = 0.7$	Input data from column D
Column J	Standard error, $a = 0.7$	Generated automatically

Use your worksheet to experiment with different values of the damping factor, selected in the Dialog Box shown in Fig. 5-21. The Exponential Smoothing tool automatically writes the formulas, computes standard errors, and plots the chart. Let's get a feeling for how EXCEL implements exponential smoothing. Cell E10 contains the formula,

$$=0.8*B9+0.2*E9$$

which takes 80% of the noiseless data in cell B9 and adds it to 20% of the previous forecast data in cell E9. This is the forecast for cell E10.

EXCEL's Exponential Smoothing tool automatically produces the error estimate in an adjacent column, (columns F, H, and J in Fig. 5-14). For example, in cell F10 you will find the formula,

$$=SQRT(SUMXMY2(B7:B9,E7:E9)/3)$$

which computes the error of the forecast (cell E10) with the actual value (cell B10). Note: SUMXMY2(B2:B5,F2:F5) is a worksheet function that returns the sum of the difference of squares of corresponding values in two arrays (see Help for this function). The square root of the difference of squares, averaged over 3, gives the mean square error.

Figure 5-23 shows an example of smoothed noiseless data, $a = 0.7$. The original signal becomes distorted. These distortions are typical of amplitude and phase errors produced by low-pass filters. Figure 5-24 shows a noiseless signal and the same signal with added noise. Figure 5-25 shows smoothing applied to a noisy signal. Note the variance reduction due to smoothing in your worksheet.

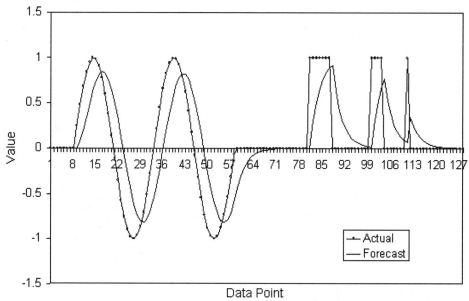

Figure 5-23. Integrating property of smoothing decreases amplitude and shifts phase of sine wave. Note tail of forecast after the actual sine wave stops. The smoother takes time to "learn" and to "forget". Pulses suffer exponential rise and decay, which gets worse with shorter pulses. The last pulse is a single point, a "delta function". The Exponential Smoothing tool acts somewhat like a low-pass filter, except for the forecast property.

Data and Noise

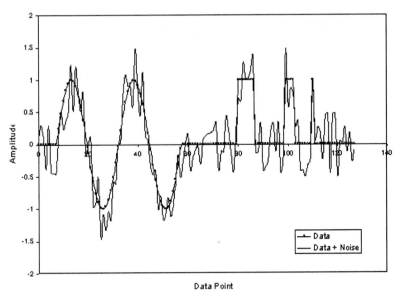

Figure 5-24. This is the same sine wave segment and pulse group shown in Fig. 5-23, but noise has been added. The noisy data are superimposed on the noise-less data. No smoothing is used. Press Function Key F9 to get new noise. The EXP-SMOOTH workbook shows the same data and noise in Figs. 5-23 and 5-24 with exponential smoothing, $a = 0.7$. Row 4 of this workbook shows variances.

✪ Special types of integrators

There are many uses for integrators in software and hardware. For example, some control systems use the integral of the input or the output as a control signal. Un-like the predictive exponential smoothing tool in EXCEL, we are now going to show you how to make a filter that produces a contemporary output y_i (not a pre-dictor) based on exponential averaging of the present input x_i and previous output y_{i-1}. Here, $k = 1/a$ (recall, a is the damping factor for EXCEL's exponential pre-dictive smoothing).

$$y_i = \frac{1}{k}x_i + \left(1 - \frac{1}{k}\right)y_{i-1} .$$ (5-19)

When k is small the exponential averager can track changing signals faster than a rectangular averaging algorithm. After the exponential averager has been running for a number of samples n much greater than k, its variance ratio is given by,

$$VR(k) = \frac{1}{2k-1} \quad \text{for } n \gg k .$$ (5-20)

This is an interesting little filter because it is much simpler to implement in a spreadsheet than a weighted averager, and because it has a *learning time* before it operates effectively. The exponential averager of Eq. (5-19) is also very simple to implement in hardware, because it requires only one storage register.

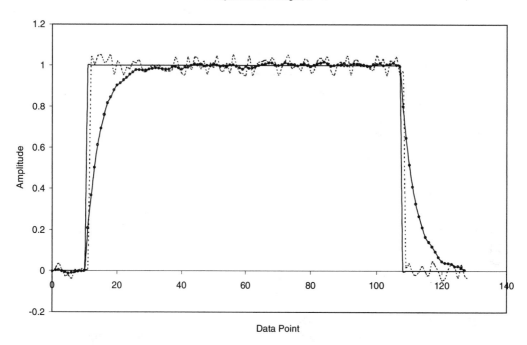

Figure 5-25. Exponential averager applied to a noisy pulse, for *k* = 5. *Dashed line:* noisy pulse. *Markers:* smoothed noisy pulse. *Solid line:* noiseless pulse.

Figure 5-25 shows the result of applying the exponential averager for *k* = 5. This is a *causal* filter, meaning that there is no output before the input starts, but the output persists after the input has stopped. We will examine filters from the FFT perspective in Chapter 12.

5.5 Savitsky-Golay functions

Savitsky-Golay functions were derived to provide a least-mean-square (LMS) error procedure for analyzing spectra, but they are valuable for general use. Although these functions originated in chemistry, they are now in commercial data analysis software and they are often included in electronic instruments. Table 5-4 compares 5-point and 7-point equal-weight and Savitsky-Golay functions (weights are rounded to 4 decimal places). Figures 5-26 and 5-27 show results.

Table 5-4. 5-point and 7-point equal-weight and Savitsky-Golay functions			
Equal-weight 5-point	Savitsky-Golay 5-point	Equal-weight 7-point	Savitsky-Golay 7-point
0.2	−0.0857	0.1429	−0.0952
0.2	0.3429	0.1429	0.1429
0.2	0.4856	0.1429	0.2857
0.2	0.3429	0.1429	0.3332
0.2	−0.0857	0.1429	0.2857
		0.1429	0.1429
		0.1429	−0.0952

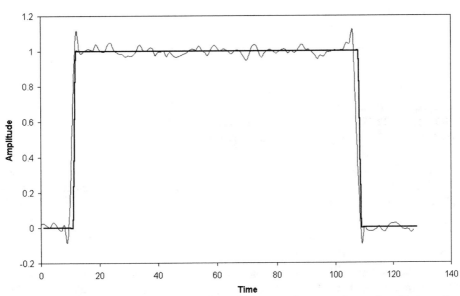

Fig. 5-26. A 5-point Savitsky-Golay function smoothes a noisy pulse. Note spikes near the pulse edges. The spikes are artifacts of the smoothing function. The original noiseless pulse is also shown.

Tip
"Outliers" are parts of data sets that are so far outside of the norm that they are removed by most smoothing operations. Be careful when you smooth experimental data. It could cost you a Nobel prize. Too much smoothing is risky because it discards outliers. Outliers may convey important information.

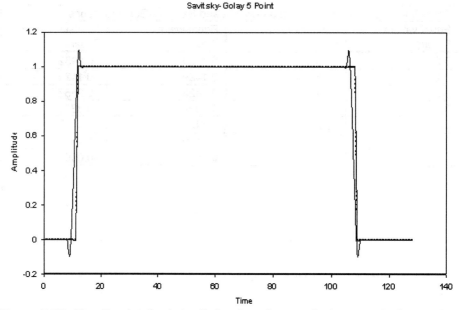

Figure 5-27. The 5-point Savitsky-Golay function applied to a noiseless pulse. Observe the spikes or overshoots at the ends of the pulse, caused by the differentiating property of this function (negative values at the ends). Nevertheless, these functions provide a least-mean-square estimate of a noisy signal.

In 1974 a group from the Stanford Linear Accelerator Center and Lawrence Berkeley Laboratory were conducting a routine study of positron-electron annihilation, as a function of energy. The total energy was incremented in 200 MeV steps and the cross-section was measured at each step. The cross-section was fairly constant except for an outlier near 3.1 GeV that was more than two standard deviations from the mean.

Recall, the probability of finding something more than two standard deviations from the mean value is less than 5 percent. Some people, and many data smoothing processes, would ignore or delete such a data point. The SLAC-LBL group did not ignore it. Careful measurements showed that they had discovered a new particle, now known to be a bound state of a charmed quark and its antiquark. In 1976 the Nobel prize in physics was awarded to Burton Richter and Samuel Chao Chung Ting for this work.

5.6 Using Trendline with noisy data

Analysis of noisy data is a common task that engineers, scientists, and ordinary mortals face every day. There is a vast body of knowledge on the subject of extraction of information from noise, and much of it involves advanced mathematics. If you have a noisy data set that you believe may be generated by a deterministic process then you can try using EXCEL's Trendline option in the Chart Wizard to estimate some of the information. This is quick and easy, and it may be productive. Click on the Chart menu, and then click on Add Trendline.

Let's demonstrate the use of Trendline. Suppose you have a single noisy data set and you believe that there is a deterministic process buried in the noise. Let's consider something simple, such as a mechanical or electrical system returning to its equilibrium state after being disturbed. This could be an automobile shock absorber or an electrical circuit with a characteristic exponential decay.

For an exponential decay process we would like to determine the time for a mechanical system to settle down to $1/e$ of its initial displacement, or for the voltage across the resistor of an RL circuit to settle to $1/e$ of its initial value. Here, e is the base of natural logarithms, 2.71828. . . This characteristic time is called the *time constant* τ (Greek letter tau). In the presence of noise it is difficult to make a measurement of the time constant or obtain a useful value for the integral under the curve over a definite range. Taking a derivative is even worse, because differentiation accentuates the noise. A moving average, exponential smoothing, or other averaging process is not helpful because of the inherent phase shift and amplitude distortion.

In Chapter 3 you learned that EXCEL's Trendline tool enables you to get a best fit of a data set to several model processes including linear, exponential, up to sixth-order polynomial, and power law. Advanced math programs have many more curve-fitting models. Open the TREND-INTEGRAL workbook and let's see how to use it. Figure 5-28 shows the Home screen and Fig. 5-29 shows results.

C9		=RAND()*$C$6-0.5*$C$6				
	A	B	C	D	E	F	G
1	**TREND-INTEGRAL.XLS**			**Using Trendline to Integrate Noisy Data**			
2	Chapter 5		Press Function Key F9 to change noise sequence.				
3			Enter Data:	Manual calculation is ON.			
4		Initial Value	5				
5		Time Constant	0.5				
6		Noise Amplitude	2				
7							
8	TIME	f(t)	Noise	f(t) + Noise			
9	0	5	0.13819	5.138188			
10	0.1	4.75615	-0.13002	4.626128			
11	0.2	4.52419	-0.49195	4.032241			
12	0.3	4.30354	-0.97775	3.325795			
13	0.4	4.09365	-0.01322	4.080431			
14	0.5	3.894	0.56259	4.456589			
15	0.6	3.70409	-0.42967	3.274422			
16	0.7	3.52344	0.63825	4.161693			

Figure 5-28. Home screen of TREND-INTEGRAL. See Section 8.9 for information about the RAND() worksheet function.

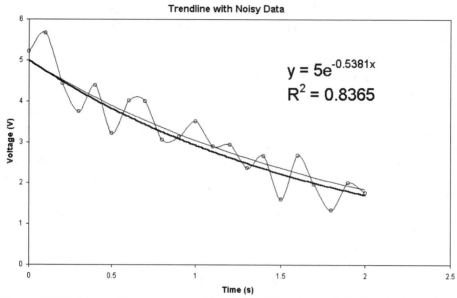

Trendline with Noisy Data

$$y = 5e^{-0.5381x}$$
$$R^2 = 0.8365$$

Figure 5-29. *Line with markers:* noisy data. *Thin line:* original noiseless data. *Thick line:* trendline estimate. The equation of the trendline is shown, together with its R^2 value (goodness of fit). Press Function Key F9 to generate new noise, new trendline, and its equation. Use the equation of the trendline to estimate the integral and derivative with analytical calculus.

This workbook generates a model noiseless exponential decay with a select-able time constant. The noise is added using EXCEL's RAND() function. The RAND() function generates a random number between 0 and 1. This is actually a *pseudo-random* number generator (to statisfy mathematicians). If you can invent a perfect random number generator you will become rich and famous, but it may be easier and quicker to eliminate all poverty and disease in the world.

5.7 Moments to remember

In *Sartor Resartus III* Thomas Carlyle (1795–1881) wrote, "It is a mathematical fact that the casting of this pebble from my hand alters the center of gravity of the universe." This quotation can be found at the St. Andrew's University web site, http://www-groups.dcs.st-and.ac.uk/~history/Quotations/Carlyle.html.
    Carlyle's statement is false. The center of gravity (actually the center of mass) does not change, but the mass *distribution* changes. According to New-ton's laws of motion *only external forces* can move the center of mass of a sys-tem. Only internal forces existed between Carlyle and the pebble. This is similar to a rocket and its exhaust (see Section 3.7).

FAQ

Q. *What is the center of mass?*
A. The center of mass represents the location of a point particle with the same mass as the entire spatially distributed mass. For equilibrium and translational motion the center of mass acts as if all of the system's mass were concentrated at that point. The center of mass is associated with the *first moment* of the mass distribution. See Equation (5-26). The center of mass of an object is similar to the geometric concept of *centroid* of an area or volume (see Internet references at the end of this Chapter).

Q. *Why do we want to compute the center of mass?*
A. The location of the center of mass is important in kinematics and dynamics because it simplifies description and analysis. For example, combined translation and rotation can be separated into two parts: translation of the center of mass and rotation about the center of mass. Furthermore, engineering tables of *moments of inertia* for common objects such as I-beams are computed for axes through the center of mass. Using the *parallel-axis transfer theorem* it is easy to find the moments of inertia about any other set of parallel axes. A moment of inertia is at its minimum value when referred to axes through the center of mass. The center of mass and centroid of area are useful for computing the area, volume, and mass of a solid of revolution using the theorems of Pappus of Alexandria (see Internet references at the end of this Chapter).

Q. *What is the difference between center of mass and center of gravity?*
A. Some people use these terms interchangeably, but they are basically different. The center of mass is independent of <u>any</u> gravitational field, but the location of the center of gravity depends on the uniformity of the local gravitational field. In a uniform field both centers are located at the same point. This will become clear when you study torque and static equilibrium. Gravity gradient stabilization is often used for Earth satellites.

Distributions and moments

The total mass M is the sum of all N individual masses m in the distribution,

$$M = \sum_{i=1}^{N} m_i \tag{5-21}$$

The moments of a distribution can be expressed in a uniform way. First, the total mass can be written as the *zero moment* of the distribution:

$$Mx^0 = \sum_{i=1}^{N} m_i \, x_i^0 . \tag{5-22}$$

Any moment can be written as:

$$Mx^n = \sum_{i=1}^{N} m_i \, x_i^n \, .$$

(5-23)

A moment to remember

The *first moment* of a one-dimensional mass distribution determines the center of mass referred to an arbitrary coordinate system:

$$M \, \overline{x} = \sum_{i=1}^{N} m_i \, x_i \, .$$

(5-24)

The first moment is simply the average value of all masses times their respective displacements from an arbitrary axis. In other words,

$$\overline{x} = \frac{\displaystyle\sum_{i=1}^{N} m_i x_i}{\displaystyle\sum_{i=1}^{N} m_i} \, .$$

(5-25)

Equation (5-25) states that if the entire mass M were located at the center of mass $\overline{x}$ then this would be equivalent to the sum of all products of each mass m_i times its displacement x_i. It is often useful to choose axes through the center of mass. For a three-dimensional mass distribution the location of the center of mass is given by,

$$\overline{x} = \frac{\displaystyle\sum_{i=1}^{N} m_i x_i}{M} \qquad \overline{y} = \frac{\displaystyle\sum_{i=1}^{N} m_i y_i}{M} \qquad \overline{z} = \frac{\displaystyle\sum_{i=1}^{N} m_i z_i}{M} \, .$$

(5-26)

Example

Figure 5-31 shows two choices for elements of area in a plane triangle and the distances of the elements from coordinate axes. Mechanical properties of elementary shapes were investigated thousands of years ago for practical reasons. For example, Archimedes built large military machines for defense against Roman ships, and the machines had to be stable in the presence of strong winds.

In Figure 5-30 we can use analytical calculus because the equation of the triangle is known, $y(x) = -x + 1$. It is often convenient to transform a mass integration into a space integration. Let the mass density of the area be ρ kg/m^2. Recall, area mass density is $\rho = dm/dA$.

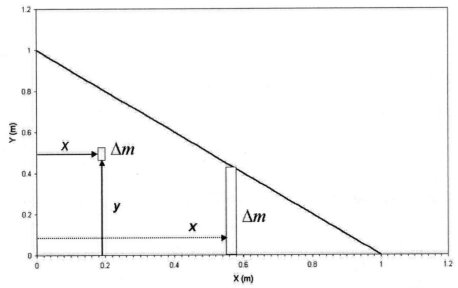

Figure 5-30. *Left:* a rectangular mass element of a triangle is shown with its co-ordinates. *Right:* a vertical strip mass element is used to compute $\bar{x}$. This Figure was composed in EXCEL using the Drawing Tool.

Now we can write the total mass (zero moment) as,

$$M = \int dm = \int \rho\, dA = \int \rho\, y\, dx \qquad (5\text{-}27)$$

where $dA = y\, dx$ is the area of the vertical strip. For the *x*-coordinate of the center of mass we now have,

$$\bar{x} = \frac{\int x \rho\, y\, dx}{\int \rho\, y\, dx}. \qquad (5\text{-}28)$$

Let's consider the simple case where the density is constant. Then the density can come out of the integrals in Eq. (5-28) and cancel. For the triangular area of Fig. 5-30 we now have,

$$\bar{x} = \frac{\int_0^1 x(-x+1)\, dx}{\int_0^1 (-x+1)\, dx} = \frac{1}{3}. \qquad (5\text{-}29)$$

By symmetry of this triangle we can see that $\bar{y} = 1/3$ also. The $\bar{y}$ of a non-symmetrical shape can be calculated using horizontal strips. Polar, cylindrical, and spherical polar coordinates can simplify computation for objects appropriate to these symmetries.

Tip

The center of mass of an arbitrary shape and density variation can be located experimentally by hanging the object from one point and then from another point and using a plumb bob. The plumb lines cross at the center of mass. This was known in ancient times, but the center of mass was generally known as the center of gravity because there was no distinction between mass and weight.

Figure 5-30 can also be used for computing moments of inertia, the second moments:

$$I_{yy} = \sum_{i=1}^{N} m_i \, x_i^2 \quad \text{and} \quad I_{xx} = \sum_{i=1}^{N} m_i \, y_i^2 . \tag{5-30}$$

Using the vertical strip, the moment of inertia with respect to the y-axis is,

$$I_{yy} = \int x^2 dm = \int x^2 \rho \, dA = \int_0^1 x^2 \rho \, y \, dx \tag{5-31}$$

$$I_{yy} = \int_0^1 x^2 \rho(-x+1) \, dx \tag{5-32}$$

Computing the moment of inertia with respect to the x-axis I_{xx} is left for you to enjoy. By symmetry in this case I_{xx} must be the same as I_{yy} but you should prove this by doing the integral using horizontal strips. Then you will be prepared to do it for non-symmetric shapes. The moment of inertia is a little more complicated than we have shown. Actually, it is a tensor that can be represented by a 3×3 matrix (see Section 6.6). The moment of inertia that we computed is one of the three diagonal components of the tensor, but don't worry about this now.

FAQ

Q. *Why do we need the second moments?*
A. Second moments arise <u>naturally</u> when we analyze rotational kinetic energy, angular momentum, torque, and the rate of change of angular momentum. Second moments are also of fundamental importance in analyzing the bending of beams. "Dynamic balancing" of an automobile wheel involves adjusting the second moment to minimize wobble.

Tip

Moments of inertia of common objects are usually tabulated with respect to co-ordinate systems through the center of mass. You can use the *parallel axis trans-fer theorem* (or *Steiner's theorem*) to find the moment of inertia about any other parallel axis. The theorem states that $I = I_{cm} + Md^2$ where I_{cm} is the moment of inertia with respect to the center of mass axis, M is the mass of the object, and d is the distance of the new axis from the center-of-mass axis. It is clear that the moment of inertia is always a minimum when referred to the center of mass.

Now let's look at the MOMENTS workbook to estimate first and second moments using numerical integration. Figure 5-31 shows the Home screen.

In column C of the MOMENTS workbook the area of the triangle is estimated by numerical integration using the trapezoidal method. In column D the mass is the product of the area × thickness × mass density. The trapezoidal method gives exact results here because we are integrating a straight line.

In Figure 5-31 the moment of inertia I_{yy} is computed by its definition, Eq. (5-30) using vertical strips.

G11		=D11*B11^2/3								
	A	B	C	D	E	F	G	H	I	J
1	**MOMENTS.XLS**		Zero, First and Second Moments of a Mass Distribution							
2	Chapter 5									
3							Report:		Exact:	% Error:
4	Enter mass density:		4500 kg/m³			Mass	22.5 kg		22.5	0.0000
5		Thickness:	0.01 m		Center of mass		0.3333 m		0.33333	-0.0100
6						I_{yy}	3.749625 kg m²		3.75	-0.0100
7						I_{xx}	3.750375 kg m²		3.75	0.0100
8					$\bar{x}$					
9					Center of					
10	X (m)	Y (m)	Area	Mass (kg)	Mass (m)	I_{yy} (kg m²)	I_{xx} (kg m²)			
11	0	1	0.005	0.225	0	0	0.075			
12	0.01	0.99	0.0099	0.4455	0.00446	4.5E-05	0.1455449			Mass Distribution
13	0.02	0.98	0.0098	0.441	0.00882	0.00018	0.1411788			
14	0.03	0.97	0.0097	0.4365	0.0131	0.00039	0.136901			
15	0.04	0.96	0.0096	0.432	0.01728	0.00069	0.1327104			
16	0.05	0.95	0.0095	0.4275	0.02138	0.00107	0.1286063			
17	0.06	0.94	0.0094	0.423	0.02538	0.00152	0.1245876			
18	0.07	0.93	0.0093	0.4185	0.0293	0.00205	0.1206536		dm	
19	0.08	0.92	0.0092	0.414	0.03312	0.00265	0.1168032			
20	0.09	0.91	0.0091	0.4095	0.03686	0.00332	0.1130357			
21	0.1	0.9	0.009	0.405	0.0405	0.00405	0.10935			
22	0.11	0.89	0.0089	0.4005	0.04406	0.00485	0.1057454			

Figure 5-31. The trapezoidal method is used to estimate the area. The parallel axis transfer theorem is used to estimate I_{xx} using the vertical strip mass element (see text). The center of mass is located at coordinates $x = 1/3$, $y = 1/3$.

An alternative calculation could have been done for I_{xx} using horizontal strips, but instead of this we have used the parallel axis transfer theorem with the same vertical strips used for I_{yy}. It is known – and you can show – that the moment of inertia of a thin rod about its center of mass is $ML^2/12$. If we translate the axis by a distance $L/2$ then the moment of inertia about the end of the rod is given by $ML^2/3$. As shown in Fig. 5-32 the formula in cell G11 is `=D11*B11^2/3`.

The first moment of objects was studied thousands of years ago because people were concerned with balancing objects and structures. Archimedes found that the center of gravity of uniform triangles corresponds to the point where the medians intersect. Figure 5-32 shows "The Law of Archimedes" $F_1 x_1 = F_2 x_2$, where F_i is the force (weight) at position x_i.

Figure 5-31. The "Law of Archimedes" is a formula that changed the face of the earth. This equation is the second condition of static equilibrium: the sum of the torques about any point is zero. A torque is a vector that is the first moment of a force.

The stamp at the left shows Archimedes using the second condition of static equilibrium to measure the volume density of a submerged object. It is said that he used this method to determine if the King's crown was pure gold.

(The first condition of equilibrium is $\Sigma \vec{F} = 0$. The sum of the forces at any point is zero.)

What's next?

EXCEL has a large collection of operators and functions called *Engineering Functions*. These functions are much more general than the name implies. We'll explore these functions in Chapter 6. In Chapter 12 you can see the *RC* integrator from the perspective of the Fourier transform in the frequency domain.

References

Galactic Industries Corporation has a discussion of topics in this chapter at their website,

http://www.galactic.com/galactic/Science/smooth.htm

P. A. Gorry, "General least-squares smoothing and differentiation by the convolution (Savitzky-Golay) Method," *Analytical Chemistry* **62**, 570–573 (1990).

J. Steiner, Y. Termonia, and J. Deltour, "Comments on smoothing and differentiation of data by simplified least square procedure," *Analytical Chemistry* **44**, No. 11, 1906–1909 (1972).

A. Savitsky and M. J. E. Golay, "Smoothing and differentiation of data by simplified least squares procedures," *Analytical Chemistry* **36**, 1627–1639 (1964).

B. Porat, *A Course in Digital Signal Processing* (John Wiley & Sons, Inc., New York, 1997).

S. K. Mitra and J. F. Kaiser, editors, *Handbook for Digital Signal Processing* (John Wiley & Sons, Inc., New York, 1993).

W. H. Press and S. A. Teukolsky, "Savitsky-Golay smoothing filters," *Computers in Physics* **4**, 689–672 (1990).

H. W. Schussler and P. Steffen, Chapter 8 in *Advanced Topics in Signal Processing*, edited by J. S. Lim and A. V. Oppenheim (Prentice Hall, Englewood Cliffs, NJ, 1988).

Mechanical integrator. A planimeter is an instrument used to determine the area of a region in the plane by tracing around its boundary. Modern planimeters are digital and connect to computers. The mechanical planimeter was invented by Jacob Amsler (1835–1912). You can find more about the planimeter and antique computers at the Computer Museum, University of Amsterdam, The Netherlands. Go to: http://www.wins.uva.nl/faculteit/museum/planimeter/plani.html

Centroid of a triangle:
http://mathworld.wolfram.com/CentroidTriangle.html

Centroids and the theorems of Pappus of Alexandria:
http://mathworld.wolfram.com/PappussCentroidTheorem.html

Test your skills

1. Rectangular integration. Integrate $1/x$ from 1 to 2 using 10 intervals. Each rectangle has a width of 0.1. Start at $x = 1$, so the numerical approximation looks like $I = 0.1(1/1 + 1/1.1 + 1/1.2 + \ldots +1/1.9)$. What is the percent error based on the exact value of the integral? Hint: do the integral

$$I = \int_1^2 \frac{dx}{x}$$

2. Do Exercise 1 using 20 intervals. Note improvement with smaller increments. What is the percent error?

3. Exercises 1 and 2 overestimate the true value of the integral because they use *outer* rectangles. Do Exercise 1 again, but now start at $x = 1.1$ so you will end at $x = 2$. In other words, use the numerical approximation $I = 0.1(1/1.1 + 1/1.2 + 1/1.3 + \ldots +1/2)$. Compare with Exercise 1. This underestimates the true value of the integral because it uses *inner* rectangles. Make a drawing to show this. Compute the percent error based on the true value of the integral.

4. Calculate the average value of the results of Exercises 1 and 3. How does the average value of the overestimate and underestimate compare with the true value? Compute percent error. Note: using the average value is equivalent to using the trapezoidal rule.

5. Trapezoidal rule. Open the workbook named TRAPEZOID. This contains discrete samples of the continuous function $\exp(-x)$. Compute the integral of this function for $0 \le x \le 1$ using 25 intervals. Repeat for 50 intervals. What is the error in each case compared to the true value of the integral?

6. Calculate the square root of the mean square of $\sin(\pi x)$ in the range 0 to 1. This is an important number; it is called the root-mean-square or r.m.s. value of the data. This is equivalent to asking "What is the constant voltage that will produce the same heating effect as the time-varying voltage?" Confirm that your result in Question 5 is the area of a rectangle with a height of $0.5\sqrt{2}$ and a width of 1. In other words, the r.m.s. value of a sine wave is approximately

0.707106781. The r.m.s. value of the voltage at a home electric outlet is 120 V. What is the maximum value of the voltage at the outlet?

7. Simpson's 1/3 rule. Repeat Question 5 using this integration rule for 50 intervals. (Remember, this rule requires an even number of intervals.) How does this compare with the trapezoidal rule?

8. Moving average. Table 5-5 contains a re-cord of observed sun spots. Compute the moving average of these data, using periods of 2 and 4 months. Planet Earth is smaller than this typical sun spot.

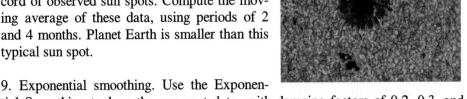

9. Exponential smoothing. Use the Exponential Smoothing tool on the sun spot data, with damping factors of 0.2, 0.3, and 0.5.

10. Exponential smoothing. The unit step function is a common test signal for mechanical, electric, and electronic systems. This test signal is designated as $u(t)$ with the property that $u(t) = 0$ for $t < 0$ and $u(t) = 1$ for $t > 0$. You can start $u(t)$ at any time t_o by using $u(t - t_o)$. Compose a worksheet with time increments of 0.1 (starting at $t = -1$) in column A, the unit step in column B, and exponential smoothing with damping factors of 0.2, 0.4, and 0.6 in columns C, D, and E. This test shows how smoothing distorts the original data.

11. Use the Moving Average tool with periods of 2, 4, and 6 on the unit step.

12. Test the equal weight and Savitsky-Golay functions in Table 5-4 with a unit step function $u(t) = 1$ for $t \geq 0$; $u(t) = 0$ otherwise.

13. Apply the Savitsky-Golay 5-point and 7-point functions to the sun spot data in Table 5-5. Compare with results of Questions 9 and 10.

Table 5-5. Observed Relative Sun Spot Numbers (see SUNSPOTS workbook)									
Year									
Month	1954	1955	1956	1957	1958	1959	1960	1961	1962	1963
1	0.2	23.1	73.6	165	202.5	217.4	143.6	57.9	38.7	19.8
2	0.5	20.8	124	130.2	164.9	143.1	106	46.1	50.3	24.4
3	10.9	4.9	118.4	157.4	190.7	185.7	102.2	53	45.6	17.1
4	1.8	11.3	110.7	175.2	196	163.3	122	61.4	46.6	29.3
5	0.8	28.9	136.6	164.6	175.5	172	119.6	51	43.7	43
6	0.2	31.7	116.6	200.7	171.5	168.7	110.2	77.4	42	35.9
7	4.8	26.7	129.1	187.2	191.4	149.6	121.7	70.2	21.8	19.6

Table 5-5, continued										
Month	*1954*	*1955*	*1956*	*1957*	*1958*	*1959*	*1960*	*1961*	*1962*	*1963*
8	8.4	40.7	169.6	158	200.2	199.6	134.1	55.8	21.8	33.2
9	1.5	42.7	173.2	235.8	201.2	145.2	127.2	63.6	51.3	38.8
10	7.0	58.5	155.3	253.8	181.5	111.4	82.2	37.7	39.5	35.3
11	9.2	89.2	201.3	210.9	152.3	124	89.6	32.6	26.9	23.4
12	7.6	76.9	192.1	239.4	187.6	125	85.6	39.9	23.2	14.9

Also see M. Waldmeir, *The Sunspot Activity in the Years 1610–1960*, (Schulthess, Zurich, 1961). The relative sun spot numbers are corrected for grouping of spots and viewing conditions of various observers who contributed to the data; this is why the sun spot numbers are not integers.

For updates, go to the home page of the Royal Observatory of Belgium, World Data Center-C1 for Sunspot Index:

http://www.oma.be/KSB-ORB/SIDC/index.html

Also, look at the National Solar Observatory (Sacramento Peak and Kitt Peak) home page: http://www.nso.noao.edu/index.html

For more about solar cycles go to: http://www.dxlc.com/solar/cycl1_20.html

14. ✪ Monte Carlo integration. Download the MONTE-CARLO workbook from this book's web site and explore the cells to learn how an approximate integral can be obtained using random numbers to generate random vectors. This workbook computes an approximate value of π using random vectors radiating from the origin to find the area of a circle of radius 1 inscribed in a square with area 4. The ratio of the number of vectors in the circle to the total number of vectors is $\pi/4$. So, counting the vectors gives an estimate of the area of the circle, and an estimate of $\pi/4$. The spreadsheet IF function is used to count the vectors. How many vectors are needed to compute π to 6 decimal places?

For more information, see S. C. Bloch and R. Dressler, "Statistical estimation of π using random vectors," *American Journal of Physics* **67** (4) 298–303 (1999). This paper contains details, background, and references for the Monte Carlo method of numerical integration. For extraordinary facts about π go to http://www.users.globalnet.co.uk/~nickjh/Pi.htm . Also, do an Internet search for "Monte Carlo integration".

. . . it leads us to the point where we can obtain numerical values, a necessary property of any such method, without which we obtain nothing but useless formal transformations.

Jean Baptiste Joseph Fourier
In *Théorie Analytique de la Chaleur* (1822)

Chapter 6
Engineering Functions

What this chapter is about

EXCEL has a useful collection named *engineering functions*. This is what they are named in Help, but these functions are more general than the name implies. We will explore the most common ones in this chapter. They comprise four categories:

- mathematical and statistical functions,

- functions for working with complex numbers,

- functions for converting values between different numbering systems, such as decimal, hexadecimal, octal, and binary systems,

- functions for converting values between different systems of measurement.

You will find the engineering functions in the Analysis ToolPak. If an engineering worksheet function is not available, run the Setup program to install the Analysis ToolPak. After you install the Analysis ToolPak, you must enable it by using the Add-Ins command on the Tools menu. For more information about how to install the Analysis ToolPak, consult Help or press Function Key F1 in EXCEL. We will also explore the matrix operations and applications in EXCEL.

6.1 Special Mathematical functions

Brief descriptions of EXCEL's special mathematical functions are listed in Table 6-1. The functions are described in detail after the Table.

EXCEL contains four types of Bessel functions. Some students think these functions were created to make life difficult. You probably won't need Bessel functions until you are doing advanced work involving circular or cylindrical boundary values, but later you may be surprised how often they appear in electrical and mechanical engineering, physics, chemistry, geophysics, and astronomy, to name a few. Entire books have been written about Bessel functions. You should be aware that there are also things called *spherical Bessel functions*; these can be found in math programs like MATHEMATICA and MATLAB.

Table 6-1. Special Mathematical Functions in EXCEL	
BESSELI	returns the modified Bessel function, which is equivalent to the Bessel function evaluated for a purely imaginary argument
BESSELJ	returns the Bessel function
BESSELK	The n-th order modified Bessel function
BESSELY	returns the Bessel function, which is also called the Weber function or the Neumann function
DELTA	tests whether two numbers are equal; the Kronecker delta function
ERF	the error function, integrated between two limits
EFRC	returns the complementary ERF function integrated between x and infinity
GESTEP	returns 1 if number ≥ step; returns 0 (zero) otherwise. Use this function to filter a set of values. For example, by summing several GESTEP functions you count values that exceed a threshold.

BESSELI

Returns the modified Bessel function $I_n(x)$, which is equivalent to the Bessel function $J_n(x)$ evaluated for purely *imaginary* arguments. (See BESSELJ. Also see Chapter 10 for more about imaginary numbers.)

Syntax

BESSELI(x,n)

x is the value at which to evaluate the function.

n is the order of the Bessel function. If n is not an integer, it is truncated.

Remarks

If x is nonnumeric, BESSELI returns the #VALUE! error value.

If n is nonnumeric, BESSELI returns the #VALUE! error value.

If n < 0, BESSELI returns the #NUM! error value.

The n-th order modified Bessel function of the variable x is:

Example

BESSELI(1.5, 1) equals 0.981666   (Note that 1.5 is imaginary and $n = 1$.)

Definition

$$I_n(x) = (i)^{-n} J_n(ix) \tag{6-1}$$

BESSELJ

Returns the Bessel function. (This is type you'll probably use most often.)

Syntax

BESSELJ(x,n)

x is the value at which to evaluate the function.

n is the order of the Bessel function. If n is not an integer, it is truncated.

Remarks

If x is nonnumeric, BESSELJ returns the #VALUE! error value.

If n is nonnumeric, BESSELJ returns the #VALUE! error value.

If n < 0, BESSELJ returns the #NUM! error value.

Definition   (Aren't you glad you have a spreadsheet to do this?)

The n-th order Bessel function of the variable x is:

$$J_n(x) = \sum_{k=0}^{\infty} \frac{(-1)^k}{k!\Gamma(n+k+1)} \left(\frac{x}{2}\right)^{n+2k} \qquad (6\text{-}2)$$

where $\Gamma(n+k+1) = \int_0^\infty e^{-x} x^{n+k}\, dx$ is the Gamma function.

Example

BESSELJ(1.9, 2) equals 0.329926

Use the workbook BESSEL to explore the four Bessel functions for different values of *n*. The Bessel function $J_1(x)$ or BESSELJ(x,1) is shown in Fig. 6-1. Figure 6-2 shows $J_{11}(x)$ for the same range.

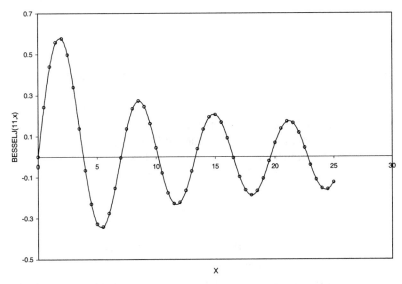

Figure 6-1. The function BESSELJ(x,1) for $0 \le x \le 25$. This looks somewhat like a damped sine wave, but it isn't. See the definition, Eq. (6-2).

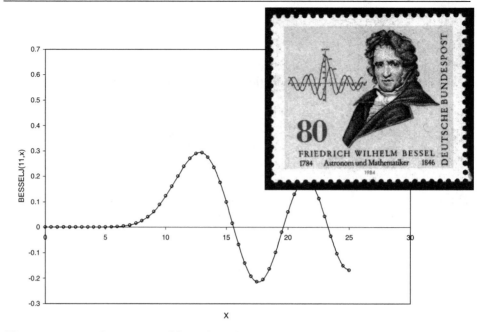

Figure 6-2. The function BESSELJ(x,11) for $0 \le x \le 25$. The graph on the postage stamp shows the real and imaginary parts of the Fourier transform of a rectangular pulse that starts at 0 in the time domain (see Chapter 11 on the CD).

BESSELK
Returns the modified Bessel function, which is equivalent to the Bessel functions evaluated for purely imaginary arguments.

Syntax
BESSELK(x,n)
x is the value at which to evaluate the function.
n is the order of the function. If n is not an integer, it is truncated.

Remarks
If x is nonnumeric, BESSELK returns the #VALUE! error value.
If n is nonnumeric, BESSELK returns the #VALUE! error value.
If n < 0, BESSELK returns the #NUM! error value.
The n-th order modified Bessel function of the variable x is:

$$K_n(x) = \frac{\pi}{2} i^{n+1} [J_n(ix) + iY_n(ix)] \qquad (6\text{-}3)$$

where J_n and Y_n are the J and Y Bessel functions, respectively.

$[J_n(ix) + iY_n(ix)]$ is often called the Hankel function of the first kind. The argument of the function can be real or imaginary. The Hankel function of the second kind is $[J_n(ix) - iY_n(ix)]$.

Example

BESSELK(1.5, 1) equals 0.277388

BESSELY

Returns the BesselY function, which is also called the Weber function or the Neumann function.

Syntax

BESSELY(x,n)

x is the value at which to evaluate the function.

n is the order of the function. If n is not an integer, it is truncated.

Remarks

If x is nonnumeric, BESSELY returns the #VALUE! error value.

If n is nonnumeric, BESSELY returns the #VALUE! error value.

If n < 0, BESSELY returns the #NUM! error value.

Definition

The n-th order Bessel function $Y_n(x)$ is:

$$Y_n(x) = \lim_{v \to n} \frac{J_v(x)\cos(v\pi) - J_{-v}(x)}{\sin(v\pi)} \qquad (6\text{-}4)$$

Example

BESSELY(2.5, 1) equals 0.145918

Tip

Like sines and cosines, Bessel functions are *orthogonal functions*. So, they are useful for series representations, like Fourier series (see Section 4.4). You'll find Bessel functions used extensively in acoustics, mechanics, electromagnetics, and quantum mechanics where circular or cylindrical boundary values are present.

The zeroes of the Bessel functions are important because they determine natural frequencies of systems, like the zeroes of sines and cosines determine the natural frequencies in rectangular coordinates. When you play tennis, baseball, soccer, or basketball you're using Bessel functions, whether you know it or not.

DELTA

DELTA tests whether two values are equal. It returns 1 if number1 = number2; and it returns 0 otherwise. Use this function to filter a set of values.

For example, by summing several DELTA functions you calculate the count of equal pairs. This function is also known as the Kronecker Delta function.

Syntax

DELTA(number1,number2)

number1 is the first number.

number2 is the second number. If omitted, number2 is assumed to be zero.

Remarks

If number1 is nonnumeric, DELTA returns the #VALUE! error value.

If number2 is nonnumeric, DELTA returns the #VALUE! error value.

Examples

DELTA(5, 4) equals 0

DELTA(5, 5) equals 1

DELTA(0.5, 0) equals 0

ERF

ERF returns the error function integrated between lower_limit and upper_limit.

Syntax

ERF(lower_limit,upper_limit)

Lower_limit is the lower bound for integrating ERF.

Upper_limit is the upper bound for integrating ERF. If omitted, ERF integrates between zero and lower_limit.

Remarks

If lower_limit is nonnumeric, ERF returns the #VALUE! error value.

If lower_limit is negative, ERF returns the #NUM! error value.

If upper_limit is nonnumeric, ERF returns the #VALUE! error value.

If upper_limit is negative, ERF returns the #NUM! error value.

Definition

$$ERF(z) = \frac{2}{\sqrt{\pi}} \int_0^z e^{-t^2} dt \qquad (6\text{-}5)$$

and

$$ERF(a,b) = \frac{2}{\sqrt{\pi}} \int_a^b e^{-t^2} dt = ERF(b) - ERF(a) \qquad (6\text{-}6)$$

Examples

ERF(0.74500) equals 0.70793

ERF(1) equals 0.84270

EFRC

ERFC returns the complementary ERF function, integrated between x and infinity.

Syntax

ERFC(x)

x is the lower bound for integrating ERF.

Remarks

If x is nonnumeric, ERFC returns the #VALUE! error value.

If x is negative, ERFC returns the #NUM! error value.

Definition

$$ERFC(x) = \frac{2}{\sqrt{\pi}} \int_x^\infty e^{-t^2}\, dt = 1 - ERF(x) \qquad (6\text{-}7)$$

Example

ERFC(1) equals 0.1573

GESTEP

GESTEP returns 1 if number ≥ step; it returns 0 (zero) otherwise. You can use this function to filter a set of values. For example, by summing several GESTEP functions you can count the number of values that exceed a selected threshold.

Syntax

GESTEP(number,step)

Number is the value to test against step.

Step is the threshold value. If you omit a value for step, GESTEP uses zero.

Remark

If any argument is nonnumeric, GESTEP returns the #VALUE! error value.

Examples

GESTEP(5, 4) equals 1

GESTEP(5, 5) equals 1

GESTEP(−4,−5) equals 1

GESTEP(−1, 0) equals 0

6.2 Complex functions

EXCEL has 18 functions that make complex math easy and convenient. This requires a lot of explanation and examples, so we'll do this in Chapter 10. Examples are the best way to understand these functions. If you can't wait, go there now.

6.3 Number conversion functions

EXCEL has 12 functions that let you convert values into different number systems. We'll show the details of binary-to-decimal, binary-to-hexadecimal, and binary-to-octal functions; see Help for the others. The 12 functions are:

BIN2DEC
BIN2HEX
BIN2OCT
DEC2BIN
DEC2HEX
DEC2OCT
HEX2BIN
HEX2DEC
HEX2OCT
OCT2BIN
OCT2DEC
OCT2HEX

BIN2DEC

BIN2DEC converts a binary number to a decimal number.

Syntax

BIN2DEC(number)

Number is the binary number you want to convert. Number cannot contain more than 10 characters (10 bits). The *most significant bit* of number is the sign bit. The remaining 9 bits are magnitude bits. Negative numbers are represented using two's-complement notation.

Remark

If number is not a valid binary number, or if number contains more than 10 characters (10 bits), BIN2DEC returns the #NUM! error value.

Examples

BIN2DEC(1100100) equals 100.

BIN2DEC(1111111111) equals –1 (The sign is the most significant bit.)

BIN2HEX

BIN2HEX converts a binary number to hexadecimal number.

Syntax

BIN2HEX(number,places)

Number is the binary number you want to convert. Number cannot contain more than 10 characters (10 bits). The most significant bit of number is the sign bit. The remaining 9 bits are magnitude bits. Negative numbers are represented using two's-complement notation.

Places is the number of characters to use. If places is omitted, BIN2HEX uses the minimum number of characters necessary. Places is useful for padding the return value with leading 0s (zeros).

Remarks

If number is not a valid binary number, or if number contains more than 10 characters (10 bits), BIN2HEX returns the #NUM! error value.

If number is negative, BIN2HEX ignores places and returns a 10-character hexadecimal number.

If BIN2HEX requires more than places characters, it returns the #NUM! error value.

If places is not an integer, it is truncated.

If places is nonnumeric, BIN2HEX returns the #VALUE! error value.

If places is negative, BIN2HEX returns the #NUM! error value.

Examples

BIN2HEX(11111011, 4) equals 00FB

BIN2HEX(1110) equals E

BIN2HEX(1111111111) equals FFFFFFFFFF

BIN2OCT

BIN2OCT converts a binary number to an octal number.

Syntax

BIN2OCT(number,places)

Number is the binary number you want to convert. Number cannot contain more than 10 characters (10 bits). The most significant bit of number is the sign bit. The remaining 9 bits are magnitude bits. Negative numbers are represented using two's-complement notation.

Places is the number of characters to use. If places is omitted, BIN2OCT uses the minimum number of characters necessary. Places is useful for padding the return value with leading 0s (zeros).

Remarks

If number is not a valid binary number, or if number contains more than 10 characters (10 bits), BIN2OCT returns the #NUM! error value.

If number is negative, BIN2OCT ignores places and returns a 10-character octal number.

If BIN2OCT requires more than places characters, it returns the #NUM! error value.

If places is not an integer, it is truncated.

If places is nonnumeric, BIN2OCT returns the #VALUE! error value.

If places is negative, BIN2OCT returns the #NUM! error value.

Examples

BIN2OCT(1001, 3) equals 011

BIN2OCT(01100100) equals 144

BIN2OCT(1111111111) equals 7777777777

6.4 Other useful functions

EXCEL has many other functions and tools that important for engineering, science, and technology although they are not included in the category of EXCEL's engineering functions (see Fig. 6-3).

Many of these useful functions and tools are described in other chapters. See Appendix 4 for Goal Seek, Solver, and Lookup Wizard. Here, we will discuss the CONVERT function and matrix algebra.

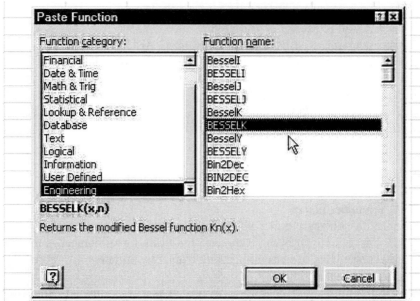

Figure 6-3. A list of all functions in the Engineering category can be viewed by clicking on the Paste Function icon. Use the scroll bar to see the full list.

6.5 CONVERT, Measurement conversion function

In Section 1.11 we introduced the CONVERT worksheet function. Now let's go into the details of this handy tool.

CONVERT

This converts a number from one measurement system to another. For example, CONVERT can translate a table of distances in miles to a table of distances in kilometers.

Syntax

CONVERT(number,from_unit,to_unit)

Number   is the value in from_units to convert.

From_unit   is the units for number.

To_unit   is the units for the result. CONVERT accepts the following text values for from_unit and to_unit.

Weight and mass	From_unit or to_unit
Gram "g"	
Slug "sg"	
Pound mass (avoirdupois) "lbm"	
U (atomic mass unit) "u"	
Ounce mass (avoirdupois) "ozm"	

Distance   From_unit or to_unit
Meter   "m"
Statute mile   "mi"
Nautical mile   "Nmi"
Inch   "in"
Foot   "ft"
Yard   "yd"
Angstrom   "ang"
Pica (1/72 in.)   "Pica"

Time   From_unit or to_unit
Year   "yr"
Day   "day"
Hour   "hr"
Minute "mn"
Second "sec"

Pressure   From_unit or to_unit
Pascal "Pa"
Atmosphere   "atm"
mm of Mercury "mmHg"

Force   From_unit or to_unit
Newton "N"
Dyne   "dyn"
Pound force   "lbf"

Energy From_unit or to_unit
Joule   "J"
Erg   "e"
Thermodynamic calorie "c"
IT calorie   "cal"
Electron volt   "eV"
Horsepower-hour   "HPh"
Watt-hour   "Wh"
Foot-pound   "flb"
BTU   "BTU"

Power From_unit or to_unit
Horsepower   "HP"
Watt   "W"

Magnetism   From_unit or to_unit
Tesla   "T"
Gauss   "ga"

Temperature   From_unit or to_unit
Degree Celsius "C"
Degree Fahrenheit   "F"
Degree Kelvin   "K"

Liquid measure   From_unit or to_unit
Teaspoon   "tsp"
Tablespoon   "tbs"
Fluid ounce   "oz"
Cup   "cup"
Pint   "pt"
Quart   "qt"
Gallon "gal"
Liter   "l"

Prefixes
The following abbreviated unit prefixes can be used as a prefix to any metric from_unit or to_unit.

Prefix	Multiplier	Abbreviation
exa	1E+18	"E"
peta	1E+15	"P"
tera	1E+12	"T"
giga	1E+09	"G"
mega	1E+06	"M"
kilo	1E+03	"k"
hecto	1E+02	"h"
dekao	1E+01	"e"
deci	1E-01	"d"
centi	1E-02	"c"
milli	1E-03	"m"
micro	1E-06	"u"

nano	1E-09	"n"
pico	1E-12	"p"
femto	1E-15	"f"
atto	1E-18	"a"

Remarks

If the input data types are incorrect, CONVERT returns the #VALUE! error value.

If the unit does not exist, CONVERT returns the #N/A error value.

If the unit does not support an abbreviated unit prefix, CONVERT returns the #N/A error value.

If the units are in different groups, CONVERT returns the #N/A error value.

Unit names and prefixes are case-sensitive.

Examples

CONVERT(1.0, "lbm", "kg") equals 0.453592

CONVERT(68, "F", "C") equals 20

CONVERT(2.5, "ft", "sec") equals #N/A

Don't forget the quotation marks (" ").

6.6 Matrix algebra

✪ Matrix algebra applications include solving systems of simultaneous linear algebraic equations in several variables and rotation of coordinate systems. The matrix algebra operations available in EXCEL are limited, but there are enough to do some useful things. If you need more advanced operations, you can use programs such as MATHCAD, MATLAB, or MATHEMATICA. A 2x2 matrix (consisting of 2 rows and 2 columns) looks like this:

$$\begin{pmatrix} a_{11} & a_{21} \\ a_{12} & a_{22} \end{pmatrix}$$

The *determinant* of a 2x2 matrix looks like this:

$$\begin{vmatrix} a_{11} & a_{21} \\ a_{12} & a_{22} \end{vmatrix} = a_{11}a_{22} - a_{12}a_{21} \tag{6-8}$$

For example,

$$\begin{vmatrix} 2 & -3 \\ 7 & 5 \end{vmatrix} = (2)(5) - (7)(-3) = 10 + 21 = 31. \tag{6-9}$$

Array formulas and how to enter them

An array formula can perform multiple calculations and then return either a single result or multiple results. Array formulas act on two or more sets of values known as array arguments. Each array argument must have the same number of rows and columns. You create array formulas the same way that you create basic, single-value formulas. Array formulas are entered in a special way:

➻ Select the cell or cells that will contain the formula, create the formula, and then press CTRL+SHIFT+ENTER to enter the formula.

MDETERM
This returns the matrix determinant of an array.
Syntax
MDETERM(array)

Array   is a numeric array with an equal number of rows and columns.

Array can be given as a cell range, for example, A1:C3; as an array constant, such as {1,2,3;4,5,6;7,8,9}; or as a name to either of these.

If any cells in array are empty or contain text, MDETERM returns the #VALUE! error value.

MDETERM also returns #VALUE! if array does not have an equal number of rows and columns.

Remarks
The matrix determinant is a number derived from the values in array. For a three-row, three-column array, A1:C3, the determinant is defined as:

MDETERM(A1:C3) equals

A1*(B2*C3-B3*C2) + A2*(B3*C1-B1*C3) + A3*(B1*C2-B2*C1)

Matrix determinants are generally used for solving systems of mathematical equations that involve several variables.

MDETERM is calculated with an accuracy of approximately 16 digits, which may lead to a small numeric error when the calculation is not complete. For example, the determinant of a singular matrix may differ from zero by 1E-16.

Examples
MDETERM({1,3,8,5;1,3,6,1;1,1,1,0;7,3,10,2}) equals 88

MDETERM({3,6,1;1,1,0;3,10,2}) equals 1

MDETERM({3,6;1,1}) equals -3

MDETERM({1,3,8,5;1,3,6,1}) equals #VALUE! because the array does not have an equal number of rows and columns.

Tip
Use your mouse to select ranges in the worksheet instead of entering individual numbers. This is faster and you won't make errors typing. See Fig. 6-4.

Open the MATRIX worksheet and explore it as we discuss these matrix operations.

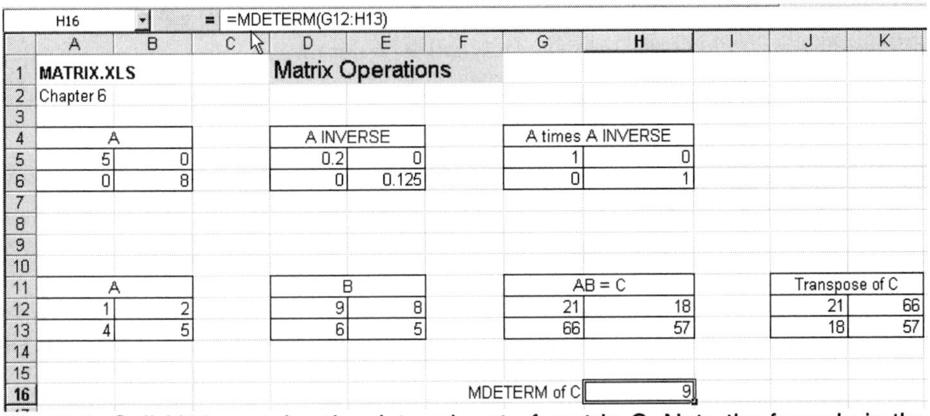

	H16		▼		**=**	=MDETERM(G12:H13)				

	A	B	C ▷	D	E	F	G	H	I	J	K
1	MATRIX.XLS			**Matrix Operations**							
2	Chapter 6										
3											
4	A			A INVERSE			A times A INVERSE				
5	5	0		0.2	0		1	0			
6	0	8		0	0.125		0	1			
7											
8											
9											
10											
11	A			B			AB = C			Transpose of C	
12	1	2		9	8		21	18		21	66
13	4	5		6	5		66	57		18	57
14											
15											
16							MDETERM of C	9			

Fig. 6-4. Cell H16 contains the determinant of matrix C. Note the formula in the cell editing box, =MDTERM(G12:H13). Here, **AB = C**.

MINVERSE
This returns the inverse matrix for the matrix stored in an array.
Syntax
MINVERSE(array)
Array   is a numeric array with an equal number of rows and columns.
Array can be given as a cell range, such as A1:C3; as an array constant, such as {1,2,3;4,5,6;7,8,9}; or as a name for either of these.
If any cells in array are empty or contain text, MINVERSE returns the #VALUE! error value.
MINVERSE also returns the #VALUE! error value if array does not have an equal number of rows and columns.
Remarks
Formulas that return arrays *must* be entered as array formulas.

You can use inverse matrices, like determinants, to solve systems of mathematical equations involving several variables. The product of a matrix and its inverse is the *identity matrix*, the square array in which the diagonal values equal 1, and all other values equal 0. A 2x2 identity matrix looks like this:

$$\begin{pmatrix} 1 & 0 \\ 0 & 1 \end{pmatrix}$$

Let's look at an example of how a two-row, two-column matrix is calculated. Suppose that the range A1:B2 contains the letters a, b, c, and d that represent any four numbers. The following table shows the inverse of the matrix A1:B2.

Table 6-2. Inverse of a 2x2 Matrix		
	Column A	Column B
Row 1	d/(a*d − b*c)	b/(b*c − a*d)
Row 2	c/(b*c − a*d)	a/(a*d − b*c)

MINVERSE is a great labor-saving spreadsheet function. Even a 2x2 matrix requires some analytical effort. For a 2x2 matrix of the form,

$$\mathbf{A} = \begin{pmatrix} a & b \\ c & d \end{pmatrix}$$

the inverse matrix is given by,

$$\mathbf{A}^{-1} = \frac{1}{|\mathbf{A}|}\begin{pmatrix} d & -b \\ -c & a \end{pmatrix} = \frac{1}{ad-bc}\begin{pmatrix} d & -b \\ -c & a \end{pmatrix}.$$

Calculating a 3x3 inverse matrix requires much more work. Fortunately these tedious tasks can be accomplished with computers in today's world. MINVERSE is calculated with an accuracy of approximately 16 digits, which sometimes may lead to very small numerical errors. Some square matrices cannot be inverted and will return the #NUM! error value with MINVERSE. The determinant for a non-invertable matrix is 0.

Examples

MINVERSE({4,-1;2,0}) equals {0,0.5;-1,2}

MINVERSE({1,2,1;3,4,-1;0,2,0}) equals {0.25,0.25,-0.75;0,0,0.5;0.75,-0.25,-0.25}

Figure 6-5 shows the use of MINVERSE in the MATRIX worksheet.

Tip

Use the INDEX function to access individual elements in a very large matrix. This is a complicated function, so if the matrix is small it is easier to examine the array visually.

MMULT

Returns the matrix product of two arrays. The result is an array with the same number of rows as array1 and the same number of columns as array2.

Syntax

MMULT(array1,array2)

(array1, array2   are the arrays you want to multiply.)

The number of columns in array1 must be the same as the number of rows in array2, and both arrays must contain only numbers. Array1 and array2 can be given as cell ranges, array constants, or references.

If any cells are empty or contain text, or if the number of columns in array1 is different from the number of rows in array2, MMULT returns the #VALUE! error value.

D5		▾		=	{=MINVERSE(A5:B6)}			
	A	B	C ⤵	D	E	F	G	H
1	MATRIX.XLS			Matrix Operations				
2	Chapter 6							
3								
4	A			A INVERSE			A times A INVERSE	
5	5	0		0.2	0		1	0
6	0	8		0	0.125		0	1

Figure 6-5. Use of MINVERSE in the MATRIX worksheet. The formula in the cell editing box {=MINVERSE(A5:B6)} is in all cells in the range D5:E6. You must select these cells and enter the array formula using Ctrl+Shift+Enter.

Remarks

The *matrix product* array a of two arrays b and c is:

$$a_{ij} = \sum_{k=1}^{n} b_{ik} c_{kj} \qquad\qquad (6\text{-}10)$$

where i is the row number, and j is the column number.
Let's look at a specific example of using Eq. (6-10):

$$\mathbf{B} = \begin{pmatrix} 2 & 3 \\ 4 & 5 \end{pmatrix} \qquad \mathbf{C} = \begin{pmatrix} 6 & 7 \\ 8 & 9 \end{pmatrix}$$

$$\mathbf{A} = \mathbf{BC} = \begin{pmatrix} 2 & 3 \\ 4 & 5 \end{pmatrix} \begin{pmatrix} 6 & 7 \\ 8 & 9 \end{pmatrix} = \begin{pmatrix} 2*6+3*8 & 2*7+3*9 \\ 4*6+5*8 & 4*7+5*9 \end{pmatrix} = \begin{pmatrix} 36 & 41 \\ 64 & 73 \end{pmatrix}$$

Formulas that return arrays *must* be entered as array formulas.

➡ Select the cell or cells that will contain the formula, create the formula, and then press CTRL+SHIFT+ENTER to enter the formula.

Examples

MMULT({1,3;7,2}, {2,0;0,2}) equals {2,6;14,4}
MMULT({3,0;2,0}, {2,0;0,2}) equals {6,0;4,0}
MMULT({1,3,0;7,2,0;1,0,0}, {2,0;0,2}) equals #VALUE!, because the first array has three columns, and the second array has only two rows.
Figure 6-6 shows the use of MMULT in the MATRIX worksheet. Open this worksheet and explore the formulas. Change the values of the matrix elements and observe the results. Experiment!

TRANSPOSE

Returns a *vertical range* of cells as a *horizontal range*, or *vice versa*. TRANSPOSE will not produce the transpose of an entire matrix in *one* operation. (You must transpose one column or one row at a time.)

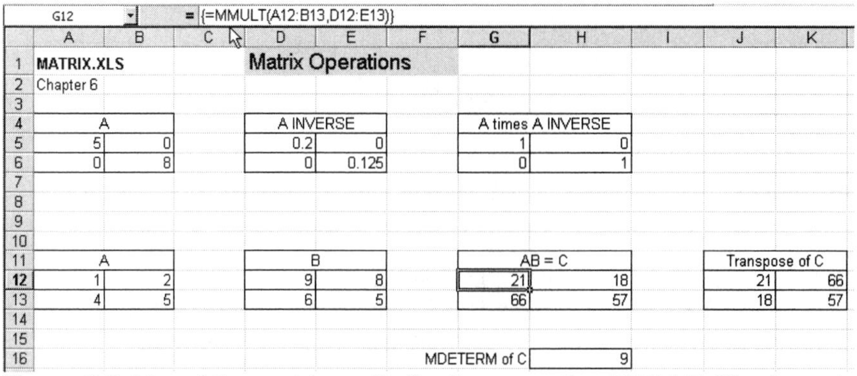

Figure 6-6. Use of the matrix multiplication operation MMULT. The formula in the cell editing box {=MMULT(A12:B13,D12:E13)} is in all cells in the range G12:H13. Remember: You must enter all array formulas using Ctrl+Shift+Enter. Select the range of cells before typing the formula. If you only see one entry, you have not selected the cells or you have only used Enter.

TRANSPOSE must be entered as an *array formula* (CTRL+SHIFT+ENTER) in a range that has the same number of rows and columns, respectively, as array has columns and rows. Use TRANSPOSE to shift the vertical and horizontal orientation of an array on a worksheet. For example, some functions, such as LINEST, return horizontal arrays. LINEST returns a horizontal array of the slope and Y-intercept for a line. The following formula returns a vertical array of the slope and Y-intercept from LINEST:

TRANSPOSE(LINEST(Yvalues,Xvalues))

Syntax

TRANSPOSE(array)

array   is an array or range of cells on a worksheet that you want to transpose. The transpose of an array is created by using the first row of the array as the first column of the new array, the second row of the array as the second column of the new array, and so on.

Figure 6-7 shows the use of TRANSPOSE in the MATRIX workbook.

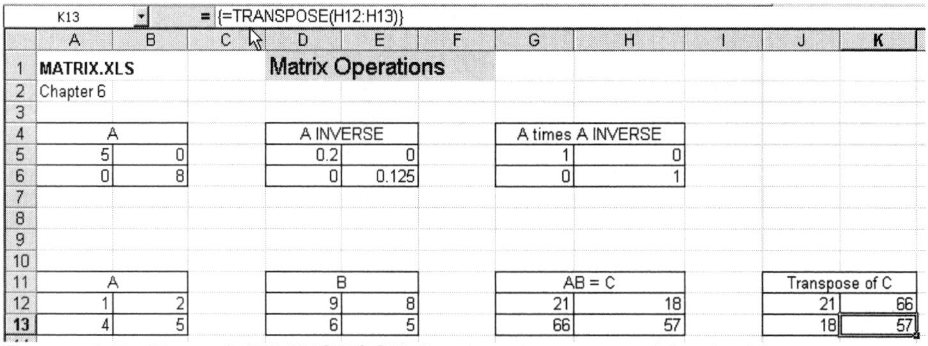

Figure 6-7. Use of TRANSPOSE in the MATRIX workbook. You must use TRANSPOSE twice to transpose a 2x2 matrix. The formula shown is in J13:K13.

Example

Suppose A1:C1 contain 1, 2, 3, respectively. When the following formula is entered as an array into cells A3:A5:

TRANSPOSE($A$1:$C$1) equals the same respective values in A3:A5

6.7 Solving simultaneous equations

Matrix algebra makes it easy to solve simultaneous equations. First, let's solve a very simple system that you can do by hand or in your head. Consider the pair of simultaneous linear algebraic equations,

$$x + 2y = 4$$
$$3x + y = 5.$$

The analytical solution to these two simultaneous equations is easily found to be $x = 1.2$ and $y = 1.4$. Now let's solve the equations using matrix methods. (This is like cracking a peanut with a sledge hammer, but it illustrates the method in a simple way.) We can rewrite the two equations in matrix form,

$$\begin{pmatrix} 1 & 2 \\ 3 & 1 \end{pmatrix} \begin{pmatrix} x \\ y \end{pmatrix} = \begin{pmatrix} 4 \\ 5 \end{pmatrix} \qquad (6\text{-}11)$$

or in symbols $\mathbf{AB} = \mathbf{C}$. Multiply from the left by $\mathbf{A}$ inverse,

$$\mathbf{A}^{-1}\mathbf{AB} = \mathbf{A}^{-1}\mathbf{C} \quad so \quad \mathbf{B} = \mathbf{A}^{-1}\mathbf{C}. \qquad (6\text{-}12)$$

Find $\mathbf{A}^{-1}$ using your spreadsheet. Then our matrix equation becomes

$$\begin{pmatrix} x \\ y \end{pmatrix} = \begin{pmatrix} -0.2 & 0.4 \\ 0.6 & -0.2 \end{pmatrix} \begin{pmatrix} 4 \\ 5 \end{pmatrix}. \qquad (6\text{-}13)$$

Carry out the indicated multiplication and you will find

$$\begin{pmatrix} x \\ y \end{pmatrix} = \begin{pmatrix} 1.2 \\ 1.4 \end{pmatrix}. \qquad (6\text{-}14)$$

This agrees with our analytical solution of $x = 1.2$ and $y = 1.4$. The power of the matrix method becomes clear when you need to solve a large number of simultaneous linear equations in many variables. Matrix operations reduce the labor to a routine operation.

As a check on your solution, remember to plug your solution back in the original equations to be sure that no error has occurred. Very small errors may creep in because the spreadsheet calculates the matrix inverse with a precision of no more than 16 decimal places. This can make 0 appear to be 2 x 10^{-16}.

6.8 Matrix application: Atwood's machine

In 1784 George Atwood of Cambridge University invented a simple machine to study Newton's laws of motion at slow speeds. Atwood's machine may be one of the most popular mechanical devices on the Internet; there are many web sites with photos and descriptions of several variations of this machine.

Analyzing the motion of the machine requires solving a system of simultaneous linear algebraic equations. Let's model this machine in two ways, first with a simple model using a massless, frictionless pulley; this requires a 2x2 matrix. (Note that massless, frictionless mechanical components are found only in textbooks.) Our second, more realistic, model requires a 3x3 matrix. Atwood's machine with a massive pulley is problem 10 at the end of this chapter.

As usual, to start the analysis draw the free-body diagrams of each object as shown in Fig. 6-8. With a massless, frictionless pulley only two free-body diagrams are necessary. Each mass has a tension force T up and a weight force Mg down. By Newton's second law of motion the sum of the external forces is equal to the mass times the acceleration. Therefore, the equations of motion are,

$$T - M_1 g = +M_1 a$$
$$T - M_2 g = -M_2 a .$$

We need to solve for the tension T and the acceleration a. Don't worry if you guess wrong about the direction of the acceleration. If you choose the wrong sign for the acceleration, the answer will have the opposite sign. We can solve this simple system of two simultaneous equations directly but we are going to use matrix methods. Let's rewrite the equations of motion for a massless pulley with the unknown quantities on the left and the known quantities on the right,

$$T - M_1 a = M_1 g$$
$$T + M_2 a = M_2 g .$$

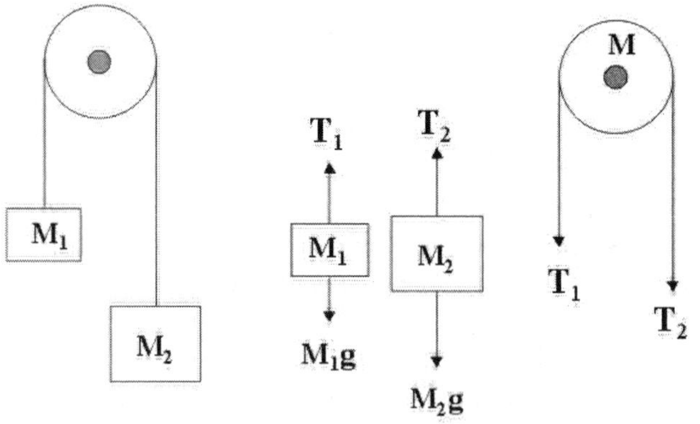

Figure 6-8. Two masses are suspended by an inextensible string passing over a frictionless pulley. Free-body diagrams show tension T and weight Mg. Tensions are equal for a massless pulley. Pulley with mass M is used in Problem 10.

Now we are ready to rewrite these equations in matrix format,

$$\begin{pmatrix} 1 & -M_1 \\ 1 & +M_2 \end{pmatrix} \begin{pmatrix} T \\ a \end{pmatrix} = \begin{pmatrix} M_1 \\ M_2 \end{pmatrix} g \; .$$

The inverse of the 2x2 matrix is found using Table 6-2 and the example in the discussion of MINVERSE on page 128,

$$\frac{1}{M_2 + M_1} \begin{pmatrix} M_2 & M_1 \\ -1 & 1 \end{pmatrix} .$$

Multiply both sides of the matrix equation from the left by the inverse of the 2x2 matrix and the problem is solved,

$$\begin{pmatrix} T \\ a \end{pmatrix} = \begin{pmatrix} 2M_2 M_1 \\ M_2 - M_1 \end{pmatrix} \frac{g}{M_2 + M_1} \; .$$

In other words,

$$T = \frac{2M_2 M_1}{M_2 + M_1} g$$

$$a = \frac{M_2 - M_1}{M_2 + M_1} g \; .$$

As a numerical example, let $M_1 = 1\,\text{kg}$ and $M_2 = 2\,\text{kg}$. Then $T = 4g/3\,\text{N}$ and $a = g/3\,\text{ms}^{-2}$. The acceleration is less than the acceleration of a freely falling mass, as expected. The mass of the pulley can be included with a bit of extra work; see Problem 10. Figure 6-9 shows this version of Atwood's machine.

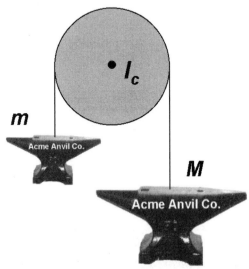

Figure 6-9. Atwood's machine including a pulley with mass. The moment of intertia of the pulley about the axis of rotation is I_c. This Figure was made using EXCEL's Drawing Tool.

What happens when the two masses are identical? Then the tension is Mg and the acceleration is zero. In other words, the system is in static equilibrium.

Frictionless pulley with mass
We can include the mass of the pulley in terms of its moment of inertia with respect to the axis of rotation. See Problem 10. For more about the moment of inertia see Section 5.7.) Figures 6-8 and 6-9 were made with EXCEL's Drawing Tool, which is useful but it cannot compete with engineering drawing software.

6.9 Rotation of coordinates

Why would you want to rotate coordinates? For one reason, it is often possible to find a simpler method of solution by rotating axes. For example, an object sliding on an inclined plane is easier to analyze in a coordinate system where one axis is parallel to the plane and one axis is perpendicular to the plane (see Section 4-3). For the inclined plane you only need to rotate about one axis to transform a two-dimensional motion problem into a one-dimensional motion problem. See Figures 6-10 and 4-2.

Matrix algebra is preferred by many people for rotation of coordinate axes because it can be done as a routine operation even for rotation about three axes in space. (In relativity you need a 4x4 matrix for rotation about four axes in space-time. This is called a Lorentz transform but don't worry about it now.)

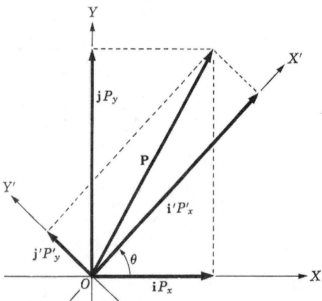

Figure 6-10. A counterclockwise rotation of a coordinate system through an angle θ. The rotation is viewed looking into the positive z-axis toward the origin. The vector **P** is constant but its projections on the axes are different.

Equation (6-15) shows a matrix equation for rotation about one axis; in this case it is the z-axis, as in Fig. 6-10. A rotation like this does not affect the z-component of vectors. Notice that the rotation matrix can be regarded as an operator that transforms the unprimed vector into the primed vector.

$$\begin{pmatrix} \cos\theta & \sin\theta & 0 \\ -\sin\theta & \cos\theta & 0 \\ 0 & 0 & 1 \end{pmatrix} \begin{pmatrix} x \\ y \\ z \end{pmatrix} = \begin{pmatrix} x' \\ y' \\ z' \end{pmatrix} \tag{6-15}$$

Because we are not changing the z-component, we can examine only the x and y components and this reduces the discussion to two dimensions. In other words, all changing vector components lie in the xy plane. In this simplified version Eq. (6-15) becomes

$$\begin{pmatrix} \cos\theta & \sin\theta \\ -\sin\theta & \cos\theta \end{pmatrix} \begin{pmatrix} x \\ y \end{pmatrix} = \begin{pmatrix} x' \\ y' \end{pmatrix}. \tag{6-16}$$

For example, suppose there is a vector with magnitude 10 along the original positive x-axis. A 45 degree rotation of the coordinate system counterclockwise to a new coordinate system can be represented by

$$\begin{pmatrix} \cos 45 & \sin 45 \\ -\sin 45 & \cos 45 \end{pmatrix} \begin{pmatrix} 10 \\ 0 \end{pmatrix} = \begin{pmatrix} 10\cos 45 \\ -10\sin 45 \end{pmatrix} = \begin{pmatrix} 7.071068 \\ -7.071068 \end{pmatrix}. \tag{6-17}$$

Notice that the vector lies in the fourth quadrant of the rotated coordinate system. Also notice that the magnitude of the vector is still 10. (Recall, the magnitude of a vector is the square root of the sum of the squares of the components.) When you apply this rotation to more than one vector you will find that the relative angles between all vectors are unchanged and all magnitudes are unchanged.

A transformation that leaves vector magnitudes and relative angles unchanged is called an *orthogonal* transformation. You can identify an orthogonal transformation because the determinant of the matrix is +1. This is obviously the case for the matrix used here because $\cos^2\theta + \sin^2\theta = +1$.

There are several exercises at the end of this chapter that will help you become skillful with matrix operations in your spreadsheet.

6.10 INDEX worksheet function

✪ This function is useful when you work with a large matrix because it returns a value, or the reference to a value, from within a table or range. Be careful: there are *two forms* of the INDEX function: array and reference. The array form always returns a value or an array of values; the reference form always returns a reference. Although it does simple things, INDEX is complicated to use.

INDEX(array,row_num,column_num) returns the value of a specified cell or array of cells within array.

INDEX(reference,row_num,column_num,area_num) returns a reference to a specified cell or cells within reference.

We repeat:

Two forms of INDEX

The INDEX function has two syntax forms: array and reference. It returns the value of an element in an array or a table, selected by the row and column number indexes. For a matrix, use the array form.

Syntax 1 (array)

The array form always returns a value or array of values; use the array form if the first argument to INDEX is an array constant.

Syntax 2 (reference)

The reference form always returns a reference.

Syntax 1 (Array form)

INDEX(array,row_num,column_num)

Array   is a range of cells or an array constant.

Values that do not change in array formulas:

A basic, single-value formula produces a single result from one or more arguments or values; you can enter either a reference to a cell that contains a value or the value itself. In an array formula, where you might usually use a reference to a range of cells, you can instead type the array of values contained within the cells. The array of values you type is called an array constant and generally is used when you do not want to enter each value into a separate cell on the worksheet.

To create an array constant, you must do the following:

Enter the values directly into the formula, enclosed in braces ({ })

Separate values in different columns with commas (,)

Separate values in different rows with semicolons (;)

For example, you can enter {10,20,30,40} in an array formula instead of entering 10, 20, 30, 40 in four cells in one row. This array constant is known as a 1-by-4 array and is equivalent to a 1-row-by-4-column reference. To represent the values 10, 20, 30, 40 in one row and 50, 60, 70, 80 in the row immediately below, you would enter a 2-by-4 array constant: {10,20,30,40;50,60,70,80}.

Items that an array constant can contain

Array constants can contain numbers, text, logical values such as TRUE or FALSE, or error values such as #N/A.

Numbers in array constants can be in integer, decimal, or scientific format.

Text must be enclosed in double quotation marks, for example "Tuesday".

You can use different types of values in the same array constant, for example, {1,3,4;TRUE,FALSE,TRUE}.

The values in an array constant must be constants, not formulas.

Array constants cannot contain $ (dollar signs), parentheses, or % (percent signs).

Array constants cannot contain cell references.

Array constants cannot contain columns or rows of unequal length.

Row_num   selects the row in array from which to return a value. If row_num is omitted, column_num is required.

Column_num   selects the column in array from which to return a value. If column_num is omitted, row_num is required.

If both the row_num and column_num arguments are used, INDEX returns the value in the cell at the intersection of row_num and column_num.

If array contains only one row or column, the corresponding row_num or column_num argument is optional.

If array has more than one row and more than one column, and only row_num or column_num is used, INDEX returns an array of the entire row or column in array.

If you set row_num or column_num to 0 (zero), INDEX returns the array of values for the entire column or row, respectively. To use values returned as an array, enter the INDEX function as an array formula in a horizontal range of cells. To enter an array formula, press CTRL+SHIFT+ENTER.

Remarks

Row_num and column_num must point to a cell within array; otherwise, INDEX returns the #REF! error value.

Examples

INDEX({1,2;3,4},2,2) equals 4

If entered as an *array* formula, then:

INDEX({1,2;3,4},0,2) equals {2;4}

What's next?

Fasten your seat belt. Chapter 7 is about differential equations using EXCEL.

References

D. Frenkel, L. Golebiowski, and R. Portugal, "Computer algebra takes on the vibrating-membrane problem," *Computing in Science and Engineering* **1** (2), 88–93 (1999). This paper is an excellent example of the use of Bessel functions, and it has graphics of the time evolution of various vibration modes of a circular membrane for different stimuli.

T. Lawson, *Linear Algebra*, (John Wiley & Sons, Inc., New York, 1996). This is a thorough treatment of matrix algebra, with computational skills and theory. You need calculus and an introduction to differential equations for this book.

MATLAB (www.mathworks.com) has EXCEL LINK and MATHEMATICA (www.wolfram.com) has MATHEMATICA LINK FOR EXCEL. MATHCAD 8 (www.mathsoft.com) has a component for data I/O with EXCEL.

Test your skills

1. Use CONVERT to express the Celsius temperature 37 degrees on the Fahrenheit scale.

2. Use CONVERT to change a pressure of 5000 Pa to a pressure in atm.

3. RAND() function. Open the RANDOM workbook and explore it to see how the RAND() worksheet function is used. (This workbook is in the Chapter 8 folder on the CD. Also see Sections 8.8 and 9.10.)

4. Inverse matrix. Use your spreadsheet to compute the inverse of the matrix,
    $$\begin{pmatrix} 5 & 6 \\ 7 & 8 \end{pmatrix}.$$

5. Multiply the matrix in Exercise 4 by its inverse to obtain the identity matrix,
    $$\begin{pmatrix} 1 & 0 \\ 0 & 1 \end{pmatrix}.$$
    (This confirms that the inverse matrix you computed in Exercise 4 is actually the inverse of the given matrix.)

6. Multiply the two matrices as shown. Notice that the result of matrix multiplication *depends on the order* of multiplication. In other words, matrix multiplication is not commutative.

    $$\begin{pmatrix} 1 & 2 & 3 \\ 4 & 5 & 6 \\ 7 & 8 & 9 \end{pmatrix}\begin{pmatrix} 9 & 8 & 7 \\ 6 & 5 & 4 \\ 3 & 2 & 1 \end{pmatrix} = ? \qquad \begin{pmatrix} 9 & 8 & 7 \\ 6 & 5 & 4 \\ 3 & 2 & 1 \end{pmatrix}\begin{pmatrix} 1 & 2 & 3 \\ 4 & 5 & 6 \\ 7 & 8 & 9 \end{pmatrix} = ?$$

7. Rotation of coordinates. Make a drawing of a two-dimensional rectangular coordinate system. On the *x*-axis draw a vector 3 cm long. Now draw a new set of axes rotated 60 degrees counterclockwise, with the same origin. (This is a rotation around the *z*-axis.) What are the lengths of the vector components in the rotated coordinate system? Measure them on your drawing and calculate them using your spreadsheet.

8. Rotation of coordinates, Section 6.9. Compose a worksheet using matrix

multiplication to compute the vector components in Exercise 7 for any angle. (Hint: enter the rotation angle in a cell at the top of the worksheet and use this as an absolute cell address for the sines and cosines. Remember: change degrees to radians! Test your worksheet with positive and negative angles.)

9. Determinant of a matrix. Show that the determinant of the rotation matrix in Exercise 8 is +1. Use MDETERM in your worksheet and also show this analytically. The value +1 shows that this is an orthogonal transformation.

10. ✪ Atwood's machine. Two objects are connected by a string of negligible mass. One object is 50 kg and the other object is 110 kg. The string passes over a frictionless pulley of mass $M = 2$ kg and radius $R = 0.3$ m. See Fig. 6-9. The moment of inertia of the pulley about its rotation axis is $I = 0.09$ kg m^2 (see Chapter 5). The objects are released from rest. The string does not slip on the pulley. From the free-body diagrams the equations of motion are,

$$T_1 - M_1 g = +M_1 a$$
$$T_2 - M_2 g = -M_2 a$$
$$T_2 R - T_1 R = (I/R)a .$$

Use the matrix method to find the tensions in the string and the acceleration. (Use $g = 9.8$ m/s^2 for the acceleration of gravity.) Compare the worksheet answers with an analytical solution.

Here is a more challenging problem: the Figure at the right shows a double Atwood's machine. For simplicity assume that the pulleys are massless and frictionless. Mass M_1 is 50 kg, M_2 is 150 kg, and M_3 is 100 kg. The system starts from rest. Find the acceleration of each mass and the tension in each string. This machine is easier to analyze using methods of advanced dynamics (Lagrange's equations) instead of using Newton's laws of motion. EXCEL's Drawing Tool was used to compose this Figure.

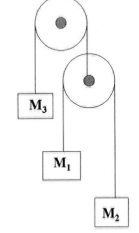

11. ✪ Entropy and the COMBIN worksheet function. Many students believe that entropy was invented to baffle them. Some people say that entropy is discussed by philosophers, used by engineers and understood by scientists. After doing this exercise you should be able to discuss it, use it, and understand some of it. Entropy was known for many years as a thermodynamic function before it was discovered that it is a measure of the disorder of systems. For example, an orderly system has low entropy and a disorderly system has high entropy. Chemical reactions occur, people get older, stars burn out and pollution increases; these are all aspects of increasing entropy be-

cause any isolated system will have an increase in entropy. Entropy is conveniently measured in units of J/K, that is, Joule/Kelvin. A *macrostate* refers to a gross description of a system. For example, a gas can be described by its pressure, temperature, and volume. A *microstate* is a specific arrangement of particles of the gas. Obviously, there can be many microstates that produce the same macrostate in a gas. The more microstates there are, the more probable the associated macrostate will be. For a simple model, consider 4 coins. There is 1 micro-state corresponding to 4 heads and 1 microstate corresponding to 4 tails. There are 4 microstates with 1 tail and 3 heads and 4 microstates with 1 head and 3 tails. However, there are 6 microstates corresponding to 2 heads and 2 tails, and this is the most probable macrostate which is the least orderly, the most random. Open the ENTROPY workbook and you will see how to use the COMBIN worksheet function to compute the possible combinations for a large number particles. Consult Help for information about COMBIN. Observe that the most probable state is much more probable than any other state. You can almost disregard other states even for 100 objects, and especially when you have a large number like 6.02 x 10^{23} (Avogadro's number). Modify the workbook to examine $n = 10$, 50 and 1000 objects.

Note: the number of ways to make k choices from n objects is

$$\frac{n!}{k!(n-k)!}$$

where $n!$ is "n factorial". The entropy S is given by

$$S = 1.38 \times 10^{-23} \ln\left(\frac{n!}{k!(n-k)!}\right) \text{ J/K.}$$

Boltzmann's constant is 1.38×10^{-23}. The Figure below is from the ENTROPY-2 workbook. For more information see D. Halliday, R. Resnick, and J. Walker, *Fundamentals of Physics*, Sixth Edition (John Wiley & Sons, Inc., New York, 2001) pages 483–504. This exercise relates to the National Science Education Standard of *conservation of energy and increase in disorder.*

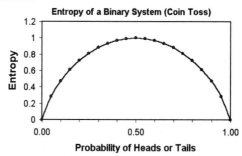

Maximum entropy is associated with maximum randomness.

Chapter 7
Differential Equations

What this chapter is about

Differential equations are important in engineering and science because we use them to describe how systems change. In this chapter we will discuss two numerical methods of solution of ordinary linear differential equations and compare them with each other. We will use simple examples so we can get exact analytical solutions and compare errors in the numerical methods.

We will also do simple, interactive examples of the powerful finite element method of solving Laplace's equation, a ubiquitous partial differential equation which appears throughout all technology and science. This method will show you how and when to use *circular references* in EXCEL, which is something you should usually avoid. Results will be displayed on a 3-D chart.

In this chapter we will discuss two general categories:

- Initial value.
  Example: $x(t) = 22$ and $dx/dt = 6$, when $t = 0$.
- Boundary value.
  Example: $y(x) = 0$, for $x = 0$ and $x = 11$.

7.1 Preliminary operations

Before using numerical methods of solution you should try to find an analytical solution. Differential equations have been studied for hundreds of years, so you may find that a solution is already known for almost any elementary – or even advanced – problem you may encounter.

The first step is to try to identify the differential equation as a known type. If the type is not known, the second step is to try to transform the equation into a known type by a change of variable. This step is similar to changing an unknown integral into a known integral by, for example, a trigonometric substitution. Naturally, this requires some experience. If you can find an analytical solution, then you can use your spreadsheet to produce tables over ranges of interest for different values of variables and constants.

Higher-order ordinary differential equations can be transformed into systems of first order equations, as we will see. This technique can often be applied even to partial differential equations. For example, in advanced dynamics a Legendre transformation is used to change Lagrange's equations (n second-order partial differential equations) into Hamilton's equations ($2n$ first-order partial differential equations). Another useful technique is *separation of variables*, which enables you to transform a partial differential equation into a system of ordinary differential equations. This is a common technique in boundary-value problems.

Extensive tables of Laplace transforms are available, so you can reduce ordinary differential equations to algebraic equations. Of course, analytical methods require considerable expertise, but this is also true for effective use of numerical methods.

Advanced mathematical programs (MAPLE, MATHCAD, MATHEMATICA, MATLAB, and so on) are more powerful than EXCEL for solving differential equations. However, they require some learning time, they are expensive, and you cannot see what the programs are doing.

FAQ

Q. *Why spend time on an analytical solution when I need a table of values? Why not go directly to a numerical solution?*
A. Numerical solutions give results over finite ranges of values. On the other hand, analytical solutions give results over all ranges of variables so you can avoid unpleasant surprises. For example, a numerical solution for a mechanical system may be stable for the values used in your numerical solution, but it may be unstable for other ranges of values. Fluid flow may be smooth and laminar for some values, but the flow may suddenly become turbulent for a small change of an independent variable or constant. You can observe this is a rising column of smoke in still air.

7.2 Example: variables-separable ODE

Variables-separable is one of the easiest types of ordinary differential equations. If you can separate the variables – putting all functions of the dependent variable on the left side and all functions of the independent variable on the right side – then the solution is reduced to computing some integrals. Tables of integrals are available to satisfy almost all of your needs. There is an integrator on the Internet that enables you type in the integrand and obtain the result (see Chapter 5, Figure 5-8). If you can't do the integrals analytically, you can use the methods of Chapter 5 to get numerical approximations to the integrals.

In this example we will solve a second-order ordinary differential equation by transforming it into two first-order ODEs, After obtaining the solutions of the two first order ODEs we will use EXCEL to produce a table of solution values.

Now let's solve a differential equation. Suppose you have an object of mass m moving in a viscous medium with a resistive force that is proportional to velocity $-R\,dx/dt$, where R is the resistive force constant. This is a one-dimensional problem so we don't need to use vectors. See Fig. 7-1. By Newton's second law of motion the product of the mass times the acceleration is equal to the sum of the external forces, $ma = \Sigma F$. So, our model equation is

$$m\frac{d^2x}{dt^2} = -R\frac{dx}{dt}. \tag{7-1}$$

We can write the velocity as $v = dx/dt$ and the acceleration as $a = dv/dt$. Now use these substitutions in Eq. (7-1) to obtain a first-order ODE,

$$m\frac{dv}{dt} = -Rv. \tag{7-2}$$

This is an equation where it is possible, and easy, to separate the variables. Let's put v on the left side and t on the right side to obtain,

$$\frac{dv}{v} = -\frac{R}{m}dt. \tag{7-3}$$

Now we can integrate both sides and find,

$$\int \frac{dv}{v} = -\frac{R}{m}\int dt + C \tag{7-4}$$

$$\ln(v) = -\frac{R}{m}t + C \tag{7-5}$$

where C is a constant of integration to be determined by the initial velocity.

Now exponentiate both sides and use the rule of logarithms $\exp(\ln x) = x$. Figure 7-2 shows this rule as "The Law of Napier" $\exp(\ln N) = N$. The result is

$$v = \exp(\ln v) = \exp\left(-\frac{R}{m}t + C\right). \tag{7-6}$$

Now use another rule of logarithms $\exp(A + B) = \exp(A)\exp(B)$,

$$v = \exp(C)\exp\left(-\frac{R}{m}t\right). \tag{7-7}$$

$$F(v) = -Rv$$

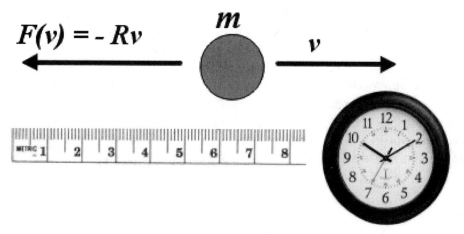

Figure 7-1. A resistive force ($-Rv$) acts on mass m moving with velocity v. The resistive force is always opposite to the velocity.

Next let's satisfy the initial condition: $v = v_0$ when $t = 0$. The final result is

$$v = v_0 \exp\left(-\frac{R}{m}t\right) \tag{7-8}$$

where we have set the initial velocity $v_0 = \exp(C)$. Equation (7-8) describes a simple exponential decay in which the system is stable for all time. The *time constant* for this exponential process is $\tau = m/R$ seconds. This is the time for the velocity to fall to $1/e$ or about 0.367879 of its initial value. To find the position as a function of time re-write Eq. (7-8) as

$$\frac{dx}{dt} = v_0 \exp\left(-\frac{R}{m}t\right). \tag{7-9}$$

We can find the displacement $x(t)$ by integrating Eq. (7-9).

$$x = \int v\, dt = v_0 \int \exp\left(-\frac{R}{m}t\right) dt + C_x . \tag{7-10}$$

The constant C_x is determined by the *initial value* of x when $t = 0$, which we will call x_0. The final result is

$$x = x_0 + \frac{v_0 m}{R}\left[1 - \exp\left(-\frac{R}{m}t\right)\right]. \tag{7-11}$$

Figure 7-2. The "Law of Napier" (Ley de Napier), a mathematical formula that changed the face of the Earth (Las 10 Formulas Matematicas que Cambiaron la Faz de la Tierra). This formula facilitated numerical calculation and celestial navigation, symbolized by the marine sextant and the Big Dipper constellation of stars on the stamp. Celestial navigation produced the first accurate maps for exploration and international trade. John Napier's work, published in 1614, was praised 200 years later by Pierre-Simon Laplace, "...by shortening the labors, doubled the life of the astronomer".

So, we have obtained the solution of a second-order ODE, Eq. (7-1), by solving two first-order ODEs. Now let's put the solution in a workbook.

Open the workbook named Drag-Force-1 and you will see the home screen as shown in Fig. 7-3. In this Figure input data are entered in cells C6:C9. These cells are referred to by the formulas in cells B12 and C12 using absolute cell addresses. The time axis is in column A, and is composed using [Edit][Fill][Series][Column]. The formula in cell B12 is Eq. (7-8) written as

`=$C$8+exp(-($C$7/$C$6)*A12)`.

The formula in cell B12 is copied to cells B13:B112. As usual, the copy operation is performed using the fill handle on the cell.
The formula in cell C12 is Eq. (7-11) written as

`=$C$9+(($C$8*$C$6)/$C$7)*(1-EXP(-($C$7/$C$6)*A12))`.

This is copied to cells C13:C112. You can see this formula in the Formula Editing Box for cell C12 in Fig. 7-3.

The velocity and position Reports are in cells G7 and G8. The cells simply refer to the velocity and position at $t = 10$ seconds. The formula in cell G7 is `=B112`, and the formula in cell G8 is `=C112`.

Columns A, B, and C are used to produce *XY* scatter graphs to view the results in different ways.

	A	B	C	D	E	F	G	H
1	**Drag-Force-1.XLS**			Object with Resistive Drag Force				
2	Chapter 7							
3								
4								
5			Enter Data:				REPORT:	
6		Mass *m*	2	kg	Velocity at 10 s		**0.247875**	m/s
7	Force Constant *R*		1.2	N s/m	Position at 10 s		**166.2535**	m
8	Initial velocity		100	m/s	Time constant tau		**1.666667**	s
9	Initial position		0	m	Velocity at tau		**36.78794**	m/s
10					Position at tau		**105.3534**	m
11	**Time**	**Velocity**	**Position**					
12	0	100	0					
13	0.1	94.17645	9.705911					
14	0.2	88.69204	18.84659					
15	0.3	83.52702	27.45496					
16	0.4	78.66279	35.56202					
17	0.5	74.08182	43.19696					

$$F = -R \, \frac{dx}{dt} \qquad \tau = \frac{m}{R}$$

$$m \, \frac{d^2 x}{dt^2} = -R \, \frac{dx}{dt}$$

Figure 7-3. Home screen of Drag-Force-1. This workbook produces a table of values using the analytical solution of a second-order ordinary differential equation. You can enter new data in cells C6:C9 and observe the new results.

The graphs are Velocity, Velocity Log (a semi-log graph), Position, Velocity and Position (using left and right *y*-axes with a common *x*-axis to display individual data), and Velocity vs. Position. The first four graphs display velocity and position as functions of time, using column A for time. Note that the semi-log graph cannot display negative values.

FAQ

Q. *The Drag-Force-1 example reminds me of a resistor-capacitor discharge. Is this analogy valid?*
A. No, because mass in a mechanical system is analogous to inductance in an electrical system. See Table 7-1 for analogous elements. The Drag-Force-1 example is analogous to a resistor-inductor discharge.

Table 7-1. Analogous Elements in Mechanical and Electrical Systems	
Mechanical	Electrical
F force	*V* electromotive force, voltage
x displacement	*q* electric charge
v velocity	*I* electric current
a acceleration	*dI/dt* rate of change of current
m mass	*L* inductance
k restoring force constant	*1/C* reciprocal of capacitance
R resistive force constant	*R* electrical resistance

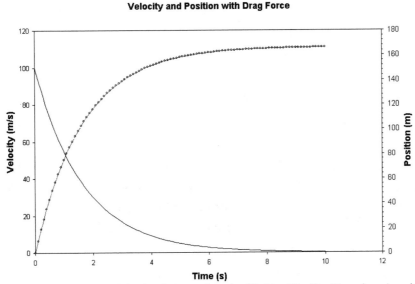

Figure 7-4. *Left axis:* Velocity (no markers). *Right axis:* Position (markers). This time evolution of the damped mass system is computed for the data shown in Fig. 7-3.

Equations (7-8) and (7-11) are *parametric equations*, with t as the parameter. The Velocity vs. Position graph shows an important feature of EXCEL: it is easy to eliminate the parameter by graphing v as a function of x.

The series for position is used as the x-axis and the series for velocity is plotted on the y-axis so you can graph *a function of a function* to find the velocity at any position instead of at any time. Parameter elimination could also be done analytically but in this case it is much easier to do it using EXCEL. Figure 7-4 shows the time evolution of the velocity and position.

7.3 Euler's numerical method

Now let's solve an ODE using purely numerical methods. Euler's method is direct and simple but it can be easily improved, as you will see later.

Leonhard Euler, one of the world's greatest mathematicians, lived in Switzerland from 1707–1783. He brought new ideas into calculus, geometry, algebra, number theory and probability. In applied mathematics, he did original work in acoustics, optics, mechanics, astronomy, artillery, navigation, statistics and finance. Let's see how Euler's method works for an object with constant acceleration. This is typical of a mass falling in a constant gravitational field with no air resistance. Astronauts did this experiment on the moon using a feather and a coin. Naturally, both fell at the same rate. Galileo was right, Aristotle was wrong.

If we know the force F on an object with mass m, then we can find the acceleration by Newton's second law, $a = F/m$. Then the velocity increment dv and displacement increment dx follow from the definitions of these quantities,

$$dv = a \, dt \qquad \qquad (7\text{-}12)$$

$$dx = v \, dt \, . \qquad \qquad (7\text{-}13)$$

For finite time intervals these equations become,

$$\Delta v = \bar{a} \, \Delta t \qquad \qquad (7\text{-}14)$$

$$\Delta x = \bar{v} \, \Delta t \, . \qquad \qquad (7\text{-}15)$$

In Equations (7-14) and (7-15) the bars over the acceleration and velocity indicate the *average values* of these quantities during the time interval Δt.

In discrete form (for discrete data) the velocity and displacement can be expressed as,

$$v_{n+1} = v_n + a_n \, \Delta t \qquad \qquad (7\text{-}16)$$

$$x_{n+1} = x_n + v_n \, \Delta t \, . \qquad \qquad (7\text{-}17)$$

As time goes by, the fundamental things apply. Time advances according to,

$$t_n = t_0 + n \, \Delta t \, . \qquad \qquad (7\text{-}18)$$

Although this method seems to be an obvious extension of calculus, there is a difficulty because calculus involves infinitesimal increments and *instantaneous values* of acceleration and velocity. Finite increments can introduce errors if increments are too large, because *average values* of acceleration and velocity are in Equations (7-14) and (7-15). This will become clear in the worksheet. A more accurate method, the *modified or improved Euler*, is also calculated in the workbook. The exact analytical solution is calculated for comparison.

The following example of constant acceleration is chosen for its simplicity to show how to implement the two methods, but it gives a dramatic indication of the improvement obtained using the modified (or improved) Euler method. You can reduce errors by using very small time increments. A large time increment is used in Fig. 7-5 to emphasize the errors in Euler and modified Euler methods.

In applications involving non-constant acceleration (like a vibrating system or a harmonic oscillator) and velocity-dependent forces the Runge-Kutta method is preferred, although it requires more work. No pain, no gain. See Section 7.4.

Open the EULER workbook and you should see the Home screen shown in Figure 7-5. Input data are in cells D5:D8. In this case, acceleration $a(0)$ is constant and is stored in cell D6.

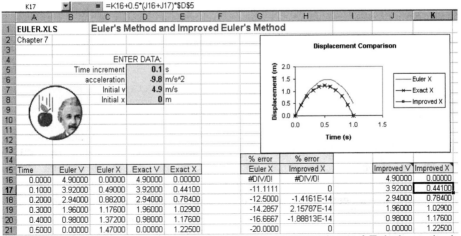

Fig. 7-5. Home screen of the EULER workbook for comparison of Euler's method, improved Euler, and the exact analytical results. The time increment is large to emphasize differences in the results.

Initial velocity $v(0)$ and displacement $x(0)$ are in cells D7 and D8. The time increment is contained in cell D5; accuracy is sensitive to the size of this increment.

Time axis:
Cell A15 contains the Time axis title.
Cell B15 contains the Euler Velocity title.
Cell C15 contains the Euler Displacement title, and so on.

Euler velocity:
Cell B16 contains the initial velocity $D$7.
Cell B17   =B16+$D$6*$D$5
Euler displacement:
Cell C16   =$D$8
Cell C17   =C16+B16*$D$5

Exact velocity:
Cell D16   =$D$7
Cell D17   =$D$7+$D$6*A16
Exact displacement:
Cell E16   =$D$8+$D$7*A16+0.5*$D$6*A16^2

Percent error, Euler displacement:
Cell G16   =(E16−C16)*100/E16
Percent error, improved Euler displacement:
Cell H16   =(E16−K16)*100/E16

Improved Euler velocity:
Cell J16   `=$D$7`
Cell J17   `=J16+$D$6*$D$5`

Improved Euler displacement:
Cell K16   `=$D$8`
Cell K17   `=K16+0.5*(J16+J17)*$D$4`

Notice that the Euler method computes the displacement using the value of the velocity from the previous point. In Exercise 3 you will change Euler's method to use the value of the velocity at the current point, and compare results with the standard method. In the EULER workbook the modified Euler method uses the *average* value of the velocity based on the previous point and the current point. This simple change produces a remarkable increase in accuracy.

Change the initial velocity and observed the results. Figure 7-6 shows the computed displacements with the data shown in cells D5:D8 in Fig. 7-4. See Fig. 7-7 for the error in the exact and modified Euler method.

Note: The formulas used in calculating the exact velocity and displacement are the standard kinematic formulas derived by calculus for constant acceleration,

$$v(t) = v_0 + at \tag{7-19}$$

$$x(t) = x_0 + v_0 t + 0.5at^2 . \tag{7-20}$$

Equation (7-19) comes from Eq. (7-12),

$$v(t) = \int dv = \int a \, dt = v_0 + at .$$

Using Equations (7-13) and (7-19) we find Eq. (7-20),

$$x(t) = \int dx = \int v \, dt = \int (v_o + at) \, dt = x_0 + v_0 t + 0.5at^2 .$$

Next, change the initial conditions in the worksheet. Instead of throwing the ball up (as shown in Fig. 7-5 with initial velocity 4.9 and initial position 0), let's just drop the ball from initial position 4.9 and initial velocity 0. This is a simple free-fall experiment, like Galileo may have done from the Leaning Tower of Pisa. Before Galileo, the philosopher Aristotle had written that heavier objects fell faster than lighter objects. Galileo showed that all objects fall at the same speed if the air resistances of the objects are the same.

With no air resistance all objects fall at the same rate. Your workbook should show something like Fig. 7-6. We know that an object will move 4.9 m in the first second of free fall, neglecting air resistance.

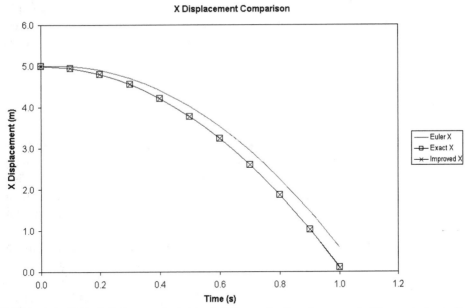

Figure 7-6. Free fall from a height of 4.9 m, starting from rest. The exact result agrees closely with the modified Euler result. The object arrives at the surface in one second. The standard Euler method has considerable error and the error increases as time goes by. Despite this, the Euler method may give acceptable results by choosing a very small increment.

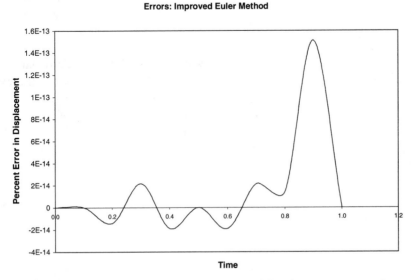

Figure 7-7. Errors in the modified Euler method for the parameters shown in Fig. 7-4. Compare errors of the standard Euler method, column G in Fig. 7-4.

Experiment with other initial positions and initial velocities. For example, don't just drop the ball. Throw it down with an initial velocity in the same direction as acceleration. You may need to adjust the chart scale, or set the scale for Automatic.

7.4 Good vibrations

Vibrating systems are found in various forms throughout engineering and science. A mechanical design may fail if it is based purely on statics and does not consider the possibility of vibration. Thousands of years ago Roman soldiers were trained to march in step. They found through experience that they had to break step and march independently as they crossed a bridge to prevent the collapse of the bridge.

On July 1, 1940, the Tacoma Narrows Bridge at Puget Sound in the state of Washington was completed and opened to traffic. The bridge was located near the city of Tacoma, Washington. The bridge began to experience oscillations. On November 7, 1940, at approximately 11:00 AM the suspension bridge collapsed in dramatic fashion because the designers did not consider the effects of wind-induced resonant vibrations. The bridge had been open for traffic only a few months.

Professor F. B. Farquharson was on the faculty at the University of Washington. He had conducted numerous tests on a model of the bridge and had assured everyone of its stability. The professor was the last man on the bridge. Even when the bridge was vibrating more than twenty-eight feet up and down, he was making engineering measurements, apparently not anticipating the collapse. When the motion increased he made his way to safety by following the line of nodes in the middle of the roadway.

The full video record of the vibrations, still photos, Professor Farquharson's escape, and the final collapse of the bridge is available on the Internet at the web site http://www.enm.bris.ac.uk/research/nonlinear/tacoma/tacoma.html .

The prototype of a vibrating system is a mass on a spring. We will start with the simple model of an undamped (no energy loss) one-dimensional system with a linear restoring force of $-kx$. We can write Newton's second law of motion $ma = \Sigma F$ for this model system as,

$$m\frac{d^2x}{dt^2} = -kx . \tag{7-21}$$

Let's rewrite this as,

$$\frac{d^2x}{dt^2} = -\frac{k}{m}x . \tag{7-22}$$

The solution of this equation can be expressed in several equivalent forms, and they are so well known that we don't need to derive them. Let's get a solution by intuition.

Look at the equation; what do you see? Of course, you see the second derivative of a function is proportional to the negative of the function. The only functions we know with this special property are sines and cosines, or their equivalent complex exponential representations (see Chapter 10). If we try a solution of the form $x(t) = A\exp(i\omega_0 t)$, where $i = \sqrt{-1}$ and $i^2 = -1$, we find $d^2x/dt^2 = -\omega_0^2 x$, so

$$-\omega_0^2 A\exp(i\omega_0 t) = -\frac{k}{m} A\exp(i\omega_0 t). \qquad (7\text{-}23)$$

This must hold for all A and all time so we find,

$$\omega_0^2 = \frac{k}{m} \qquad (7\text{-}24)$$

where ω_0 is the natural frequency of the system expressed in rad/s. Note how the natural frequency of the system is controlled by the ratio of the energy storage parameters: the potential energy is proportional to k and the kinetic energy is proportional to m. In this simple model no energy is dissipated.

Because Eq. (7-22) is a linear equation the sum of two solutions is also a solution and we can write,

$$x(t) = A\cos(\omega_0 t) + B\sin(\omega_0 t) \qquad (7\text{-}25)$$

where A and B are constants determined by the initial conditions. The initial displacement $x(0)$ determines A and the initial velocity $v(0)$ determines B.

A more complicated, but more realistic, model is a system with energy loss and external energy input through a force. We can write this model equation as,

$$m\frac{d^2x}{dt^2} = -kx + R\frac{dx}{dt} + F(t). \qquad (7\text{-}26)$$

Now there are three forces on m. We used the restoring force $-kx$ in Eq. (7-21), the resistive force was used in Eq. (7-1), and now we have added a general external driving force $F(t)$. Four types of external forces are commonly used in test and measurement of the dynamic properties of systems: impulse (delta function), step function (Heaviside function), sinusoidal, and random noise. The sinusoidal force is the easiest to generate in laboratory measurements, and it is the easiest to use with elementary mathematics. Let's put Eq. (7-26) in standard form,

$$\frac{d^2x}{dt^2} + 2K\frac{dx}{dt} + \omega_0^2 x = F(t) \qquad (7\text{-}27)$$

where $K = R/2m$ is the *damping constant*, the reciprocal of the time constant. The damping constant is related to the time constant τ for a non-oscillatory system by $\tau = 1/2K$. Recall, we found for the damped mass system of Section 7.1, $\tau = m/R$. Again we see that, the larger the mass, the longer the decay time and the larger the dissipative force factor, the shorter the decay time.

Naturally, the specific form of $F(t)$ will determine the form of the solution that describes the motion of the system. If $F(t)$ is periodic, then it is often useful to express it as a Fourier series (Section 4.4) so the problem is reduced to sinusoidal forces. Because the system is linear, the total response is the sum of the responses to each Fourier component.

The solutions of Eq. (7-27) are well known, and they can be separated into three categories that depend on the system parameters:

- Over-damped, $\omega_0 < K$
- Critically damped, $\omega_0 = K$
- Under-damped, $\omega_0 > K$.

An over-damped system sags toward equilibrium relatively slowly, like a pendulum in heavy motor oil. A critically-damped system has the desirable property of returning to equilibrium in the shortest time. An under-damped system is oscillatory with an exponential decay envelope. When damping is small the amplitude of the system can become very large near its resonant frequency. Recall the Tacoma Narrows bridge collapse.

Let's look at a solution for the interesting case of an under-damped system returning to equilibrium after the external force has been removed. One useful way of expressing the solution is,

$$x(t) = e^{-Kt}\left[x_0 \cos(\omega_u t) + \{(v_0 + kx_0)/\omega_u\}\sin(\omega_u t)\right] \qquad (7\text{-}28)$$

where $\omega_u = \sqrt{\omega_0^2 - K^2}$ is the frequency that is down-shifted due to damping. Because the amplitude is changing it would be more accurate to say that the under-damped oscillator does not have a single frequency; it is not *isochronous*. Equation (7-28) has a spectrum that is spread due to damping. The more the damping, the greater will be the spread in the spectrum (see Chapter 11).

Vibrating electromechanical systems on microchips using quartz crystals can detect bacteria and viruses. See *Scientific American* **286** (3) 20–21 (March 2002).

Figure 7-8 shows the return to equilibrium of an under-damped system. The $1/e$ line intercepts the exponential envelope at the time constant. Figure 7-9 shows a self-graphing system that is driven by random impulse forces.

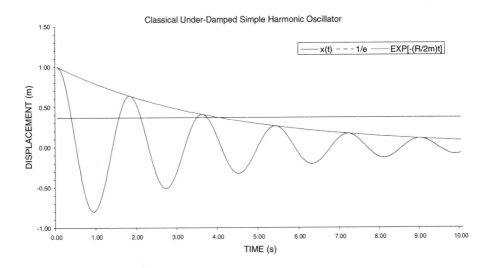

Figure 7-8. Under-damped vibration with amplitude envelope and 1/*e* line.

Figure 7-9. Self-graphing mass on a spring with random impulse driving forces. See Equation (7-27). Note that the rats must be running backwards. (Courtesy of PASCO Scientific, Roseville, California. www.pasco.com.)

7.5 Runge-Kutta method

Runge-Kutta is more accurate than Euler's method, and it is more powerful because it works with velocity-dependent forces like magnetic force on a moving electric charge. It requires more computation, but it is often worth it.

The Runge-Kutta method is designed to approximate Taylor series methods, but RK has the advantage of not requiring explicit evaluations of the derivatives in Taylor series. Instead of calculating derivatives, the Runge-Kutta method consists of computing some auxiliary quantities; details are given in the references at the end of this chapter. Let's illustrate the method for fourth-order RK with the generic differential equation,

$$\frac{dx}{dt} = f(x,t) \quad \text{with} \quad x(t_0) = x_0 \tag{7-21}$$

Here, $f(x,t)$ is some function of x and t. This is what we have called an *initial value* problem. Let h be the step size. Now we must calculate the k gradients,

$$k_1 = hf(x_n, t_n)$$
$$k_2 = hf(x_n + 0.5h, \ t_n + 0.5k_1)$$
$$k_3 = hf(x_n + 0.5h, \ t_n + 0.5k_2)$$
$$k_4 = hf(x_n + h, \ t_n + k_3)$$

and these gradients are used to calculate x at the next time increment,

$$x(t_n + h) = x_n + \frac{1}{6}(k_1 + 2k_2 + 2k_3 + k_4). \tag{7-22}$$

So, you can see this is more complicated than the Euler method. With a spreadsheet you can use very small increments so you can get good results even with the Euler method, and the improved Euler method is even better. Recall, you have a column of 65,536 cells, and 256 columns, and 256 worksheets! In many situations you do not need a complicated method.

Sir Isaac Newton advised us that "Truth is ever to be found in the simplicity, and not in the multiplicity and confusion of things."

Professor Albert Einstein (Nobel Prize 1921) said, "Everything should be made as simple as possible, but not simpler".

Fourth-order Runge-Kutta is one of several popular methods of numerical solution, but it should be used with caution:

"For many scientific users, fourth-order Runge-Kutta is not just the first word on ODE integrators, but the last word as well. In fact, you can get pretty far on this old workhorse, especially if you combine it with an adaptive step-size algorithm. Keep in mind, however, that the old workhorse's last trip may well be to take you to the poorhouse: Bulirsch-Stoer or predictor-corrector methods can be very much more efficient for problems where very high accuracy is a requirement. Those methods are the high-strung race horses. Runge-Kutta is for plowing the fields. However, even the old workhorse is more nimble with new horseshoes . . ."

W. H. Press, S. A. Teukolsky, W. T. Vetterling, and B. P. Flannery,
Numerical Recipes in C: the Art of Scientific Computing, page 712,
(Cambridge UP, Cambridge, 1992)

Here are some web sites that will instruct you on using the Runge-Kutta method:
http://www.nacse.org/sc96/DIFFEQ/mydif2/index.html
http://csep.acns.colostate.edu/csep/ODE/NODE7.html

7.6 Finite element method: Laplace

Now we come to an entirely different class of differential equations, and an entirely different method of numerical solution. Here we will learn about *circular references* and turning off Automatic Calculation in EXCEL.

Ordinary differential equations (ODEs) use total derivatives to describe processes in engineering and the sciences. You will undoubtedly take an entire course in this subject, and you'll learn specialized methods of solutions in conjunction with applications in other courses. However, total derivatives are not sufficient to describe processes involving functions of several variables. Partial differential equations (PDEs) are required to describe advanced dynamics, fluid mechanics, thermodynamics, heat transfer, and electrodynamics, to name just a few things.

The statement that "the sum of the second partial derivatives is zero" is known as Laplace's equation. This equation appears in so many things that the sum of the second partial derivatives is given a special symbol ∇^2. This is called the Laplacian operator, and it is often pronounced "del-squared". It can operate on scalar and vector functions. In Cartesian coordinates with a scalar function Laplace's equation looks like,

$$\frac{\partial^2 V(x,y,z)}{\partial x^2} + \frac{\partial^2 V(x,y,z)}{\partial y^2} + \frac{\partial^2 V(x,y,z)}{\partial z^2} = 0 \qquad (7\text{-}23)$$

or in any coordinate system x_1, x_2, x_3,

$$\nabla^2 V(x_1, x_2, x_3) = 0. \qquad (7\text{-}24)$$

Equations (7-23) and (7-24) describe many physical systems; common examples are the equilibrium temperature in a solid or the electrostatic field in a volume of space where there is no electric charge density. Analytical solutions to Laplace's equation have been studied thoroughly with different boundary conditions and different coordinate systems, for many years. Fourier series, hyperbolic functions, Bessel functions, polynomials, and all sorts of wonderful things pop up in these solutions. Sometimes the math is difficult.

The first thing you notice about Laplace's equation is that the sum of three things is zero. This means that one of them must be of opposite sign to the other two. Something that is not so obvious, but is easy to prove, is that Laplace's equation implies that the solution at a point is the *average value* of the solution around that point. This is the key for our spreadsheet application.

We are not going to discuss analytical solutions, which can be mathematically challenging. Instead, we will use EXCEL to develop a numerical solution using the extraordinarily powerful *finite element method* (FEM). Using this method you can get numerical solutions that might be impossible to obtain analytically because we do not know all of the functions in the universe.

Let's begin by using the FEM in a one-dimensional example so you can see the simplicity of the concept. We will find the temperature distribution in a long, thin, thermally insulated metal rod. One end will be held at one temperature, say 100 C in steam, and the other end will be fixed at another temperature, say 0 C in ice. Figure 7-10 shows the model of this experiment with constant-temperature heat baths at both ends and five temperature sensors attached to the rod.

Open the workbook TEMPERATURE and you will see the Home screen in Figure 7-11. The temperature distribution is far away from the steady state in this Figure. Imagine that the metal rod has 7 temperature sensors evenly spaced along its length, including the constant temperature heat baths at the ends.

The FEM is probably analogous to how Nature works. When electric charges are placed on a conductor they push each other around until they arrive at a minimum potential energy configuration.

As you use the TEMPERATURE and LAPLACE workbooks you can observe their scalar fields as they change until they reach stable configurations – the final solutions – when no further changes occur. Nature is faster than EXCEL; charges on a good conductor adjust themselves in about 10^{-14} seconds or less. Nature is also slower than EXCEL; charges may take years to adjust themselves on the surface of a good insulator like quartz.

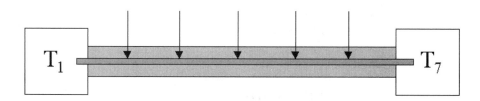

Figure 7-10. Thermally insulated conducting rod is placed between two constant-temperature heat baths. Temperature sensors are equally spaced along the rod. This is similar to Ångstrom's classic experiment in the 1800s. This Figure was made using EXCEL's Drawing Tool.

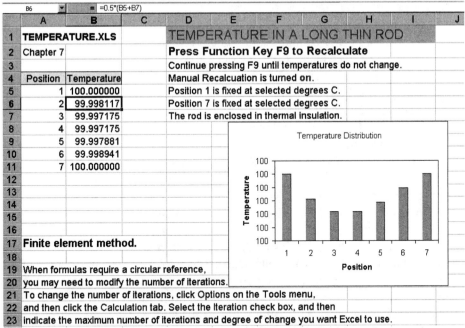

Figure 7-11. The temperature distribution has not settled into the steady state. Press Function Key F9 repeatedly until the temperatures stop changing.

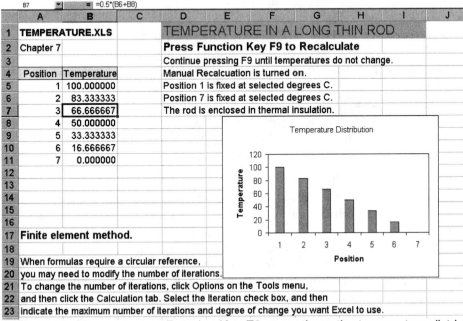

Figure 7-12. After you press Function Key F9 many times the temperature distribution eventually achieves the steady-state values shown here.

This workbook has three new features:

- First, usually you should avoid using a *circular reference*, that is, a formula that refers back to its own cell. EXCEL designers knew that some engineering and scientific applications require circular references, and they provided for this. (For more, look in Help for *circular*.)
- The second new feature in this workbook is that we are going to turn off Automatic Calculation and turn on Manual Calculation to facilitate circular references.
- The third new feature is the use of 3-D charts for display of results.

Let's see how to use the FEM to find the electric potential, or the temperature, in a two-dimensional situation. Open the worksheet named LAPLACE and you will see a sketch of a box (see Fig. 7-13). The empty box has a tight-fitting top that is insulated from the sides of the box. The top is a conductor maintained at a potential difference of 100 volts with respect to the sides and bottom. For temperature, think of the box as being filled with a thermal conductor and with the temperature of the top maintained at a temperature difference of 100 degrees C with respect to the sides and bottom. For example, the sides and bottom could be in contact with ice and the top could be in contact with steam.

The first step in FEM is to discretize the area or volume into a grid. Here, we are going to use a rectangular grid in two dimensions, 5 by 5. The more grid points you use, the better the results will be.

When you open the workbook it may be in a final state. To start it again, change one of the boundary values. For example, change one of the 100 volt values to 0 and press Function Key F9. Continue pressing F9 until the solution stops changing. You may need to press F9 more than 50 times before the solution becomes stable. The final state is shown in Fig. 7-13.

Now change the 0 back to 100 and press Function Key F9. The field will be distorted, something like Fig. 7-14. Continue pressing F9 until the field achieves a stable configuration. Because of the symmetry of the boundary conditions, the field inside the box should show a symmetrical pattern.

More on circular references

Examine the formulas in cell D6 (Fig. 7-13) and cell D5 (Fig. 7-14). The formula in cell D6 refers to cell D5 and the formula in cell D5 refers to cell D6. This is a circular reference and usually you will get a nasty warning from EXCEL (see Fig. 7-15) if you do not use Manual Recalculation and check the Iteration box.

When a formula refers to its own cell, either *directly* or *indirectly*, it is called a circular reference. To calculate such a formula, EXCEL must calculate each cell involved in the circular reference once by using the results of the previous iteration. Unless you change the default settings for iteration, EXCEL stops calculating after 100 iterations or after all values in the circular reference change by less than 0.001 between iterations, whichever comes first.

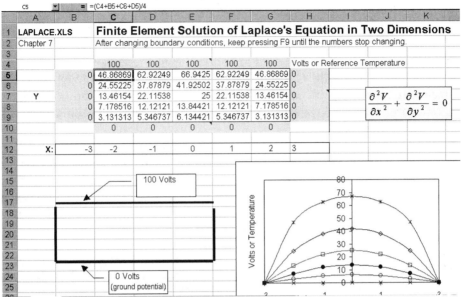

Figure 7-13. Home screen of LAPLACE. The formula for cell C5 is shown in the formula editing box. Note that the formula is the average value of the cells around cell C5. The worksheet is shown in its final state, the FEM solution.

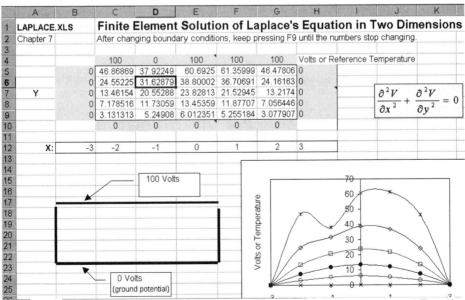

Figure 7-14. The value of boundary cell D4 has been changed to 0 and Function Key F9 has been pressed once. Note the distorted field pattern; compare with Fig. 7-13. Press Function Key F9 repeatedly until the numbers do not change. You may have to press the key about 50 times.

EXCEL cannot resolve formulas with circular references by using normal calculation. When you type in a circular reference, a message will warn you that a circular reference is present (Fig. 7-15).

If the circular reference is accidental, click OK. The Circular Reference toolbar displays, and tracer arrows point to each cell that is referenced by the circular reference. You can use the Circular Reference toolbar to move through each cell in the reference so that you can redesign the formulas or logic to break the circular reference. Some scientific and engineering formulas require circular references. The FEM is one of them.

Since some formulas *require* a circular reference, you may need to change the number of iterations. To change the number of iterations, click Options on the Tools menu, and then click the Calculation tab. Select the Iteration check box, and then indicate the maximum number of iterations and degree of change you want EXCEL to use (see Fig. 7-16). The Exercises at the end of this chapter will give you some practice in handling circular references.

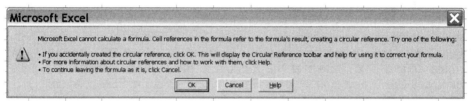

Figure 7-15. This is the circular reference warning. In the LAPLACE worksheet we are intentionally using circular references. When you do *not* want to use circular references, click OK and EXCEL will bring up the Circular Reference toolbar to guide you in debugging the circular reference.

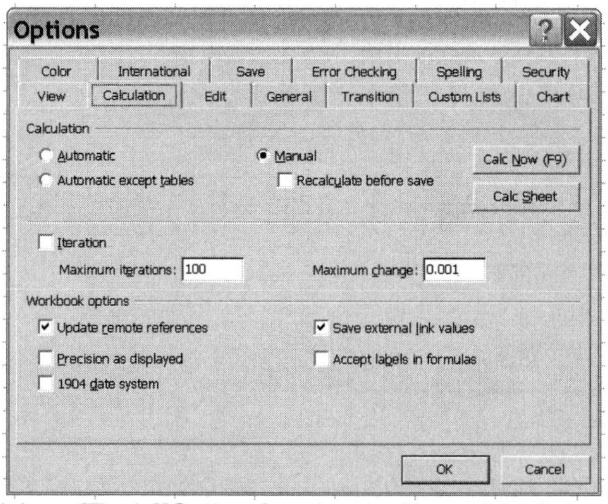

Figure 7-16. Click on [Tools][Options] and you will see this dialog box. The Iteration box is shown checked and a maximum of 100 iterations is selected.

> **Tip**
> It is often possible to transform a PDE into a system of ODEs using the method of *separation of variables*. For example, with Laplace's equation in three dimensions, you can solve three second-order ODEs after the variables are separated. It is often easier to solve two or three ODEs than one PDE. See Section 7.7.

It is instructive and useful to view two-dimensional data in three-dimensional charts as shown in Figs. 7-17 and 7-18. These Figures are on the worksheet tabs.

Look back at Fig. 3-16 in Chapter 3. This is the 3-D dialog box that lets you control the viewing angle of the 3-D and surface charts. Just click on a chart and use your mouse to grab a corner. Move the mouse to rotate the chart.

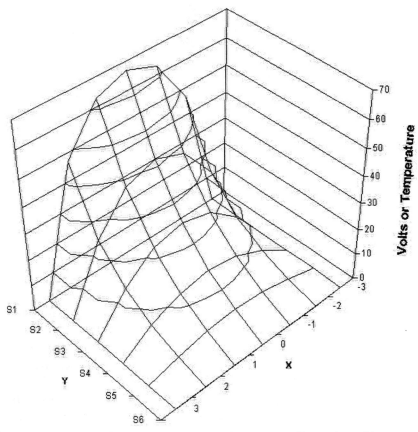

Figure 7-17. FEM solution to Laplace's equation in two dimensions. You can view this chart by clicking on the 3-D tab at the bottom of the LAPLACE workbook. Notice the use of a vertical title for "Volts or Temperature." You can control the orientation of titles with the Alignment option. This Figure was produced with only a 5 x 5 grid. It would look much smoother with more elements.

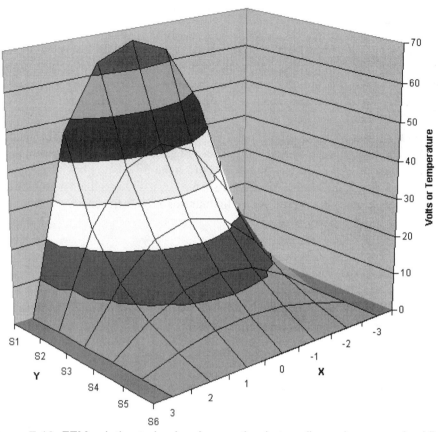

Figure 7-18. FEM solution to Laplace's equation in two dimensions, *x* and *y*. View this chart by clicking on the Surface tab on the worksheet. You can see this in color on your monitor; note the improvement in graphical clarity.

7.7. PDE separation of variables

✪Let's look at an example of *separation of variables* to transform a PDE into a system of ODEs. Schrödinger's equation is the PDE that gave us the transistor, the laser, Silicon Valley, and the PC that you are using. Erwin Schrödinger won a Nobel Prize in 1933 for his equation, which is one of the basic formulations of quantum mechanics. Schrödinger's equation will not help you to build bridges or automobiles, but it will help you to produce better steel and other materials with which to build bridges and automobiles. We will find modes of oscillation of an electron that will remind you of the vibrations shown in the movie of the Tacoma Narrows bridge just before it collapsed.

We will apply Schrödinger's PDE to a mass located in a rectangular potential well. This is a simplified model of an electron trapped in a quantum well on a microchip, which makes a little laser. Unlike a laser diode, a quantum well's frequency is determined by the size of the well. FEM is often used to solve more complicated quantum problems.

Schrödinger's equation is based on two bits of information. Max Planck (Nobel Prize 1918) found by experiments that energy E is quantized as $E = \hbar\omega$, where $\hbar$ is Planck's constant divided by 2π and ω is the radian frequency (rad/s). The experimental value of the fundamental physical constant $\hbar$ is 1.052×10^{-34} Joule-s. In his Ph.D. dissertation Prince Louis Victor de Broglie (Nobel Prize 1929) suggested that mechanical momentum mv is associated with a *de Broglie* wavelength λ by the simple relation $\lambda = h/mv$. The value of h is 6.63×10^{-34} Joule-s.

Prince de Broglie's formula was quickly confirmed by experiments at Bell Laboratories (now Lucent Technologies), and it is considered to be one of ten formulas that changed the face of the Earth. See Figure 7-19. It is also the basis of the electron microscope, because an electron's wavelength can be much smaller than visible light and λ can be tuned with a voltage. Ernst Ruska won the Nobel Prize in 1986 for his invention of the electron microscope.

If there is a wavelength, what is the wave equation? Schrödinger put the two bits of information from Planck and de Broglie together and formed his equation,

$$-\frac{\hbar^2}{2m}\nabla^2\Psi + V\Psi = i\hbar\frac{\partial\Psi}{\partial t} \tag{7-25}$$

where Ψ is the wave function that describes the mass m, $i = \sqrt{-1}$ and V is the potential energy function, used here as an operator on Ψ. (See Chapter 10 for more about i.) The solution of Eq. (7-25) is very sensitive to the form of V. Equation (7-25) looks difficult, but let's apply it to our simple system of a one-dimensional rectangular potential well. In the well V is zero except at the walls. At the walls V can be assumed to be very large or even infinite. With these simplifying assumptions inside the well Eq. (7-25) reduces to,

$$-\frac{\hbar^2}{2m}\frac{\partial^2\Psi}{\partial x^2} = i\hbar\frac{\partial\Psi}{\partial t}. \tag{7-26}$$

Now let's do the separation. Let $\Psi(x,t) = \psi(x)T(t)$. In other words, we are assuming that the function of two variables can be represented as the product of two other functions. One of these new functions (ψ) depends only on x, and the other new function (T) depends only on t. Substitute the product $\psi(x)T(t)$ in Eq. (7-26) and you will find,

$$-\frac{\hbar^2}{2m}T(t)\frac{d^2\psi(x)}{dx^2} = i\hbar\,\psi(x)\frac{dT(t)}{dt}. \tag{7-27}$$

Figure 7-19. Prince Louis Victor de Broglie's equation is a formula that changed the face of the Earth. This stamp shows the application of $\lambda = h/mv$ to the electron microscope. The circles symbolize electron diffraction and interference.

In Equation (7-27) we have changed partial derivatives to total derivatives because each function in the product is a function of only one variable. Now divide both sides of this equation by $\psi(x)T(t)$,

$$-\frac{\hbar^2}{2m}\frac{T(t)}{\psi(x)T(t)}\frac{d^2\psi(x)}{dx^2} = i\hbar\frac{\psi(x)}{\psi(x)T(t)}\frac{dT(t)}{dt} \qquad (7\text{-}28)$$

and cancel functions to obtain,

$$-\frac{\hbar^2}{2m}\frac{1}{\psi(x)}\frac{d^2\psi(x)}{dx^2} = i\hbar\frac{1}{T(t)}\frac{dT(t)}{dt} \; . \qquad (7\text{-}29)$$

Now the left side is only a function of x and the right side is only a function of t. How can a function of only one variable be equal to a function of another variable? This can be true only if both functions are equal to a constant. This is what we call the *separation constant*. Let the separation constant be E. You can choose anything you want for the constant, but let's call it E because I know what's coming and this choice will simplify things later. The separation constant E will turn out to be the energy.

So, we have completed a major task. Instead of one complicated PDE we now have a system of two simple ODEs that we saw earlier in this chapter:

$$\frac{d^2\psi(x)}{dx^2} = -\frac{2mE}{\hbar^2}\psi(x) \qquad (7\text{-}30)$$

$$\frac{dT(t)}{dt} = \frac{E}{i\hbar}T(t) \ . \tag{7-31}$$

To save printer's ink we can let $2mE/\hbar^2 = k^2$ and $E/i\hbar = -i\omega$. Note that $E/i\hbar = -i\omega$ is just Planck's law again. With these changes let's rewrite the two ODEs as,

$$\frac{d^2\psi(x)}{dx^2} = -k^2\psi(x) \tag{7-32}$$

$$\frac{dT(t)}{dt} = -i\omega T(t) \ . \tag{7-33}$$

Equation (7-32) is our old harmonic oscillator model equation that we examined in Section 7.4 but now we have a vibration in space x, not time t. Furthermore, Eq. (7-33) looks like our exponential decay model in Section 7.1, except for the i.

Let's put in the two boundary conditions $\psi(0) = 0$ and $\psi(L) = 0$, which are appropriate for a potential well that starts at $x = 0$ and has a width of L. For the time equation let's set $T(0) = T_0$.

Equation (7-33) is an ODE of the variables-separable form that we have seen before, and we can write it as,

$$\frac{dT}{T} = -i\omega \, dt \tag{7-34}$$

with the solution,

$$T(t) = T_0 e^{-i\omega t} \ . \tag{7-35}$$

Now let's see what the harmonic oscillator equation tells us. The solution is,

$$\psi(x) = A\cos(kx) + B\sin(kx). \tag{7-36}$$

The boundary condition at $x = 0$ requires $A = 0$ because,

$$0 = A\cos(k0) + B\sin(k0) \ . \tag{7-37}$$

The boundary condition at $x = L$ is more interesting:

$$0 = B\sin(kL). \tag{7-38}$$

If $B = 0$ we have no solution, so Eq. (7-38) can only be useful if,

$$kL = n\pi \qquad n = 0,1,2,3,\cdots. \tag{7-39}$$

We can ignore $n = 0$ because, as we will see shortly, this corresponds to the case in which the probability of finding the object in the well is zero. So we have,

$$k_n = \frac{n\pi}{L}, \quad n = 1, 2, 3, \cdots .$$
(7-40)

We have put a subscript n on k to identify k with its associated value of n. Note that this is what we would have found for vibrations of the Tacoma Narrows bridge or a violin string, except that $\hbar$ is hidden in Eq. (7-40).

The integer n is called a *quantum number*. It is worth noting that this quantum number appeared when boundary conditions were imposed.

Recall that we used $2mE/\hbar^2 = k^2$ so we must put a label on E and then we find,

$$\frac{2mE_n}{\hbar^2} = k_n^2 = \frac{n^2\pi^2}{L^2} .$$
(7-41)

We finally have the quantized energy levels:

$$E_n = \frac{n^2\pi^2\hbar^2}{2mL^2} .$$
(7-42)

Let's summarize several important points:

- The energy levels are quantized – only special energies are allowed.
- The energy levels are not evenly spaced; the energy levels increase as n^2.
- Integers (quantum numbers) arise when boundary conditions are imposed, as in classical mechanics.
- The energy of each level increases rapidly as L decreases. In other words, confining an electron produces quantized energy levels and squeezing an electron increases its energy!

We need to go back and label each frequency ω with n to associate it with its own energy level, $E_n = \hbar\omega_n$. Now we can write the complete solution for one energy level as,

$$\Psi_n(x,t) = B_n \sin(k_n x)T_0 \exp(-i\omega_n t) = B_n \sin(k_n x)\exp(-i\omega_n t)$$
(7-43)

where we have absorbed the constant T_0 into the constant B_n.

How do we find the value of B_n? Max Born (Olivia Newton-John's grandfather) won the Nobel Prize in 1954 for answering this question. Professor Born interpreted Ψ as the *probability amplitude* associated with the object of mass m.

Today almost everyone believes that this statistical interpretation is correct, because it works so well.

The probability of finding mass m in the whole potential well is 1, so we can normalize the wave function to 1. We can't go into the details here, but let me say that the *probability density* is $\Psi^*\Psi$ where Ψ^* is the *complex conjugate* of Ψ. (See Chapter 10 to learn about the complex conjugate. In Chapters 10 and 11 you will see that the *power spectral density* of a classical mechanical system has an analogous mathematical form.) The probability density is like other more familiar densities – mass density, for example. You have to integrate mass density over space to determine how much mass is present. Similarly for probability,

$$1 = \int_0^L [B_n \sin(k_n x)\exp(+i\omega_n t)][B_n \sin(k_n x)\exp(-i\omega_n t)]\, dx \qquad (7\text{-}44)$$

so we can find,

$$B_n^2 = \frac{1}{\int_0^L \sin^2(k_n x)\, dx} = \frac{2}{L}. \qquad (7\text{-}45)$$

After we do the integral in Eq. (7-45) we have a complete wave function,

$$\Psi_n(x,t) = \sqrt{\frac{2}{L}}\, \sin(k_n x)\exp(-i\omega_n t) . \qquad (7\text{-}46)$$

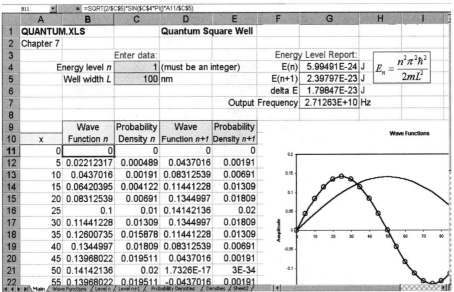

Figure 7-20. Home screen of the QUANTUM workbook. The wave functions for energy levels 1 and 2 are shown. The output frequency shown is in the microwave region of the electromagnetic spectrum.

Open the QUANTUM workbook and you will see the Home screen shown in Fig. 7-20. Note how Eq. (7-45) is entered in cell B11. In this workbook you can input data on the width L of the well and the quantum number n. This workbook is set up for an electron mass, and it produces values of the energy levels and the frequency of the light for a transition between levels n and $n + 1$. Graphs of the wave functions and probability densities are shown.

FAQ

Q. *How can I compute the frequency of the light from the confined electron?*
A. For electric dipole radiation the distribution of the electron charge q must change in some non-symmetrical way, like a dipole radio antenna. Note that only integral numbers of electron half-waves are allowed. The lowest level is a half wave. The second level is a full wavelength. (This is the de Broglie wavelength, not the photon wavelength.) The end result is that when you compute the electric dipole moment qx connecting different energy levels you find that dipole transitions can occur between *adjacent levels* because they have alternating symmetry. The frequency of the light is proportional to the *difference* in the energies. For example, between the first two levels the frequency of the photon is $\omega_2 - \omega_1$. This comes out of the math even if you can't visualize the physical argument. This is the same thing that Niels Bohr (Nobel Prize 1922) found earlier in his semi-classical theory of the hydrogen atom, $E_{n+1} - E_n = \hbar(\omega_{n+1} - \omega_n)$, where n is an integer. See Figure 7-21. Also see cells G4:G7 in Fig. 7-20.

Figure 7-21. The quantum of energy is $h\nu$ where h is Planck's constant and the frequency in Hz is represented by the symbol ν, the Greek letter *nu*. The italic Roman letter v (vee) looks very much like the Greek letter ν.

What's next?

In Chapter 8 we will explore some of the applications in the Analysis ToolPak. The ToolPak is loaded with useful features but it would take many chapters to explain all of them. So, we're going to look at a few of the ones you'll use most often and you can learn the rest when – and if – you need them.

References

ODE Architect, the Ultimate ODE Power Tool, CD (John Wiley & Sons, Inc., New York, 1999).

J. A. Roberson and C. T. Crowe, *Engineering Fluid Mechanics*, Sixth Edition (John Wiley & Sons, Inc., New York, 1997). Laplace's equation pp. 660–664, finite difference method pp. 642–649.

J. Jin, *The Finite Element Method in Electromagnetics*, (John Wiley & Sons, Inc., New York, 1993).

M. Abramowitz and I. A. Stegun, *Handbook of Mathematical Functions with Formulas, Graphs, and Mathematical Tables*. (Dover Publications, New York, 1974). Pages 875-899 refer to methods in this chapter. This book is also available in hardcover from the U. S. Government Printing Office at the web site http://www.gpo.gov . Stock Number: 003-003-00279-8. This is the famous National Bureau of Standards Applied Mathematics Series 55. 10th printing, 1972, with corrections; reprinted 1984. It provides engineers and scientists with a comprehensive, self-contained summary of mathematical functions and methods that are needed in physical and engineering problems. (The National Bureau of Standards is now named the National Institute of Science and Technology, or NIST. The web site is http://www.nist.gov . This is a great web site; you should explore it.)

G. Arfken, *Mathematical Methods for Physicists*, 3rd Edition (Academic Press, Orlando, Florida, 1985) pp. 492-493.

J. H. E. Cartwright and O. Piro, "The Dynamics of Runge-Kutta Methods." Int. J. Bifurcations Chaos **2**, 427-449 (1992).
                    http://formentor.uib.es/~julyan/TeX/rkpaper/root/root.html.

J. D. Lambert and D. Lambert, *Numerical Methods for Ordinary Differential Systems: The Initial Value Problem*, (John Wiley & Sons, Inc., New York, 1991). Chapter 5.

W. H. Press, B. P. Flannery, S. A. Teukolsky, and W. T. Vetterling, "Runge-Kutta Method" and "Adaptive Step Size Control for Runge-Kutta." Sections 16.1 and 16.2 in *Numerical Recipes in C: The Art of Scientific Computing*, second edition (Cambridge University Press, Cambridge, England, 1992). pp. 704-716.

Applications of Euler and Feynman algorithms:
http://www.kw.igs.net/~jackord/j6.html
http://www.kw.igs.net/~jackord/bp/f1.html

Use of Euler and Runge-Kutta to solve first-order and second-order ODEs:
http://www.nacse.org/sc96/DIFFEQ/mydif2/index.html
http://csep.acns.colostate.edu/csep/ODE/NODE7.html

http://www.shu.ac.uk/schools/sci/maths/ssuser/
The Spreadsheet User journal.

http://www-math.mit.edu/~djk/18_013a/chapter26/sections.html
Notes on numerical analysis of ordinary differential equations.

L. N. Long and H. Weiss, "The Velocity Dependence of Aerodynamic Drag: A Primer for Mathematicians," American Mathematical Monthly, **106**, 127 – 133 (February 1999). The appendix contains a model of re-entry of the space shuttle into Earth's atmosphere, which has a closed-form solution.

Test your skills

1. Improved Euler's method. Show that the ordinary differential equation

$$\frac{dy}{dx} = x - y$$

has the exact solution $y(x) = 2e^{-x} + x - 1$, for the initial condition $y = 1$, $x = 0$. Use the improved Euler's method to get a solution for $y(x)$ for $x = 1$ to 5 in steps of 0.1. Compute and graph the errors compared to the exact solution.

2. Compute Question 1 with a step size of 0.01. Compute and graph the errors between Euler, improved Euler, and the exact solution.

3. Laplace's equation. Compose a worksheet to perform a one-dimensional finite element solution with Laplace's equation for the temperature distribution in a long thin wire or rod. Both ends of the rod are fixed at 0 C in an ice bath. The rod is thermally insulated except at the ends. The center of the rod can be heated using a laser and fiber optics. Use 11 equally spaced temperature sensors along the rod for temperature calculations. Use 6 decimal places for the temperature col-

umn. At time $t = 0$ the laser is switched on and the temperature at the center of the rod (at sensor number 6) quickly rises to 100 C. Determine the temperature distribution and graph the data. *Hint:* turn on Manual recalculation. Continue pressing Function Key F9 until the temperature distribution does not change.

This experiment is currently a standard measurement method using a laser or a pulsed current through a resistor to apply a transient heat pulse to a wire or thin rod. This relates to the National Science Education Standard *energy and heat*.

4.✪ Heat flow equation. The classical heat flow equation studied by Joseph Fourier and others in the 1800s can be written as,

$$\nabla^2 H = \frac{\rho c}{k}\frac{\partial H}{\partial t}, \qquad \text{or in one space dimension for a wire,} \qquad \frac{\partial^2 H}{\partial x^2} = \frac{\rho c}{k}\frac{\partial H}{\partial t},$$

where H is the heat flow per unit area per unit time, ρ is the mass density, c is the specific heat capacity, and k is the thermal conductivity. This has the same form as Schrödinger's equation except that i is missing. Using the method of separation of variables in Section 7.7 find the general solution for the experiment of Question 3. The initial conditions are: both ends fixed at 0 C, the center temperature at 100 C, and the temperature distribution has the shape of an isosceles triangle. At time $t = 0$ the laser is switched off. Compose a workbook to compute the first five Fourier components as functions of time. Use a 3-D graph to show the temperature distribution as it changes to a uniform distribution.

5.✪ Do you have your parachute? The physical situation that we are going to model is a mass of 200 kg falling in a resistive medium with a resistive force constant of 63 N s/m. This is like a parachute or a falling cat. The system can be modeled as a second order ODE using Newton's second law $ma = \Sigma F$,

$$200\,\frac{d^2 y}{dt^2} = 200g - 63v.$$

This can be transformed to two first order ODEs by means of the substitution $\frac{dy}{dt} = v$ which requires solution of $\frac{dv}{dt} = g - \frac{63}{200}v$ and, of course, $\frac{dy}{dt} = v$.

Let the initial conditions be $y = 0$, $v = 0$, for $t = 0$. Down is positive, up is negative. (Also see the paper by L. N. Long and H. Weiss in the References section.)

(a) The *terminal velocity* is achieved when the resistive force $-63v$ is equal to the weight $200g$. Show that the terminal velocity is $200g/63$ m/s.

(b) Show that the exact solution for the velocity v is given by the equation,

$$v(t) = \frac{200g}{63}[1 - \exp(-\frac{63}{200}t)].$$

Note that the terminal velocity is achieved after a long time, $t \gg \dfrac{200}{63}$.

(c) Show that the exact solution for the displacement y is

$$y(t) = \frac{200g}{63}\left\{t + \frac{200}{63}[\exp(-\frac{63}{200}t) - 1]\right\}.$$

These equations enable you to design a landing system for other planets by inserting the appropriate value of g. For example, for a Mars lander $g = 3.72$ m/s^2. Compare with Earth, $g = 9.8$ m/s^2. The resistive force depends on the parachute and the atmosphere.

(d) Compose a worksheet to compute y and v for the first 5 seconds, in steps of 0.2 seconds, using the improved Euler method.

(e) Calculate the percent error relative to the exact solution at each time increment. Make a graph of the percent error at each time increment.

(f) Make graphs showing the numerical solutions for x and v, and the exact solutions for visual comparison. To avoid graphic clutter, make one chart for y and another chart for v.

This exercise relates to the National Science Education Standard *position and motion of objects – motions and forces*.

Cats can be seriously injured if they fall less than seven or eight floors from a building. Injury *decreases* if a cat falls more than seven or eight floors. There is a record of a cat that fell 32 floors and suffered slight injury. See W. O. Whitney and C. J. Mehlhaff, "High-rise syndrome in cats," *The Journal of the American Veterinary Association*, **191**, 1399–1401 (1987). For more about parachutes and falling cats, see D. Halliday, R. Resnick, and J. Walker, *Fundamentals of Physics*, sixth edition, pages 104–105 (John Wiley & Sons, Inc., New York, 2001).

The science of mechanics, my dear Hermodorus, has many important uses in practical life, and is held by philosophers to be worthy of the highest esteem, and is zealously studied by mathematicians, because it takes almost first place in dealing with the nature of the material elements of the universe. For it deals generally with the stability and movement of bodies about their centers of gravity, and their motions in space, inquiring not only into the causes of those that move in virtue of their nature, but forcibly transferring others from their own places in a motion contrary to their nature. . .

Pappus of Alexandria (about 290–350)

Mechanics is the paradise of mathematical sciences. Mechanical science is most noble and useful beyond all others, since by means of it all animated bodies that have motion perform all their operations.

Leonardo DaVinci (1452–1519)

Chapter 8
Analysis ToolPak

What this chapter is about

The Analysis ToolPak is one of 15 Add-ins included with EXCEL. The ToolPak has 19 tools that can make your life easier. We will list them here for ready reference. To access the Analysis ToolPak, click on [Tools][Data Analysis].
In alphabetical order, the contents of the Analysis TookPak are:

- Anova: Single Factor
- Anova: Two-Factor with Replication
- Anova: Two-Factor without Replication
- Correlation
- Covariance
- Descriptive Statistics
- Exponential Smoothing (See Section 5.4)
- F-Test Two-Sample for Variances
- Fourier Analysis (See Chapter 11)
- Histogram
- Moving Average (See Section 5.3)
- Random Number Generation
- Rank and Percentile
- Regression
- Sampling
- t-Test: Paired Two Sample for Means
- t-Test: Two-Sample Assuming Equal Variances
- t-Test: Two-Sample Assuming Unequal Variances
- z-Test: Two Sample for Means

You may never use some of these tools but you should be aware of them because one of them may be just what you need to get some results. We will discuss some of the tools in detail, because they are usually important in engineering and science. In particular, Chapter 11 is devotedly entirely to Fourier Analysis because EXCEL's user manual and Help are not of much help for this tool, which is the most powerful one in EXCEL. It can be argued that the Fast Fourier Transform (FFT), which is really what EXCEL's Fourier Analysis tool is about, is the most important mathematical event of the last hundred years for practical purposes, although the proof of Fermat's last theorem was the subject of more news on TV and in print. (Fermat's last theorem is important for theoretical purposes, but it is not known at this time that it has any practical applications.)

Tip
You can consult Help for information on applying the statistical tools, but you must be careful. Getting meaningful results with statistics requires more knowledge about these tools than you will find in Help. This warning is often repeated in Help. Remember what your grandmother said, "Statistics don't lie, but statisticians do."

Section 1.7 has a brief discussion of the Analysis Tool-Pak. Now let's go into more detail. Click on the Tools menu and you will see Fig. 8-1. If Data Analysis does not appear on the drop-down menu, you will have to install the ToolPak (see Help, Section 1.7, and the next page).

Figure 8-1. Data Analysis will be on the Tools drop-down menu if the Analysis ToolPak is installed.

If you do not see Data Analysis, it is easy to install the ToolPak:

On the Tools menu, click Add-Ins.

If Analysis ToolPak is not listed in the Add-Ins dialog box, click Browse.

Locate the drive, folder name, and file name for the Analysis ToolPak add-in. The file may be named `Analys32.xll`. This is usually located in the Library/Analysis folder. Or, run the Setup program if it isn't installed.

Select the Analysis ToolPak check box. For more, consult Help.

Note:

To add or remove components of Microsoft OFFICE or EXCEL on Windows NT Workstation 3.51, start EXCEL Setup or OFFICE Setup in the same way you first installed EXCEL. Follow instructions on your monitor.

If you installed Microsoft OFFICE or EXCEL from a CD-ROM and you have mapped your CD drive to a new drive letter since you originally installed the program, you must run Setup again from the CD-ROM. If you are running any OFFICE or EXCEL files from the CD-ROM, you must uninstall the program and then install OFFICE or EXCEL again from the CD-ROM.

Now, when you click on Data Analysis you will see the upper dialog box in Fig. 8-2. Scroll down and you will see the lower dialog box in Figure 8-2.

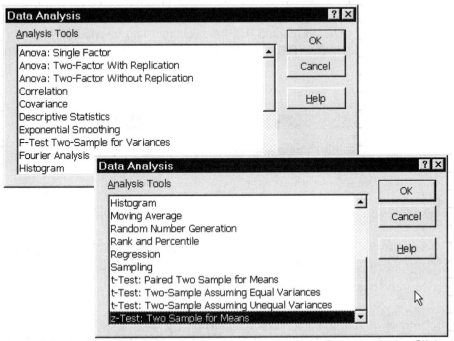

Figure 8-2. Alphabetical listing of the Analysis Tools in Data Analysis. Click on Correlation to see Fig. 8-3.

8.1 Correlation

What is it?

This is a statistical tool that lets you investigate possible relationships between data sequences. For example, if you are in Las Vegas and you suspect the roulette wheels are fixed, you might collect data to see if certain numbers are related.

Edwin Hubble was at the Mount Wilson Observatory in California when he collected data on the distances of stars and galaxies and their Doppler shifts. Hubble discovered evidence that implied the universe is expanding, because the Doppler shift (relative velocity) is correlated with distance. The more distant cosmic objects are receding faster. Similarly, if you watch a horse race you will find that the distance of a horse from the starting gate is correlated with its speed.

What does it do?

The correlation tool returns a number that indicates how values in one data set are related to values in another set. A correlation of 1 indicates that they are definitely related, and as values in one set increase, values in the other set increase. This is *positive correlation*. A correlation –1 indicates that they are definitely related, but as one set increases the other decreases. This is *negative correlation*. A correlation of 0 indicates that there is no statistical relationship. In Chapter 12 we will discuss the *correlation function*, which is a function, not a single number. The correlation function is often a function of time or space.

Click on the Correlation Analysis Tool and you will bring up the dialog box shown in Fig. 8-3. The correlation will be calculated and inserted in your worksheet. Open the CORRELATION workbook and you will see the Home screen shown in Fig. 8-4.

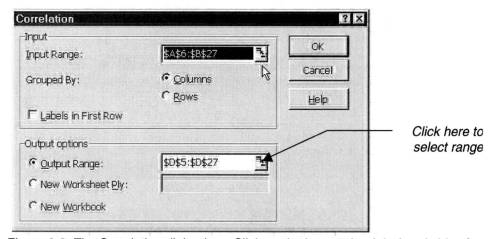

Figure 8-3. The Correlation dialog box. Click on the icon at the right-hand side of a range box to select the range using your mouse.

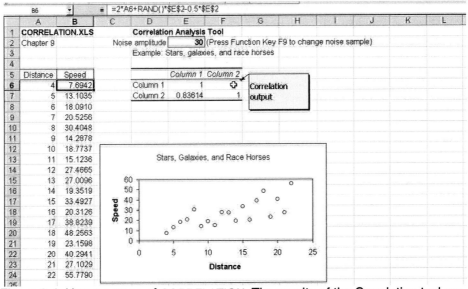

Figure 8-4. Home screen of CORRELATION. The results of the Correlation tool are shown automatically in selected output cells. Note the formula used in constructing this model. The RAND() function produces a random number between 0 and 1, and the formula modifies this with a selected noise amplitude.

In the Correlation output cells, notice that Column 1 is perfectly correlated with itself, and column 2 is perfectly correlated with itself. Column 2 has a correlation coefficient of 0.83614 with respect to Column 1.

About the Correlation dialog box

Input Range

Enter the cell reference for the range of data you want to analyze. The reference must consist of two or more adjacent ranges of data arranged in columns or rows.

Grouped By

To indicate whether the data in the input range is arranged in rows or in columns, click Rows or Columns.

Labels in First Row/Labels in First Column

If the first row of your input range contains labels, select the Labels in First Row check box. If the labels are in the first column of your input range, select the Labels in First Column check box. This check box is clear if your input range has no labels; EXCEL generates appropriate data labels for the output table.

Output Range

Enter the reference for the upper-left cell of the output table. EXCEL populates only half of the table because correlation between two ranges of data is independent of the order in which the ranges are processed. Cells in the output table with matching row and column coordinates contain the value 1 because each data set correlates exactly with itself.

New Worksheet Ply

Click to insert a new worksheet in the current workbook and paste the results starting at cell A1 of the new worksheet. To name the new worksheet, type a name in the box.

New Workbook

Click to create a new workbook and paste the results on a new worksheet in the new workbook.

✪ How does the Correlation analysis tool work?

This analysis tool and its formulas measure the relationship between two data sets that are scaled to be independent of the unit of measurement. The population correlation calculation returns the covariance of two data sets divided by the product of their standard deviations:

$$\rho_{X,Y} = \frac{COV(X,Y)}{\sigma_X \, \sigma_Y} \tag{8-1}$$

where $COV(X,Y)$ is the covariance (see Section 8.3) and where,

$$\sigma_X^2 = \frac{1}{n} \sum (X_i - \mu_x)^2 \tag{8-2}$$

is the square of the standard deviation in X, n is the number of data points, and μ_X is the mean. Similarly, for Y we have

$$\sigma_Y^2 = \frac{1}{n} \sum (Y_i - \mu_Y)^2 . \tag{8-3}$$

You can use the Correlation tool to determine whether two ranges of data move together, that is, whether large values of one set are associated with large values of the other (positive correlation), whether small values of one set are associated with large values of the other (negative correlation), or whether values in both sets are unrelated (correlation near zero). For more information about options in the Correlation dialog box, see Help.

Note: To return the correlation coefficient for two cell ranges, you can also use the CORREL worksheet function.

✪ CORREL

This function returns the correlation coefficient of the array1 and array2 cell ranges. Use the correlation coefficient to determine the relationship between two properties. For example, you can examine the relationship between a location's average rainfall and the number of cases of malaria.

Syntax
CORREL(array1,array2)
Array1   is a cell range of values.
Array2   is a second cell range of values.

Remarks
The arguments must be numbers, or names, arrays, or references that contain numbers.

If an array or reference argument contains text, logical values, or empty cells, those values are ignored; however, cells with the value zero are included.

If array1 and array2 have a different number of data points, CORREL returns the #N/A error value.

If either array1 or array2 is empty, or if s (the standard deviation) of their values equals zero, CORREL returns the #DIV/0! error value.

The formula for the correlation coefficient is given in Eq. (8-1).

Example
CORREL({3,2,4,5,6},{9,7,12,15,17}) equals 0.997054

8.2 Covariance

What is it?
This function returns covariance, which is the average of the products of deviations for each data point pair. Covariance is like an un-normalized Correlation. Recall, In Eq. (8-1) the Correlation is normalized with respect to the standard deviations.

What does it do?
You can use covariance to determine if there is a statistical relationship between two data sets. For example, you can examine whether atmospheric ozone levels are related to population density (people per square kilometer). Covariance is used in calculating the Correlation.

How does it work?

Syntax
COVAR(array1,array2)
Array1   is the first cell range of integers.
Array2   is the second cell range of integers.

Remarks
The arguments must be either numbers or names, arrays, or references that contain numbers. If an array or reference argument contains text, logical values, or empty cells, those values are ignored; however, cells with the value zero are included.

If array1 and array2 have different numbers of data points, COVAR returns the #N/A error value. If either array1 or array2 is empty, COVAR returns the #DIV/0! error value.

The covariance formula is:

$$COV(X,Y) = \frac{1}{n}\sum(x_i - \mu_x)(y_i - \mu_y) \qquad (8\text{-}4)$$

Example
COVAR({3, 2, 4, 5, 6}, {9, 7, 12, 15, 17}) equals 5.2

8.3 Descriptive Statistics

What is it?
The Descriptive Statistics is a tool that you can use to obtain information about the central tendency and variability of your data.

What does it do?
It generates a report of univariate statistics for data in the output range.

About the dialog box
Figure 8-5 shows the Descriptive Statistics dialog box in the CORELATION workbook.

Input Range
Enter the cell reference for the range of data you want to analyze. The reference must consist of two or more adjacent ranges of data arranged in columns or rows.

Grouped By
To indicate whether the data in the input range is arranged in rows or in columns, click Rows or Columns.

Labels in First Row/Labels in First Column
If the first row of your input range contains labels, select the Labels in First Row check box. If the labels are in the first column of your input range, select the Labels in First Column check box. This check box is clear if your input range has no labels; EXCEL generates appropriate data labels for the output table.

Confidence Level for Mean
Select if you want to include a row in the output table for the confidence level of the mean. In the box, enter the confidence level you want to use. For example, a value of 95 percent calculates the confidence level of the mean at a significance of 5 percent.

Kth Largest
Select if you want to include a row in the output table for the kth largest value for

each range of data. In the box, enter the number to use for k. If you enter 1, this row contains the maximum of the data set.

Kth Smallest
Select if you want to include a row in the output table for the kth smallest value for each range of data. In the box, enter the number to use for k. If you enter 1, this row contains the minimum of the data set.

Output Range
Enter the reference for the upper-left cell of the output table. This tool produces two columns of information for each data set. The left column contains statistics labels, and the right column contains the statistics. EXCEL writes a two-column table of statistics for each column or row in the input range, depending on the Grouped By option selected.

New Worksheet Ply
Click to insert a new worksheet in the current workbook and paste the results starting at cell A1 of the new worksheet. To name the new worksheet, type a name in the box.

New Workbook
Click to create a new workbook and paste the results on a new worksheet in the new workbook.

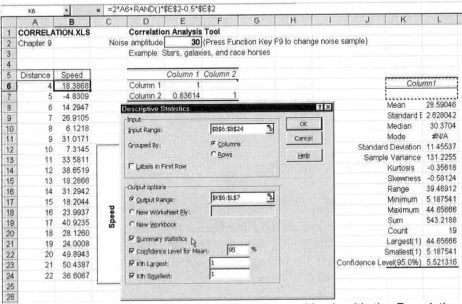

Figure 8-5. Home screen of the CORRELATION workbook with the Descriptive Statistics dialog box. The output of the Descriptive Statistics tool is in columns K and L. Figure 8-6 shows a larger view of the dialog box.

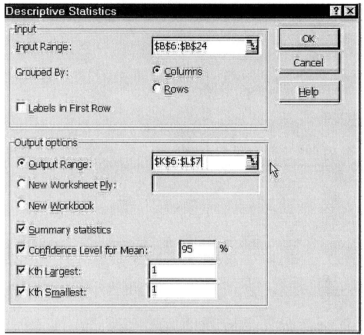

Figure 8-6. The Descriptive Statistics dialog box. The checked boxes produce the outputs shown in columns K and L on the right-hand side of Fig. 8-5.

Summary statistics
Check the boxes on the dialog box if you want EXCEL to produce one field for each of the following statistics in the output table: Mean, Standard Error (of the mean), Median, Mode, Standard Deviation, Variance, Kurtosis, Skewness, Range, Minimum, Maximum, Sum, Count, Largest (#), Smallest (#), and Confidence Level. These are shown in Fig. 8-5.

8.4 Exponential smoothing

What is it?
Exponential smoothing is a form of integration from the present data point back through all previous data points, with an exponential weight assigned to data. In other words, exponential smoothing treats older data with exponentially decreasing importance. This tool is discussed in detail in Section 5.4.

8.5 Fourier Analysis

What is it?

As we said earlier, the Fourier Analysis tool is the most powerful tool in EXCEL. It is actually a form of the Fast Fourier Transform or FFT. See Chapters 11 and 12 (on the CD) for details of how to apply this tool in the frequency domain. Many important operations can be done more simply, quickly, and easily in the frequency domain than in the original data domain.

8.6 Histogram

What is it?

This analysis tool calculates individual and cumulative frequencies for a cell range of data and data bins.

What does it do?

This tool generates data for the number of occurrences of a value in a data set. For example, in a class of 163 students, you could determine the distribution of scores in letter-grade categories. A histogram table presents the letter-grade boundaries and the number of scores between the lowest bound and the current bound. The single most-frequent score is the *mode* of the data. Consult Help for more information about options in the Histogram dialog box shown in Fig. 8-7. An example of the Histogram output is shown in Fig. 8-8.

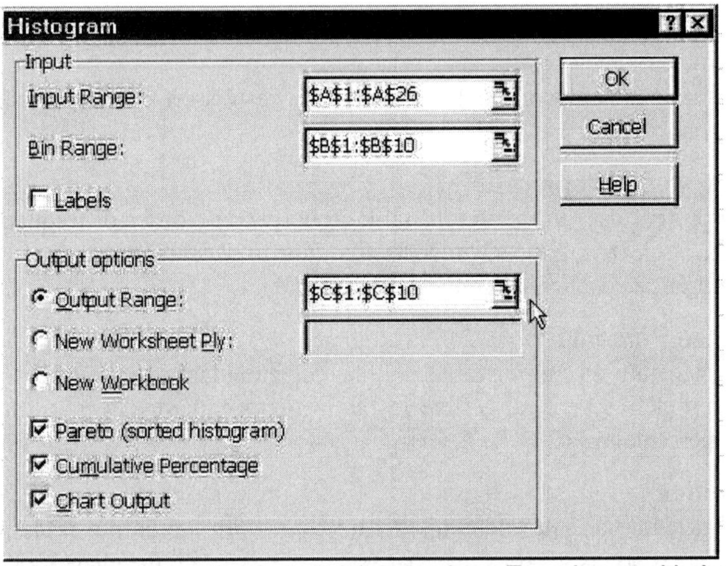

Figure 8-7. The Histogram Analysis Tool dialog box. Experiment with the options.

About the Histogram dialog box

Input Range
Enter the reference for the range of data you want to analyze.

Bin Range (optional)
Enter the cell reference to a range that contains an optional set of boundary values that define bin ranges. These values should be in ascending order. EXCEL counts the number of data points between the current bin number and the adjoining higher bin, if any. A number is counted in a particular bin if it is equal to or less than the bin number down to the last bin. All values below the first bin value are counted together, as are the values above the last bin value.

If you omit the bin range, EXCEL creates a set of evenly distributed bins between the data's minimum and maximum values.

Labels
Select if the first row or column of your input range contains labels. Clear this check box if your input range has no labels; EXCEL generates appropriate data labels for the output table.

Output Range
Enter the reference for the *upper-left cell* of the output table. EXCEL automatically determines the size of the output area and displays a message if the output table will replace existing data.

New Worksheet Ply
Click to insert a new worksheet in the current workbook and paste the results starting at cell A1 of the new worksheet. To name the new worksheet, type a name in the box.

New Workbook
Click to create a new workbook and paste the results on a new worksheet in the new workbook.

Pareto (sorted histogram)
Select to present data in the output table in descending order of frequency. If this check box is cleared, EXCEL presents the data in ascending order and omits the three rightmost columns that contain the sorted data.

Cumulative Percentage
Select to generate an output table column for cumulative percentages and to include a cumulative percentage line in the histogram chart. Clear to omit the cumulative percentages.

Chart Output
Select to generate an embedded histogram chart with the output table. (This embedded chart is not as good as one that you can make with the chart tool.)

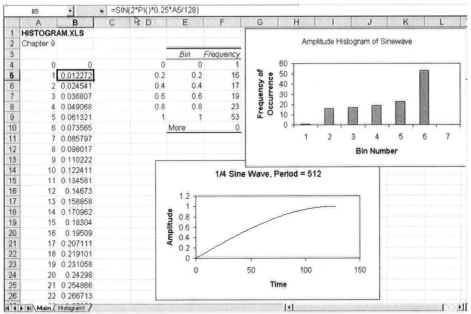

Figure 8-8. Workbook for Histogram. Columns E and F have the generated histogram data. The automatically generated histogram chart is at upper right.

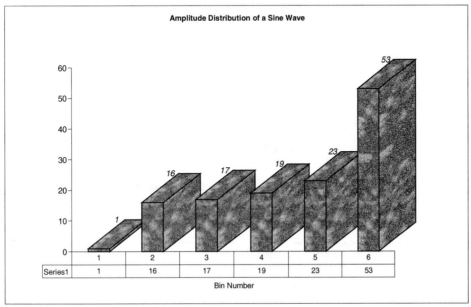

Figure 8-8. Customized histogram of data shown in Fig. 8-8. Compare with the histogram chart in Fig. 8-8. This chart with data table is a standard EXCEL type.

The histogram follows our intuition for a sine wave. There are more points near the top than near the zero-crossing. Try the following in the lab, or visualize it. Get a signal generator and an oscilloscope, and use a sine wave as the input to the scope. When you see the sine wave, turn off the horizontal sweep and lower the beam intensity. The vertical line on the screen is much brighter at the ends than at the center because the beam spends more time at the ends. That is what Figs. 8-8 and 8-9 tell us.

For another experiment, use a camcorder to videotape a pendulum. In each frame of the video, measure the displacement from the lowest point and plot the histogram. It will also look like Fig. 8-8 and 8-8. Note that the form of a histogram is sensitive to the bin size.

8.7 Moving average

What is it?
See Section 5.3 for a complete discussion of this analysis tool, its dialog box, and examples of its application to data.

What does it do?
This analysis tool and its formula project values in the forecast period, based on the average value of the variable over a specific number of preceding periods. Each forecast value is based on the formula,

$$F_{t+1} = \frac{1}{N} \sum_{j=1}^{N} A_{t-j+1} \tag{8-5}$$

where,

N is the number of prior periods to include in the moving average,

A_j is the actual value at time j,

F_j is the forecasted value at time j.

The default value of N is 3, but you may want to use more or less depending on how fast the data are changing. It is advisable to try the moving average several times with different values of N. See the Exercises at the end of this chapter.

8.8 Random number generation

What is it?
This analysis tool does what its name says: it generates random numbers according to some selected parameters. Actually, it generates pseudo-random numbers,

because a perfect random number generator has not yet been invented or discovered. Even if a perfect random number generator existed, it would be too valuable to publish the details about it because random number generators are used in low-observability radar and cryptography. For more, see the References at the end of this chapter.

What does it do?

This analysis tool fills a range with independent random numbers drawn from one of seven selected distributions. You can characterize subjects in a population with a probability distribution. For example, you might use a normal distribution to characterize the population of individuals' heights, or you might use a Bernoulli distribution of two possible outcomes to characterize the population of coin-flip results. The Random Number Generation dialog box is shown in Fig. 8-10 and results are shown in Fig. 8-11 (uniform distribution). For more information about options in this dialog box, see Help. EXCEL has two related worksheet functions:

- Use the RAND worksheet function to return an evenly distributed random number greater than or equal to 0 and less than 1 every time the worksheet is calculated.

- Use the RANDBETWEEN worksheet function to return a random number between numbers you specify every time the worksheet is calculated.

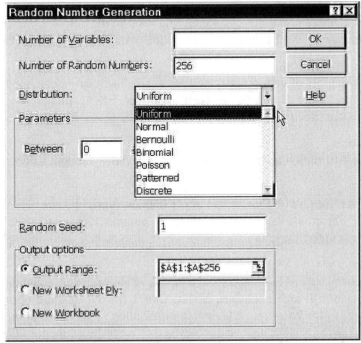

Figure 8-10. Dialog box for the Random Number Generator tool.

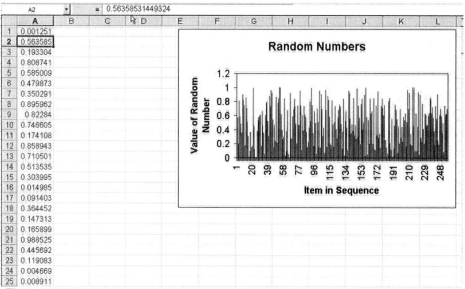

Figure 8-11. A sequence of 256 random numbers based on the uniform distribution. In an Exercise at the end of this chapter you can do a histogram of this.

About the Random Number Generation dialog box

Number of Variables
Enter the number of columns of values you want in the output table. If you do not enter a number, EXCEL fills all columns in the output range you specify.

Number of Random Numbers
Enter the number of data points you want to see. Each data point appears in a row of the output table. If you do not enter a number, EXCEL fills all rows in the output range you specify.

Distribution
Click the distribution method you want to use to create random values.

Uniform
This is characterized by lower and upper bounds. Variables are drawn with equal probability from all values in the range. A common application uses a uniform distribution in the range $0\cdots1$.

Normal
This is characterized by a *mean* and a *standard deviation*. A common application uses a mean of 0 and a standard deviation of 1 for the standard normal distribution. This is also known as a Gaussian distribution. This distribution is available in EXCEL as the NORMDIST and NORMSDIST worksheet functions (see Help).

Bernoulli

This is characterized by a probability of success (p-value) on a given trial. Bernoulli random variables have the value 0 or 1. For example, you can draw a uniform random variable in the range $0 \cdots 1$. If the variable is less than or equal to the probability of success, the Bernoulli random variable is assigned the value 1; otherwise, it is assigned the value 0.

Binomial

This is characterized by a probability of success (p-value) for a number of trials. For example, you can generate number-of-trials Bernoulli random variables, the sum of which is a binomial random variable.

Poisson

This is characterized by a value λ (lambda), equal to 1/mean. The Poisson distribution is often used to characterize the number of events that occur per unit of time. This distribution can describe discrete, rare, physical events that occur in an interval of time or space. A practical measure of rare events is that, in at least 50 trials, the number of trials times the probability of an event occurring is less than about 5. For examples, the average rate at which electrons arrive at a collector or the average rate of counts by a Geiger counter can often be described by a Poisson distribution. The characteristics of the Poisson distribution are:

- The probability of a single event is directly proportional to the size of the interval.
- The probability of two or more events in an interval is very small if the interval is sufficiently small.
- Events are independent in intervals that do not overlap.

This distribution is available in EXCEL as the POISSON worksheet function.

Patterned

This is characterized by a lower and upper bound, a step, repetition rate for values, and repetition rate for the sequence.

Discrete

This is characterized by a value and the associated probability range. The range must contain two columns: The left column contains values, and the right column contains probabilities associated with the value in that row. The sum of the probabilities must be 1.

Parameters

Enter a value or values to characterize the distribution selected.

Random Seed

Enter an optional value from which to generate random numbers. You can reuse this value later to produce the same random numbers.

Output Range

Enter the reference for the upper-left cell of the output table. EXCEL automatically determines the size of the output area and displays a message if the output table will replace existing data.

New Worksheet Ply

Click to insert a new worksheet in the current workbook and paste the results starting at cell A1 of the new worksheet. Type a name in the box, if desired.

New Workbook

Click to create a new workbook and paste the results on a new worksheet in the new workbook.

8.9 Regression

What is it?

This analysis tool performs linear regression analysis by using the *least squares* method to fit a line through a set of observations. Also, see Help for the FORECAST worksheet function, which produces a forecast based on linear regression. Figure 8-12 shows the dialog box.

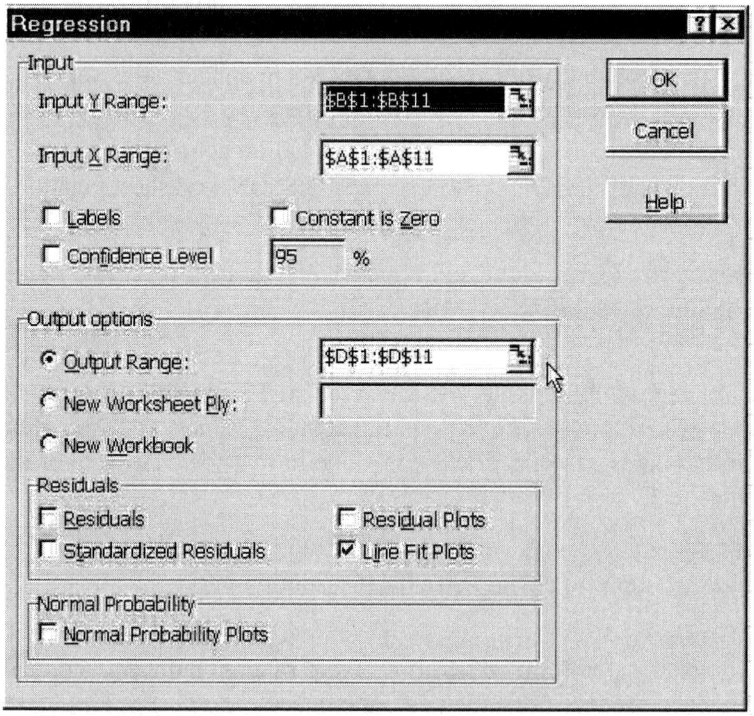

Figure 8-12. Dialog box for the Regression worksheet tool.

What does it do?

You can analyze how a single dependent variable is affected by the values of one or more independent variables. For example, you can investigate how the performance of a swimmer or runner is affected by age, height, and weight. You can assign shares in the performance measure to each of these three factors, based on a set of performance data, and then use the results to predict the performance of a new, untested athlete. (Try this with the performance of integrated circuits, and with stock market prices of corporations and their financial performance data.) The Regression tool is not magic; it must be used carefully after you have studied statistical analysis. Figure 8-13 shows the results of the Regression tool. For more information about options in the Regression dialog box, see Help.

About the Regression dialog box

Input Y Range

Enter the reference for the range of dependent data. The range must consist of a single column of data.

Input X Range

Enter the reference for the range of independent data. EXCEL orders independent variables from this range in ascending order from left to right. The maximum number of independent variables is 16.

Labels

Select if the first row or column of your input range or ranges contains labels. Clear if your input has no labels; EXCEL generates appropriate data labels for the output table.

Confidence Level

Select to include an additional level in the summary output table. Enter the confidence level you want applied in addition to the default 95 percent level.

Constant is Zero

Select to force the regression line to pass through the origin.

Output Range

Enter the reference for the upper-left cell of the output table. Allow at least seven columns for the summary output table, which includes an anova table, coefficients, standard error of y estimate, r2 values, number of observations, and standard error of coefficients.

New Worksheet Ply

Click to insert a new worksheet in the current workbook and paste the results starting at cell A1 of the new worksheet. To name the new worksheet, type a name in the box.

New Workbook
Click to create a new workbook and paste the results on a new worksheet in the new workbook.

Residuals
Select to include residuals in the residuals output table.

Standardized Residuals
Select to include standardized residuals in the residuals output table.

Residual Plots
Select to generate a chart for each independent variable versus the residual.

Line Fit Plots
Select to generate a chart for predicted values versus the observed values.

Normal Probability Plots
Select to generate a chart that plots normal probability.

An application of the Regression analysis tool to noisy data is shown in Fig. 8-13. Note the formula used in this model of distance to galaxies from our planet; the random error increases with time. The charts shown on the Main sheet are generated automatically together with the tabular information. Figures 8-14, 8-15, and 8-16 show the charts named on the tabs at the bottom of the worksheets.

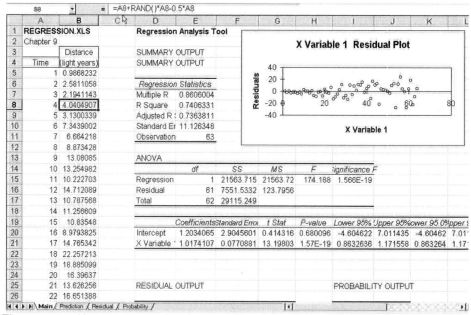

Figure 8-13. Home screen showing results of the Regression analysis tool with the options selected in Fig. 8-12. Scroll to the right and down to see more.

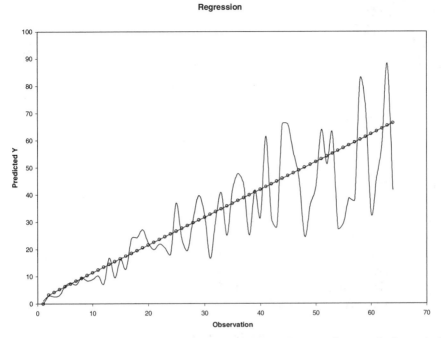

Figure 8-14. *Line with markers:* prediction of the Regression analysis tool. *Line without markers:* raw data.

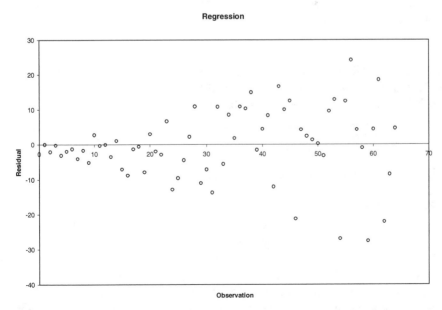

Figure 8-15. Residuals of the Regression analysis tool for the data shown in Fig. 8-13.

What's next?

Chapter 9 will show you how to import data into EXCEL and how to use EXCEL with typical student laboratory data acquisition and analysis hardware and software. The software package named MEASURE from National Instruments (www.natinst.com) is specifically designed to work with EXCEL, transforming it into a general-purpose laboratory instrument. It can be used to get data into EXCEL, to generate signals, and to control experiments.

References

Silicon Graphics, Inc., has a web site (http://lavarand.sgi.com) with new blocks of random numbers generated every minute for public use. Random numbers are available in octal and base-10 systems. The random numbers are generated by six Lava Lite® lamps, converted to digital video, and further processed by the Secure Hash Algorithm (SHS or SHA-1) of the National Institute of Standards and Technology (http://www.nist.gov).

J. J. Collins, M. Fanciulli, R. G. Hohlfield, D. C. Finch, G. v. H. Sandri, and E. S. Shtatland, "A random number generator based on the logit transform of the logistic variable," *Computers in Physics* **6** (6) 630–632 (1992).

A web site at the University of Salzburg contains tests for random numbers, random number generators, the latest news in the field, and a virtual library of related literature. http://random.mat.sbg.ac.at/ .

S. C. Bloch and R. Dressler, "Statistical estimation of π using random vectors," *American Journal of Physics* **67** (4) 298–303 (1999). This contains a brief discussion of random number generators, many references, and Internet links.

Test your skills

1. Use the Correlation tool on the data shown in the Table for Exercise 7 in Chapter 3.
2. The workbook named SWIM-RECORDS is shown in Fig. 8-16. This workbook contains data on FINA-Masters Long Course Meters free-style swimming records for women. Make an XY chart of the data in a similar workbook. Add a trendline to the chart, using Options of equation display and zero intercept. What happens if you do not select zero intercept? Is the linear trendline the best fit? (Hint: look at the R-squared value.) Use the Internet links to download the latest data. Are swimmers becoming faster? Compare free-style speeds with other swimming styles.

	A	B	C	D	E	F	G	H	I
1									
2	SWIM-RECORDS.XLS			Records as of May 1, 1999					
3	Chapter 8			**FINA-Masters Women's Long Course Meters**					
4				http://www.fina.org/masterswldrecords.html					
5		Women's		http://www.fina.org/masterswomenlcmcomplete.html					
6		Free Style		http://www.fina.org/masterswomenlcmcomplete.html					
7	Meters	Time, s							
8	50	26.2							
9	100	58.22							
10	200	120.19							
11	400	240.46							
12	800	540.28							
13	1500	1020.65							

Figure 8-16. Women's Long Course swim records (free style).

3. Use the Correlation tool for the data in SWIM-RECORDS. What is the correlation coefficient? Is this amazing? Remember, records were made by different swimmers.

4. Use the Regression tool for the data in SWIM-RECORDS. Compare this tool with the linear trendline selection in Question 1.

5. Apply the Covariance tool for the data in SWIM-RECORDS. What is the covariance for the data?

6. Apply the Descriptive Statistics tool for the data in SWIM-RECORDS.

7. Use the Random Number Generation tool to generate a random sequence of 256 numbers with a uniform distribution. Make a graph of the sequence. Use the Histogram tool to examine the frequency distribution of the sequence. Experiment with different bin sizes. Press Function Key F9 to change the numbers, retaining the same statistics.

8. Use the Random Number Generation tool to generate a random sequence of 256 numbers with a normal distribution. Make a graph of the results and observe how this compares with the uniform distribution (Question 7). Turn off Automatic Recalculation. Now the numbers will not change until you press Function Key F9.

9. Open the workbook named FREE-FALL in the Chapter 7 workbook folder. This contains data on the velocity of a freely falling object near the Earth's surface. Use numerical differentiation to obtain the acceleration and save it in column D adjacent to the velocity. Use numerical integration to obtain the displacement of the object and save it in column E adjacent to the acceleration. Make graphs of the velocity, acceleration, and displacement. Use Trendline analysis to determine the best fit, and Descriptive Statistics to analyze the data. Use power law and polynomial trendlines on the displacement. Which is the best fit?

10. Open the workbook named EKG in the folder named Workbooks. This contains experimental data on a human electrocardiogram. Use the Moving Average analysis tool with periods of 2, 3, and 5. Use the Histogram tool to make a histogram of the raw data and the result of the Moving Averages. This is a periodic waveform that we will use in Chapter 11 with the Fourier Analysis tool to determine the spectrum of the electrocardiogram and related frequency-domain attributes.

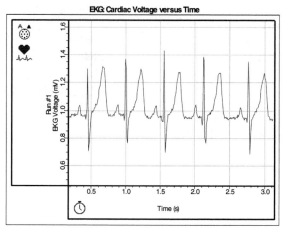

11. Open the workbook named TITRATION in the Chapter 3 Workbook folder. This contains experimental results of a solution of NaOH dripping into a solution of HCl, as the pH is monitored. Make an XY chart of the data. Add a trendline to the graph using Moving Average with a period of 2. Compare this with the result of using the Moving Average analysis tool. Experiment with different periods. Use numerical differentiation to determine the maximum slope.

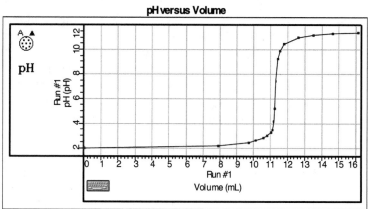

Chapter 9
EXCEL in the Lab

What this chapter is about

EXCEL is the spreadsheet chosen by the majority of engineers and scientists for laboratory experiments. EXCEL can acquire data and analyze it; by using Visual Basic for Applications (VBA) you can enable EXCEL to take control of experiments and run them. VBA can be installed using [Tools][Add-ins] and clicking on [Analysis Toolpak-VBA]. However, one chapter could not do justice to automating experiments with VBA; the subject would fill an entire book. This chapter is about typical laboratory skills that beginners need.

In this chapter you will learn how to import data from:

- data files produced by other applications,

- laboratory instruments,

- data acquisition boards.

You will also learn how to create macros to automate tasks, and how to enhance laboratory data by signal averaging (single-sweep and multi-sweep modes). We will compare results of signal averaging with other filters.

9.1 Importing data

Automatic, real-time data import is most convenient when you have the proper hardware and software, but off-line data import is often necessary. Off-line data import can be done by the following methods.

- The most obvious way you can enter data into EXCEL is using the keyboard. This is slow and subject to error. Also, entering by keyboard means that you had to acquire the data in some way, like reading an instrument display or printed matter.

- You can also enter data using voice recognition software in Microsoft OFFICE XP (or Dragon Systems, IMSI, L&H Kurzweil, IBM ViaVoice and others). Entering data by voice requires considerable practice and a microphone recommended by the voice recognition software provider.

- Optical character recognition (OCR) programs (like Textbridge and Caere) are often very useful for entering printed data. For example, you can use a copier with a Table of data you find in a book, scan it with your OCR program, save it as an ASCII text file, and then import it into EXCEL using the method described below.

The Text Import Wizard makes it easy to import a data file from another application. These are the steps to import an entire data text file into EXCEL:

1. Click the Open File icon 📁 or click on [File][Open].
2. In the *Look in* box, locate the drive, folder, or Internet location that contains the file you want to open. (See Fig. 9-1.)
3. In the *Files of type* box, click Text Files.
4. Double-click the file you want to import.
5. Follow the instructions in the Text Import Wizard to specify how you want to divide the text into columns.

Let's follow these instructions to import a data file named OZONE located in the folder named POLLUTION. This folder is on the CD-ROM.

Figure 9-1 shows this file with Text Files chosen in the *Files of type* box. Notice the Look In box; the selected folder is POLLUTION and the file OZONE appears in the contents. Click on Open and you will see Fig. 9-2 which shows Step 1 of the Text Import Wizard.

The Text Wizard has automatically detected the OZONE file as a delimited Windows (ANSI) text file. You can choose which row of the file to start the import process. A preview of the file is shown in the window; scroll down to see more of the file in case you want to start the import at a particular row.

After you have made your selections click Next and Fig. 9-3 will appear with Step 2. Now you can set the delimiters according to your desires, and see a preview of the file as it will appear when it is imported. Separate text from data with the Text Qualifier.

After you are satisfied with the appearance, click Next and Fig. 9-4 will appear with Step 3. Here you can separate dates, numbers, and text automatically by choosing General under Column Data Format, and you can choose to skip one or more columns in the import process.

If you want to make any changes in this process, click Back. If everything is OK, click Finish and you will see Fig. 9-4.

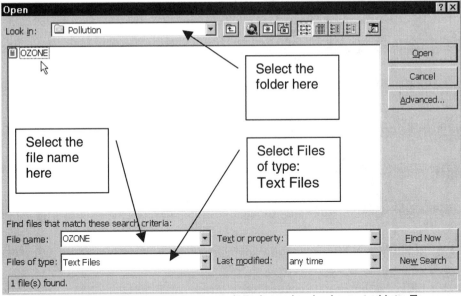

Figure 9-1. The Text File named OZONE is selected to be imported into EXCEL.

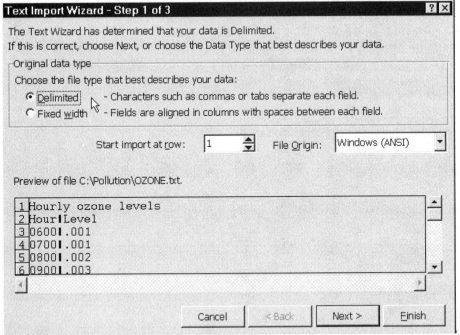

Figure 9-2. Step 1 of the Wizard automatically determines the file type and gives a preview.

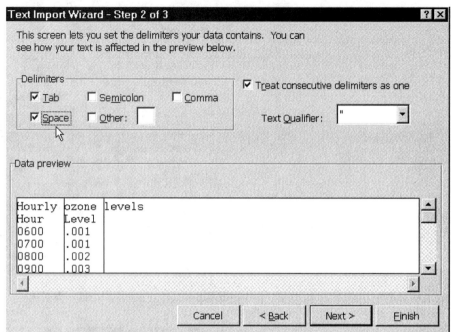

Figure 9-3. Step 2 of the Wizard lets you choose delimiters. Use your worksheet to experiment with Tab and Space delimiters.

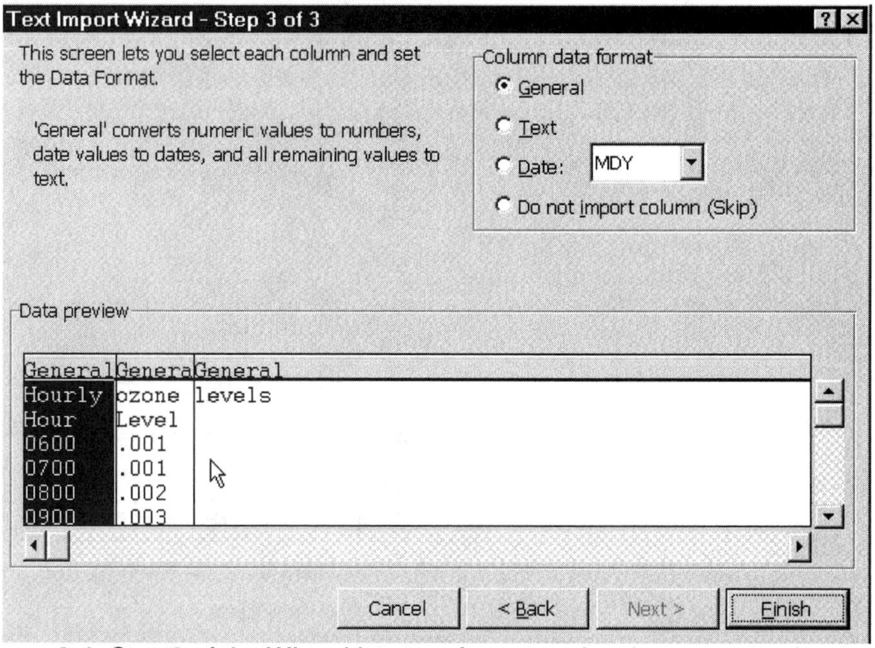

Figure 9-4. Step 3 of the Wizard lets you format each column, or stop import of selected columns.

If all goes well, you'll see Fig. 9-5 when you click on Finish. After the file is into EXCEL you can apply any final touch-ups to improve the appearance.

	A	B	C	D	E	F	G	H	I
1	Hourly	ozone	levels						
2	Hour	Level							
3	600	0.001							
4	700	0.001							
5	800	0.002							
6	900	0.003							
7	1000	0.004							
8	1100	0.004							
9	1200	0.005							
10	1300	0.004							
11	1400	0.004							
12	1500	0.003							
13	1600	0.002							
14	1700	0.002							
15	1800	0.001							
16									

Figure 9-5. This is the completed data import. It is now ready for analysis and making a chart.

9.2 Creating a macro to automate a task

A repetitive task can be done automatically by creating a *macro* in EXCEL. The easiest way to compose a macro is to use the Record Macro tool; this records each key stroke and mouse click so you can repeat the operation by making a keyboard Shortcut (like CTRL J). The Shortcut is convenient if you use it often, but if your use is infrequent you probably will not remember it. Your Shortcut will override any standard EXCEL Shortcut with the same name while the workbook that contains your Shortcut is open. You can also use your mouse to select your macro in the [Tools][Macro][Macros] menu. If you want to get fancy, you can make a customized button on a toolbar to run your macro, or create a hotspot on a graphic object that you can click. Consult Help for these methods.

Tip
To be able to use the macro Recorder you must check the box by Analysis Tool-Pak–VBA in the [Tools][Add-ins] menu. See Fig. 9-6. After this is selected you can record a macro using [Tools][Macro][Record New Macro]. See Fig. 9-7.

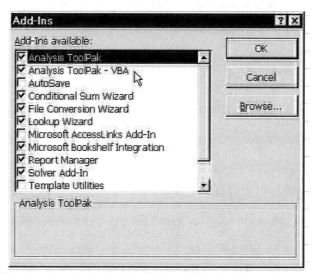

Figure 9-6. The box by Analysis ToolPak – VBA is checked using a left mouse click. Use this dialog box to add or delete Add-Ins.

The dialog box shown in Fig. 9-6 has several important Add-Ins that you should explore when you have time. The *Solver* Add-In is particularly useful because it can solve for a value to maximize another value.

Use *Solver* to determine the maximum or minimum value of one cell by changing other cells. For example, you may want to maximize the volume of a container by changing its dimensions, while constraining some dimension. The cells you select must be related through formulas in the workbook. If they are not related, changing one cell will not change the others. For information about the algorithms used by *Solver*, look in EXCEL's Help.

The *Lookup Wizard* can be a time-saver because it lets you find a specific value in a list. You can create a formula that finds a value by using row and column labels in a list. For example, if you have an inventory list that contains part numbers for microchips, descriptions, and prices, you can create a formula that finds the description or the price of a part by looking for a specific part number. The *Lookup Wizard* helps you write the formula you need.
1. Click a cell in the list.
2. On the Tools menu, point to Wizard, and then click Lookup.
3. Follow the instructions in the Wizard.
EXCEL also has a LOOKUP function that returns a value from a one-row or one-column range, or from an array. The *vector form* of LOOKUP looks in a one-row or one-column range (known as a vector) for a value and returns a value from the same position in a second one-row or one-column range. The *array form* of LOOKUP looks in the first row or column of an array for the specified value and returns a value from the same position in the last row or column of the array.

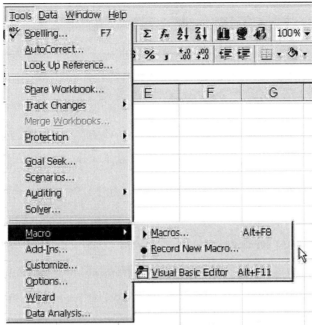

Figure 9-7. You can run a macro or record a new macro using the Tools menu. Note that you can also activate the Visual Basic Editor here to modify a macro that you have already created. Note the keyboard Shortcuts, like Alt+F8.

Figure 9-8 shows the Record Macro dialog box. If the macro name is not completely descriptive, include more information in the Description box. It can be frustrating if you are confronted later with a mysterious macro that you created! Figure 9-9 shows the Macro dialog box for selection and editing.

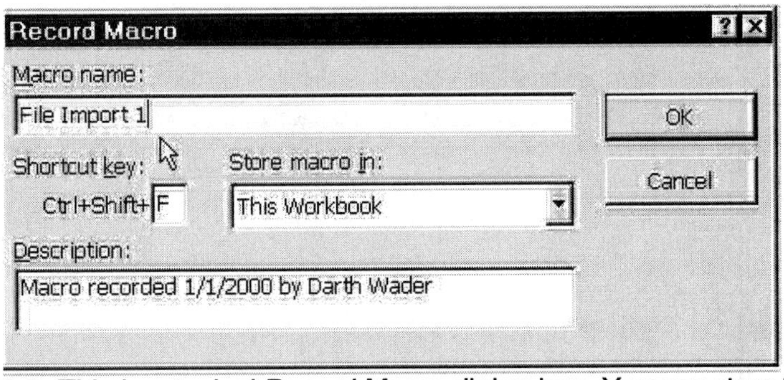

Figure 9-8. This is a typical Record Macro dialog box. You can store the macro in This Workbook, New Workbook, or Personal Macro Workbook. By storing in a Personal Macro Workbook you can easily call up the macro to use in any workbook. Choose the Shortcut key with or without Shift; it will over-ride any existing Shortcut with a similar name while the workbook is open.

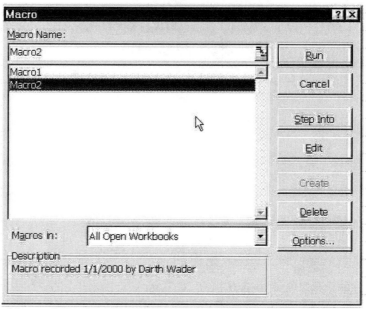

Figure 9-9. Macro dialog box. Use this as an alternative to a Shortcut to select a macro. This box also provides options for editing.

Figure 9-10 shows the Visual Basic Editor (see Fig. 9-7). You can also access this using the Shortcut by pressing ALT+F11.

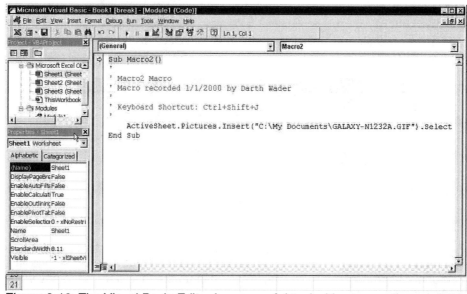

Figure 9-10. The Visual Basic Editor is a powerful tool with many options, but it is easy to use it to modify a macro that you have previously created.

9.3 Using EXCEL with PASCO Science Workshop

The basic way of getting data into EXCEL is with the keyboard, but this is tedious, time consuming, and open to errors in typing. Modern laboratory data acquisition software usually has provision for exporting and saving data files. Moving data directly from a data acquisition program into EXCEL or a word processor is often facilitated by using the Windows Copy operation. This is a great help in producing lab reports that look professional. Let's see how this is done with a popular student laboratory program for computer-assisted experiments.

The interface of the PASCO Science Workshop is shown in Fig. 9-11. With this software interface you can automatically connect and configure analog and digital inputs; just click and drag one of the input plugs into a selected channel. Note that there are three analog channels and four digital channels. This system can also be used as a signal generator; the OUT connector on the right-hand side is a low-level signal of a selected waveform that can be amplified for further use.

This software will produce a graph and a data table, and while these are good for quick looks during an experiment, they can be enhanced by exporting into EXCEL. Notice that this software has the FFT (Fast Fourier Transform) available for spectrum analysis. Again, this is good for a quick look but using EXCEL's FFT produces greatly improved results and lets you have control over the process (See Chapter 11). All of the FFT options are fixed in the Science Workshop software, except for selecting the number of data points (which must be an integer power of 2, like 256 or 512). Chapter 11 will show you how to use zero-padding to handle data sets that are not an integer power of 2.

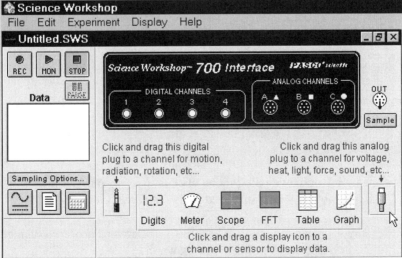

Figure 9-11. Interface of the PASCO Science Workshop. No channels are selected in this Figure. The Scope is like the Graph, but it operates on faster data. The analog and digital meters are useful for viewing during an experiment.

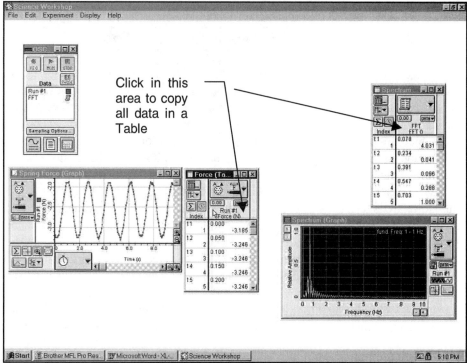

Figure 9-12. In this experiment a mass on a spring was suspended from a strain gauge force sensor and the mass was set in motion. The resulting oscillation was recorded on a graph and in a Table (left) and analyzed with the built-in FFT to obtain the spectrum. Click in the area shown to copy data to Windows clipboard.

Let's look at a completed experiment with a data table, in Fig. 9-12. It is easy to copy the entire experimental data into EXCEL if you know where to click. Notice the position of the mouse pointer in the Force Table in Fig. 9-12.

- Click on this area and the entire table and graph will be shown in reversed black and white. See Fig. 9-13. (If you click on a particular data entry in the table, only that point will be copied.)

- Now move the mouse pointer to the upper left and click on [Edit] on the menu bar.

- In the drop-down [Edit] menu click on [Copy] and all the data in the table will be transferred to the Windows clipboard.

- Now you can put the data into EXCEL or a word processor using [Paste]. The result in EXCEL is shown in Fig. 9-14.

The data in tables must be copied one table at a time.

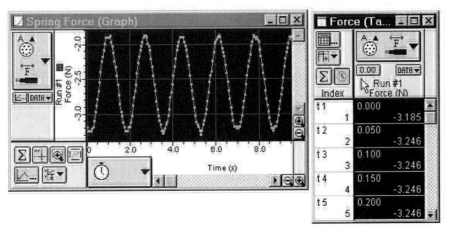

Figure 9-13. Click on the area where the mouse pointer is located and you will put all data in this Table in the Windows clipboard when you select [Edit][Copy]. Reversed black and white shows the result of a click on the Table named Force.

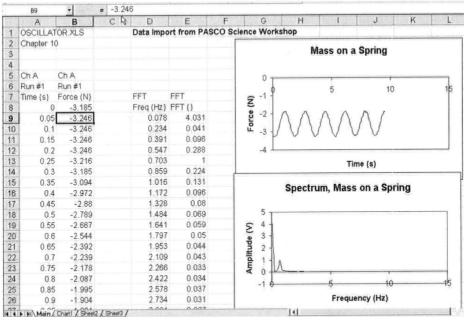

Figure 9-14. The entire Force data table shown in Fig. 9-13 has been success-fully pasted into Excel. Also, in a second Copy operation the FFT data have been copied and pasted, and charts have been constructed. The spectrum chart needs adjustment because of the spike near zero frequency. A log axis also would help graphical clarity of the spectrum analysis. These modifications are shown in Figs. 9-15 and 9-16.

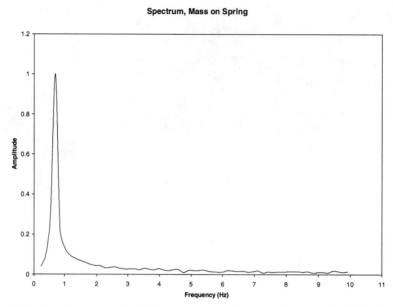

Figure 9-15. Modified chart of the spectrum imported from PASCO Science Workshop. Compare with the spectrum in Fig. 9-14; the "dc" spike at 0.078 Hz is an artifact and has been deleted. The spectral line is at 0.703 Hz. In EXCEL, place the mouse pointer on the graph to read the frequency and amplitude.

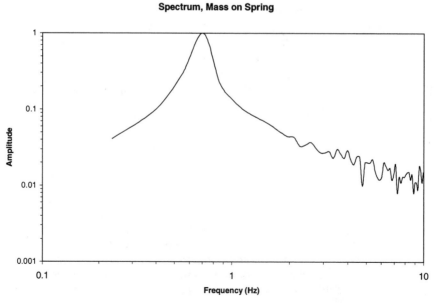

Figure 9-16. The data in Fig. 9-15 are shown here in a log-log chart format.

The width of the spectrum line in Figs. 9-15 and 9-16 is not a good estimation of the true width, and therefore not a good measure of the Q of the oscillator. The reason for this is that the FFT used here is good for a quick look, but the rectangular data window used produces extra spread in the line. (Chapter 11 will discuss better data windows). Using EXCEL with the original time data (that is, the waveform) can produce a much more accurate spectrum shape by employing other FFT techniques. We'll see how to do this in Chapter 11, but let's compare preliminary results here in Fig. 9-17. Note the sharper spectrum in the FFT produced by EXCEL.

9.4 Using EXCEL with Vernier Multi-Purpose Lab Interface

This interface, based on a standard (ISA) board with a 12-bit, 3-input, analog-to-digital converter, is intended for student labs. The maximum data-collection rate is 75,000 samples per second. Three software selectable ranges are supported, and analog output and digital I/O lines are also available.

MultiPurpose Lab Interface Box
This external box has three 8-pin DIN sockets (Channels A, B, and C) that allow quick connection to a wide range of sensors. Inside the box is a 16-pin DIP socket for use by experimenters and a prototyping area where circuits can be built.

MultiPurpose Lab Interface Software
Each input channel can be calibrated to display any type of input signal; for example, channel A can read temperature, channel B can read pH, and channel C can read pressure. Data from each of the three analog input channels can be collected, graphed, and saved on disk. Real-time graphing, histogram, oscilloscope-like display, and Fourier analysis are available. The program includes a mode which turns the computer into a digital, single-channel, storage oscilloscope that does standard Y vs. t and Y vs. X plotting.

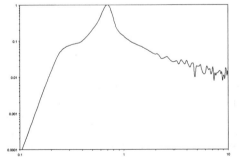 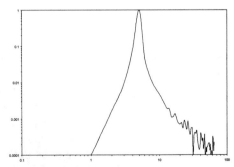

Figure 9-17. *Left:* Spectrum using the PASCO Science Workshop FFT. *Right:* Spectrum using the EXCEL FFT with waveform data from the PASCO Science Workshop. Both charts are in log-log format. Note reduced spectrum leakage.

The MPLI Program for Windows allows fast data collection on real-time graphs, oscilloscopes, and meters. The sampling rate can be as high as 75,000 samples/second or slow enough so that data can be collected over several days.

The data tools include an analysis tool, tangent lines, integration, FFT windows, histogram windows, calculated columns, and curve fitting. The MPLI Program for Windows supports automatic curve fitting to a wide variety of functions, including linear, polynomial, logarithmic, and trig . It also supports manual curve fitting, where the students type in values and try to match data to a mathematical model.

It is easy to copy data from the MPLI program into EXCEL or a word processor. Typical window arrangements are shown in Figs. 9-18 and 9-19. The MPLI windows can be re-sized and deleted; additional windows can be added.

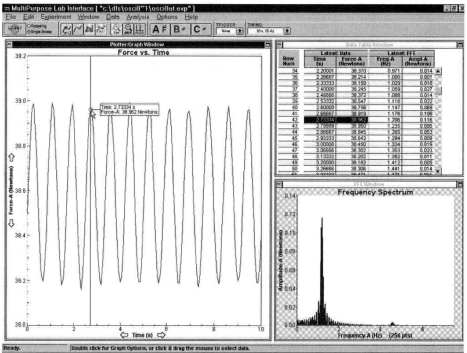

Figure 9-18. MPLI configured with graph, data table, and spectrum (FFT) windows. This experiment is a mass oscillating in air, suspended by a spring from a force sensor. The output of the force sensor is graphed. Note the cursor on the graph. It reads out time and force, and corresponds to the highlighted portion of the data table. The cursor can also measure time differences and force differences. The FFT shown here uses 256 points; the number of points is adjustable but must be an integer power of 2, like 128, 256, 512, and so on. To transfer a data table into EXCEL, click on the top of the table and then click on [Edit][Copy].

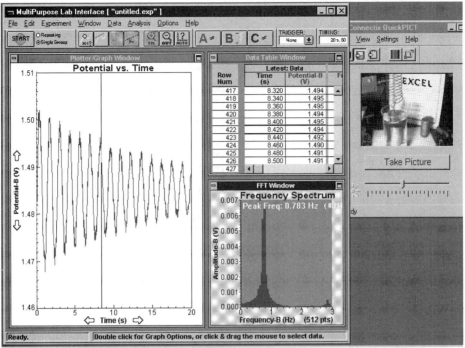

Figure 9-19. A cylindrical mass suspended from a spring is submerged in a beaker of water. The spring is suspended from a force sensor. Oscillations are damped due to motion in the water. The force is noisy because of turbulence in the water and some secondary oscillations in the spring.

Tip
Click on the heading of a data table on the MPLI screen to select the entire table. Then click on [Edit][Copy Data] on the top menu bar. This places the data table contents on the Windows clipboard. Open an EXCEL workbook, select a cell, and click on the [Paste] icon. You should see a result like Fig. 9-20.

You can also copy an entire window in MPLI by using [Edit][Copy Window] on the top menu bar. This is useful if you want to place an MPLI graph in a word processor or worksheet.

MPLI contains several useful analysis tools. For example, you can create a histogram of a waveform to examine the amplitude distribution. Ten types of manual and automatic curve fitting of experimental data can be performed.

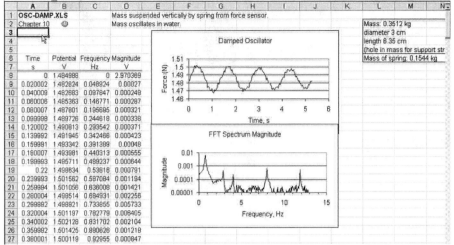

Figure 9-20. Data from Fig. 9-19 have been imported into Excel. The spectrum has been plotted here as a semi-log chart to enhance visibility of low amplitude parts of the spectrum. The water container has an inside diameter of 5.9 cm. Turbulence occurs when the 3 cm diameter mass oscillates while submerged in the water.

9.5 Using EXCEL with National Instruments MEASURE

The software package named MEASURE is a versatile industrial-strength Add-in that enables EXCEL to acquire laboratory data, control experiments, and generate signals. MEASURE has three parts: Serial, GPIB (General Purpose Interface Bus), and DAQ (National Instruments data acquisition). With this Add-in you can:

- acquire analog data and control instruments with EXCEL,

- configure your input/output (I/O) operations with easy-to-use dialog boxes,

- place data directly into worksheet cells, with no programming and no conversion algorithms,

- automate your experiments with VBA macros.

With the Serial and GPIB Add-ins you can control compatible instruments and acquire data directly with EXCEL using instruments connected to the serial port or GPIB card in your computer.

- With the Serial Add-in you can control any instrument with an RS-232 or RS-485 interface, such as electronic scales, analyzers, spectrographs, calipers, and remote I/O modules in your lab or anywhere in the world on the Internet.

- The GPIB Add-in enables you to access any GPIB instrument such as multimeters, oscilloscopes, and function generators. (GPIB is the acronym for General Purpose Interface Bus. This bus lets instruments and computers talk to each other; the instruments must have GPIB cards.)

- The DAQ Add-in works with industry-standard PCI, ISA, and PCMCIA cards that plug into slots in your computer to acquire data, generate signals, operate relays, and so on. Data acquisition with DAQ is typically from 100,000 to 300,000 samples/s, much faster than with the Serial port.

When MEASURE is installed and activated you will see additional items on the top menu bar of EXCEL. For example, in Chapter 1, Fig. 1-4, you can see the Serial menu between the Data and Window menus at the top of the worksheet. The Serial and GPIB Add-ins are accessed through these drop-down menus which are automatically added to EXCEL when you install MEASURE. You can disable these menus using the [Tools][Add-ins] menu.

First you must configure instrument-specific settings such as COM port connection, baud rate, and data bits for a serial instrument, or the GPIB address for a GPIB instrument. Then you can create specific tasks to send commands or capture data from a connected instrument, and you can specify parsing algorithms. Figure 9-21 shows the drop-down menu for the Serial Add-in.

Click on [Serial][Instruments] and you will see Fig. 9-22 which starts the instrument setup. In this example, an electronic balance is selected. The electronic balance has a 9-pin RS-232 connector on the back. A standard serial cable is used to connect the electronic balance to Com Port 1 on the computer.

On the left side of Fig. 9-22 you will see three buttons: New, Delete, and Test. When you click on Test you will see Fig. 9-23, the Instrument Test dialog box. Click on Send Data and Read Serial Port. After the instrument has been set up and tested, click on Tasks. The Capture Task dialog box is shown in Fig. 9-24.

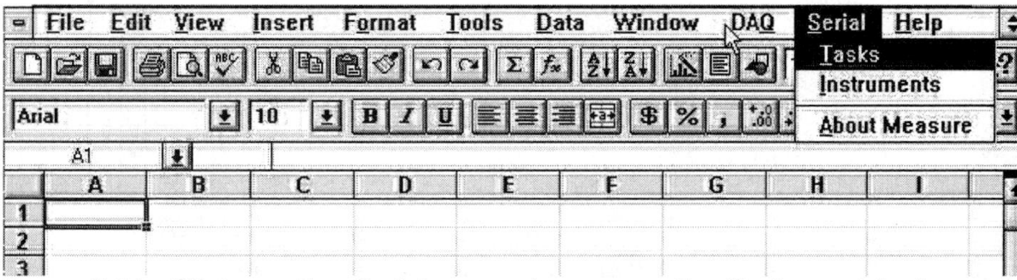

Figure 9-21. Click on the Serial menu to access the Tasks and Instruments menus.

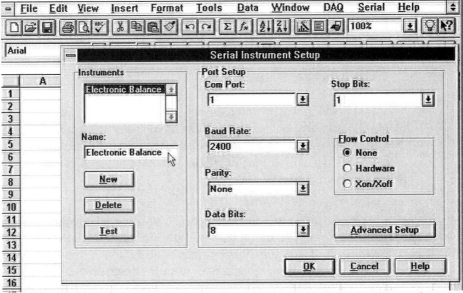

Figure 9-22. The Serial Add-in is configured for automatic data input from an electronic balance. This dialog box is in the Instruments menu.

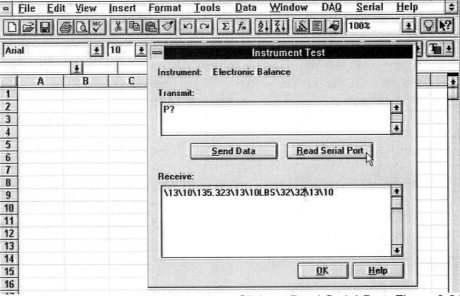

Figure 9-23. Instrument Test dialog box. Click on Read Serial Port. Figure 9-24 shows the Capture Task dialog box and a reading imported into EXCEL.

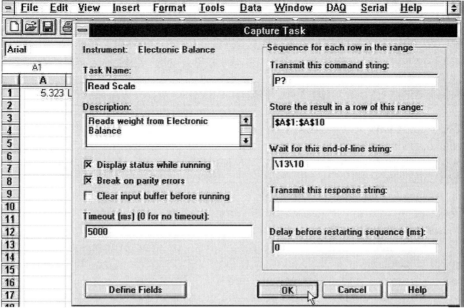

Figure 9-24. Capture Task dialog box sets capture parameters. Note that captured data are to be stored in the range $A1:$A10, as shown in Fig. 9-25.

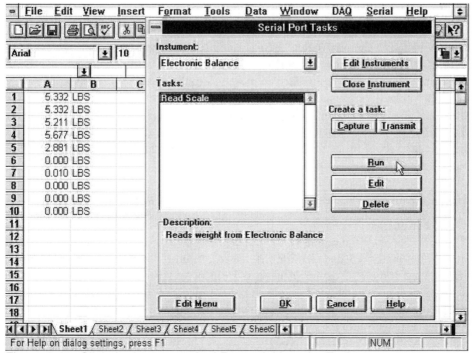

Figure 9-25. Click the button marked Run to initiate the Task.

Open the workbook named INSERT-MOVIE and you will see a typical 9-pin connector on the back of an electronic balance. You can connect a standard cable between this connector and a COM port (also 9-pin) on your computer to establish a Serial connection to transfer data and commands via RS-232 protocol.

9.6 Using Excel with TAL Technologies SOFTWAREWEDGE

You do not have to type data into your application software from the display of your instruments or key in hand-written values if the devices have RS232 (Serial) ports. WINWEDGE, part of the SOFTWAREWEDGE family, is another solution to data collection, which is a fully customizable Serial I/O device driver.

Basically, WINWEDGE inputs data from any device attached to one of a PC's Serial ports into any Windows application program in real-time. Add-on Serial boards with 2 and 4 ports are available.

All the information viewed on the displays of your instruments (and often more) is available over the Serial port. WINWEDGE extracts the information you require from the Serial data coming into a PC from any instrument. It immediately inserts the data into your application programs (EXCEL, ACCESS, statistical or math software) or any Windows 3.x, 95, 98 or NT program. You can collect data directly from electronic scales, gages, bar code scanners, flow meters, pH meters, spectrometers, analyzers, densitometers, sensors, data loggers, controllers, Global Positioning System (GPS), or any instrument, directly into fields or cells in spreadsheets or databases for real-time graphing and analysis.

In the simplest mode, WINWEDGE converts the incoming serial data to "keystrokes" so that the data enters into your application program just like typed-in data. Alternatively, a more sophisticated mode transmits the serial data via DDE (Dynamic Data Exchange) to defined locations in the destination application.

WINWEDGE can input data from any instrument, no matter how complex the output. It also supports up to 100 serial ports simultaneously and has support for TCP/IP communications for the Internet. This allows data to be collected from devices connected to an Ethernet or the Internet, in addition to serial ports. For more information, see Section 9.8.

Here are two examples of data acquisition and analysis with EXCEL:

Ozone layer
The ozone layer is the region of the upper atmosphere, between approximately 10 and 20 miles (or 15 and 30 kilometers) in altitude, which contains a relatively high concentration of ozone (a natural form of oxygen O_3). This layer absorbs solar ultraviolet radiation in a wavelength range not screened by other atmospheric components and helps protect us from the harmful effects of the sun.

Harvard University's Department of Earth and Planetary Science has developed a method of analyzing the ozone layer. The research involves tracking carbon dioxide in the atmosphere, which offers insight into how air pollution migrates and what might be effecting our ozone layer.

The Department developed a system that utilizes a carbon dioxide meter whose data are captured by a data logger. Instruments are attached to a balloon. The data from the balloon are telemetered to a receiving station on the ground where it is transferred to the Serial port of a PC running Windows 95 and SOFTWAREWEDGE 32-bit Pro version (WINWEDGE 32). WINWEDGE parses and filters the data and transfers it via dynamic data exchange (DDE) into EXCEL. The data are automatically analyzed and graphed by EXCEL.

The perfect golf ball

Golfers around the world realize that it's important to find that perfect ball that suits their game – not too soft, not too hard, and just the right amount of spin.

Choosing that perfect golf ball is not an easy task. The United States Golf Association has about 1,900 balls on its "conforming" list. There are two-piece balls, three-piece balls, balata and Surlyn balls, wound balls, liquid-center balls, titanium-center balls, "senior" balls, "ladies" balls, balls that offer "extra distance" or "extra spin" and thanks to R&D in the golf ball industry, there are many hybrid balls that combine these characteristics.

One golf ball manufacturer, long regarded as the most prestigious brand name in the $1 billion-per-year golf-ball industry, offers an array of golf ball types for almost every type of golfer. The manufacturer makes so many different types of balls and so many compressions, they are confusing even to professional golfers. For the average hit-and-hope golfer, is there really a ball out there that will improve the game?

The manufacturer's Research and Development Department has the responsibility to continually improve the quality and composition of their golf balls and to expand their product lines. One of the critical elements of a golf ball is the core composition. The core is the golf ball's primary source of potential and kinetic energy storage. Differences in core construction affect spin rate (control), initial velocity (distance) and compression (feel).

Typical core constructions, either wound or solid, can produce significant differences in control and feel. Wound balls have three parts: center, winding and cover. Wound balls offer more spin and control but typically less distance. Solid balls consist of two parts, a solid core and cover. Solid, or two-piece balls, provide more distance but less spin and control. The core is generally a compound of natural and synthetic rubbers (polymers).

The R&D Department conducts core compression experiments to improve the interior design of their golf balls. The Department uses rheometers, an instrument for measuring the flow of viscous liquids, made by Monsanto, to measure different heating cycles of the polymers that comprise a golf ball's center. Measuring different heating cycles simulates part of the actual process of developing the ball's core. By simulating the process with the rheometer, the Department can adjust the heating and compression process to improve the golf ball's core, and hence, overall control and feel of the ball.

Monsanto, the manufacturer of the rheometer, offers its own software to analyze the output of the device. However, the Department had a need to overlay curves for different heating cycles which the custom software package would not allow. By using SOFTWAREWEDGE Professional version (WINWEDGE Pro) to interface the rheometer to their PC running Windows 95, they could overlay the heating curves and analyze their results in EXCEL. The R&D team preferred to use EXCEL because it is familiar, easy to use, and has powerful statistical analysis capabilities.

The rheometer is connected via a Serial cable to a PC running EXCEL and WINWEDGE. WINWEDGE parses and filters the data from the rheometer and directs it to EXCEL. The data are then graphed in real time in EXCEL.

9.7 DATAQ serial port data acquisition

Unlike MEASURE and SOFTWAREWEDGE, this device and its associated software do not require an RS-232 Serial source for its data. The module features two, single-ended, bipolar analog inputs (maximum measurement range ±5 volts) and a digital input port for remote stop/start or remote event marker control. It also features an onboard waveform generator that can be used as an input signal to an external device. The kit includes WINDAQ/Lite recording software and WINDAQ Waveform Browser playback and analysis software.

The DI-190 kit provides a taste of the exceptional power and speed possible with WINDAQ software for Windows. The software will easily import and export data with EXCEL. A *free* download demonstrates the WINDAQ Waveform Browser, the associated playback and analysis software (see Section 9.10), but to get a hands-on demo of the data recording and display capabilities of WINDAQ/Lite, you need the DI-190 Starter Kit.

When connected to your PC's Serial port the DI-190 Starter Kit allows you to record, display, and analyze data using your own signals. The DI-190 Starter Kit consists of a portable, two-channel, 2x3-inch A/D module and a serial communications cable, enabling you to connect to the serial port of any PC (open the workbook DATA-INPUT to see two photos).

Data acquisition rates up to 240 samples per second are supported at 12 bits of resolution with either WINDAQ/Lite or WINDAQ Serial Acquisition for Windows. This is fast enough for things like thermistors and slow mechanical measurements, but remember that 240 samples/s means that the highest frequency you can know with confidence is 120 Hz (see Chapter 11 for a discussion of the Nyquist frequency.) Faster speeds and up to 240 input lines are available with other DATAQ devices. Figure 9-26 shows the circuit diagram of the input box. The box takes its power from the PC.

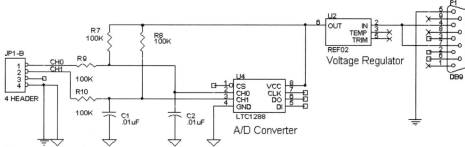

Figure 9-26. Circuit diagram of the input module. The four connections at the left are input screw terminals. The DB9 Serial connector at the right accepts a cable to a COM port connector on your PC. Power is supplied by the COM port.

Figure 9-27 shows the waveform of an irregular heartbeat. A section of the waveform is to be selected for export to EXCEL. The cursor is set at the start of the section and Function Key F4 is pressed. Then the cursor is set at the end of the section. Figure 9-28 shows a waveform imported into EXCEL.

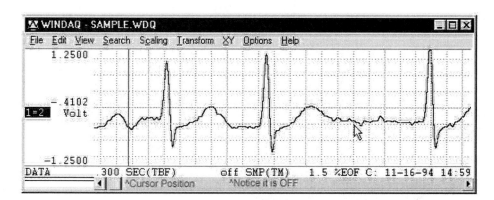

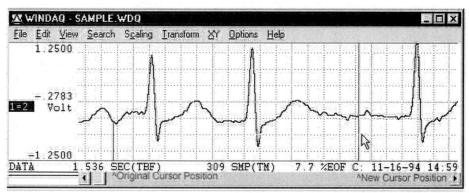

Figure 9-27. *Top:* Start of irregular heartbeat waveform is selected with cursor. *Bottom:* End of waveform section is selected with cursor. Note menu items.

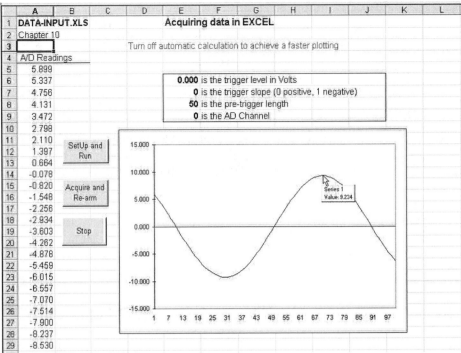

Figure 9-28. A sine wave has been acquired and imported into EXCEL. The Analog-to-Digital (A/D) output is in column A. The three rectangular buttons control VBA macros. When you open this workbook you are given the option of disabling the macros. You should disable the macros if you do not have WINDAQ installed. The three buttons require WINDAQ hardware and software to operate.

9.8 Parallel port data acquisition

Your PC's parallel port can be used to acquire relatively slow data streams with a PC Analog Data Sampler. Several models are available; we'll describe an inexpensive sampler.

A typical A/D sampler monitors voltage changes ranging from milliseconds to months, and is powered through the parallel port. The unit is packaged in a DB-25 extended case and looks like the connector at the end of a printer's parallel cable. It is switch-selectable to 2V or 20V full scale ranges.

The sampler can be used as a low frequency digital "scope" to look at audio and other signals up to 5 kHz. The unit requires no battery or external power sources and comes with Windows software. You can plot charts of acquired data and you can save data as text files to allow import into a spreadsheet (See Section 9.12, Marlin P. Jones & Associates, Analog Data Samplers.)

9.9 Universal Serial Bus (USB) data acquisition

The speed of USB 2.0 is 480 Megabits per second (Mbps), 40 times faster than USB 1.1. To put this in perspective, you can back up a gigabyte of data from your PC hard drive in less than a minute on USB 2.0 versus about a half-hour on USB 1.1.

The parallel port or printer port has a forward direction transfer rate of 150 KBps. The reverse direction data rate on parallel port is one third of the forward rate, 50 KBps. The RS-232 serial port has a maximum limit of 38400 bps. The USB 1.1 port on the back of older systems has a maximum throughput of 12 Mbps for full speed devices. Nevertheless, the new version is compatible with the old version.

In addition to high bandwidth, another advantage of USB is that only one IRQ is required by the USB controller, which can handle up to 127 devices. The USB bandwidth is shared among all devices. There are no annoying jumper configurations or hardware settings on USB devices. Configuration is painless.

The USB is extremely useful for data acquisition for several reasons.

- Equipment can obtain power from the USB port; it doesn't need to be battery powered or plugged into the wall. This makes USB ideal for portable data acquisition with a notebook computer.
- By using a USB hub you can connect many devices to one USB port, so you can easily expand your system.
- USB ports are provided on most new PCs so there is no need to open the computer and install adapter cards.
- You can plug in and unplug your equipment without switching off your computer or even restarting Windows.
- The USB cable can be up to 5 m long. However, by using USB hubs between cables you can reach 30 m.
- You can use USB devices with other data acquisition equipment (such as cards that you installed in your PC or instruments that plug directly into the RS-232 serial port).

If you have an older PC that does not have a USB port you can use a PCI-based card that provides one. However, you need to be running Windows 98 or later. (Early releases of Windows 95 do not support USB. Later releases have some support but it's preferable to use Windows 98 or newer versions.) You can test whether your PC is USB compatible by visiting http://www.usb.org and downloading their evaluation utility program. Another solution for an older computer is to use a USB-to-serial adapter, such as the Keyspan Twin USB to Serial Adapter, part #USA-28X. Contact info@keyspan.com and www.keyspan.com.

In new computers the USB will probably replace serial and parallel ports. Educational and industrial USB data acquisition devices are now widely available, and the technology is changing rapidly. Do an Internet search for "USB data acquisition" to get the latest information. Also, see References, page 233.

9.10 Ensemble averaging of experimental data

Data acquired from experiments are naturally noisy. As you repeat an experiment you will get slightly different results, if you look closely enough. There are many experiments in which you cannot even see the data because they are buried in noise. Fortunately, there are several methods that enable you to extract signals from noise. If you can repeat an experiment many times, and if each data record is sufficiently long, then *ensemble averaging* is simple, effective, and useful. (We have already considered the *moving average* in Section 5.3.) Ensemble averaging has some advantages over the usual high-pass, low-pass, and band-pass filtering:

- There is no phase shift (or phase distortion, a time delay artifact) using ensemble averaging,

- Variance is reduced (random noise is diminished) as the number of records increases. (See page 93.)

Variance reduction is a figure of merit for an averaging process; recall that the variance is the difference between the mean square and the square of the mean, so it is the square of the standard deviation. Variance reduction is related to noise reduction but in some types of filters it is also related to information reduction!

If S_1 is a signal + noise and S_2 is the processed output signal, there will be variances V_1 and V_2 associated with these data. The variance ratio V_2 / V_1 is a measure of the noise reduction.

TIP

Variance is related to power, that is, the square of the standard deviation, so it is necessary to use the square root of the variance ratio when you do analysis based on voltage measurements.

In many experiments, you will find that the random noise increases as the square root of the number of records N in the ensemble, and the signal increases as N. Therefore, the signal/noise ratio increases as $\sqrt{N}$. For example, 100 records produce a ten-fold improvement and 10^4 records produce a hundred-fold improvement. This occurs if each record is an independent measurement, that is, there is no noise correlation among records. Very low frequency noise may produce correlations, so it is important that each record be as long as is convenient. The longer the records, and the greater the number of records N, the better the results will be.

The key to success with coherent (phase-preserving) ensemble averaging is that the noise, characterized by random amplitudes and phases, tends to increase more slowly than the signal information with each additional observation. Unsynchronized coherent signals are diminished because they occur with a different phase in each data sequence. See Chapter 11 for incoherent averaging.

Because coherent ensemble averaging is based on repetitive measurements, it is important that the timing (or phase) of the signal be synchronized precisely (or strobed) with the data acquisition system. Time-jitter in the synchronization will reduce signal enhancement because of blur; this can be serious when the leading or trailing edge of the signal carries important information but jitter also reduces the effectiveness of signal averaging during the entire process.

In contrast with convolutional filtering processes (Chapter 12), ensemble averaging with tight synchronization does not broaden, smear, shift, or blur spectral lines when spectra are averaged. The price that you must pay is in time, acquiring repetitive records.

Although we have emphasized that ensemble averaging is only useful with repetitive signals, there are some special cases in which it can be used for a non-repetitive signal. For example, in deep-space communication from a space vehicle to Earth a single data sequence had to be transmitted but it was buried in noise. By sending a command to the space craft to transmit the signal many times the Earth station used ensemble averaging to recover the data.. In other words, a non-repetitive signal was made repetitive, and the signal was the same on every transmission but the noise was different.

Ensemble averaging can be performed in two modes, *single-sweep* and *multi-sweep*. These are easy to implement in a spreadsheet. Let's examine each and see what are their advantages and disadvantages.

Single-sweep mode

In this mode all records are acquired and then the entire ensemble is averaged. The averaging process is done at the same data point for every record. (See Fig. 9-29. Explore the worksheet formulas with your mouse.)

Table 9.1 Single-sweep ensemble average	
Advantages	*Disadvantages*
Computation is required only at the end of data acquisition	Ensemble average is not available until the end of data acquisition
Easy to implement in digital or analog form	Decisions are delayed until ensemble average is completed
Long integration times and long sweep times are possible	May not be effective in reducing 1/f noise
Time resolution is good	Maximum usable frequency is limited by sampling pulse width. Shorter pulse is required for higher usable frequency
All original data are stored for possible later use	Large memory is required for large ensemble

Multi-sweep mode

In this mode a weighted average is computed after each record is acquired. For example, when the fourth record is acquired it is combined with the average of the first three records. The average of the first three records is weighted three times more than the fourth record, and so on. In the multi-sweep mode you can see the signal rising out of the noise as each new record is acquired. Compare Table 9.2 with Table 9.1.

Table 9.2 Multi-sweep ensemble average	
Advantages	*Disadvantages*
Updated ensemble average is always available	Computation is necessary after each record is acquired
Signal-to-Noise ratio increases with each new record	Time resolution is limited by available memory
Improved 1/f noise reduction	More and faster computing is required
Less memory is required. Previous data can be discarded after up-dated ensemble average is computed	Maximum usable frequency is limited by the Sampling Theorem. Sampling rate must be two times the maximum usable frequency

Figure 9-29 shows a micro-tutorial worksheet that demonstrates both modes of ensemble averaging. Note the cells that report variances; both modes have the same variance reduction and the same ensemble average.

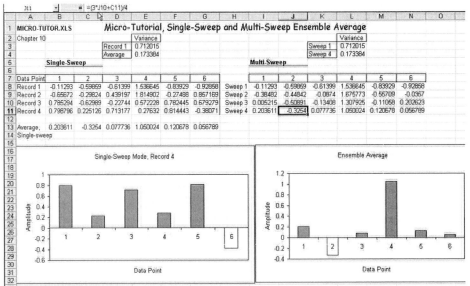

Figure 9-29. Single-sweep and multi-sweep ensemble average micro-tutorial. The noiseless signal is a pulse with amplitude of 1, located at data point 4. On the charts, negative values are not shaded (this is selected on the chart wizard).

The micro-tutorial shows the two modes applied to a scalar ensemble consisting of four records of a noisy signal, a single pulse of amplitude 1 at data point 4. Open the workbook MICRO-TUTOR and explore the formulas in the cells. In the single-sweep mode all records are raw data. Press Function Key F9 to change the noise sample.

Single-sweep section

The formula in cell B13 is =AVERAGE(B8:B11). This is copied to cells C13:G13. Note that this copy operation involves cells with *relative* cell addresses, so each average refers to its own column.

The formula in cell E3 is =VARP(B8:G8). This displays the population variance of Record 1. The formula in cell E4 is =VARP(B13:G13), and it displays the population variance of the single-sweep ensemble average.

Note that the single-sweep average (cell E4) is identical to the final multi-sweep average (cell L4). Also, the single-sweep ensemble average (cells B13:G13) is identical to Sweep 4 (cells I11:N11) of the multi-sweep section.

Multi-sweep section

The formulas in the multi-sweep mode require a little more explanation. In this version of the multi-sweep method all records are equally weighted. For example, Sweep 3 is the average of three records, so it is weighted three times more than the fourth incoming record (see explanation for formula in Sweep 4 below).

Sweep 1 is simply the first incoming data, identical to Record 1 of the single-sweep method.

Sweep 2 computes the average of Sweep 1 and the second incoming record. A typical cell formula is =(J8+C9)/2 in cell J9.

Sweep 3 computes the average of Sweep 2 and the third incoming record. A typical cell formula is =(2*J9+C10)/3 in cell J9.

Sweep 4 computes the average of Sweep 3 and the fourth incoming record. A typical cell formula is =(3*J10+C11)/4 in cell J11. This formula is displayed in the cell editing box in Fig. 9-29.

You can invent unequal weighting formulas so the ensemble "forgets" older data. This is useful for relatively slowly changing incoming data.

Tip

These examples demonstrate ensembles of scalar data. It is a simple extension to operate on vector data. For a vector ensemble, compose a worksheet section for in-phase data and another section for the quadrature data. As an alternative, you can compose a worksheet section for the vector magnitude and another section for the vector phase. Vector (phase-preserving) ensemble averaging is often called *pre-detection averaging* because of its use in telecommunications and radar. Similarly, scalar ensemble averaging is called *post-detection averaging*.

Figures 9-30 and 9-31 show the screens of the ENSEMBLE workbook. Nine records and nine sweeps are shown in the sheet tab named **Single & Multi**, but you can add more. This workbook also demonstrates the use of hyperlinks *inside* the workbook to jump to another screen. While viewing the Home screen (Fig. 9-30) click on <u>Go To Multi-Sweep Average</u> and you will see Fig. 9-31.

Now click on <u>Go To Single-Sweep Average</u> and you will jump back to the Home screen. Right-click on one of the hyperlinks to activate a pop-up menu, then left-click on [Hyperlink] and you will see the hyperlink editing menu. Look at [Edit Hyperlink] and you will see that <u>Go To Multi-Sweep Average </u>refers to cell AM4. You can change the cell reference in this dialog box. Of course, you can also use hyperlinks to refer to other files on your computer or to URLs on the Internet.

Tip

You can enhance your workbooks with different fonts. The title in Fig. 9-30 uses the font named Comic Sans MS in 16-point size. Note that EXCEL automatically re-sizes the row to accommodate the larger font.

If you really want to impress your laboratory instructor, click on the [Drawing] icon on the top menu, then click on the [Insert WordArt] icon on the Drawing menu that appears at the bottom of your screen and use your artistic creativity.

C10		= =VARP(B29:Z29)														
	A	B	C	D	E	F	G	H	I	J	K	L	M	N	O	
1	ENSEMBLE.XLS				SINGLE-SWEEP and MULTI-SWEEP ENSEMBLE AVERAGE											
2	Chapter 10															
3											Click:					
4	Enter noise amplitude		2			Noise sample	-0.83269			Go To Multi-Sweep Average						
5																
6	Single-Sweep Ensemble															
7		Variances														
8	Noiseless	0.201600				Press Function Key F9 for new noise										
9	Sample 1	0.407628														
10	Ensemble Average	0.270207														
11																
12	Data Point	1	2	3	4	5	6	7	8	9	10	11	12	13	14	
13	Noiseless	0	0	0	0	0	0	0	0	0	0	1	1	1	1	
14	Sample:															
15	1	0.991574	0.152329	0.002453	-0.20752	-0.00792	0.130351	-0.04595	0.460175	0.083086	0.098801	0.97634	1.277545	1.206191	0.993096	0.5
16	2	0.668664	0.44494	0.513341	0.339862	0.633602	0.598989	-0.85203	-0.19585	0.41377	0.745501	1.060242	1.191246	0.428015	1.62061	0.4
17	3	-0.63277	0.178643	-0.05507	0.258206	-0.96836	-0.90421	0.594467	0.9416	0.059077	-0.01377	1.061102	1.64489	1.956575	0.438958	1.4
18	4	-0.05745	0.87424	-0.40721	0.260535	0.193743	0.174224	0.682772	-0.12552	0.613646	-0.8499	1.502838	0.88869	1.941304	1.785261	0.5
19	5	0.208019	0.329919	-0.81682	-0.86206	-0.8273	-0.52069	-0.07796	-0.2632	-0.9555	-0.48575	1.799078	0.251116	1.971839	1.471836	1
20	6	-0.6225	0.560437	0.450576	0.120859	-0.50298	0.722943	0.814519	-0.44179	0.44319	-0.10932	1.168055	0.635732	1.851125	1.327112	0.4
21	7	0.863229	0.476784	-0.46654	-0.61993	0.682253	0.445254	-0.18374	-0.43832	0.989007	0.774747	1.892952	1.946427	0.316888	1.992068	0.2
22	8	0.197114	0.919644	0.557605	0.130464	0.833689	-0.73333	-0.05868	-0.34551	-0.54115	-0.7909	1.106462	0.283817	0.582372	0.522329	0.6
23	9	0.279577	0.24983	0.661172	-0.28555	0.085094	0.402966	0.156607	-0.81991	-0.24135	-0.9749	0.988681	1.790936	1.900679	0.213065	0.7
24	10															
25	11															
26	12															
27	13															
28	14															
29	Average:	0.210606	0.465196	0.048834	-0.09613	0.013536	0.035167	0.114446	-0.13648	0.095974	-0.17839	1.283961	1.101156	1.350554	1.151371	0.7
30	(Single Sweep)															

Figure 9-30. Home screen of the ENSEMBLE workbook. Note variances and the hyperlink to the Multi-Sweep Average screen. Compare the variances of the Single-Sweep ensemble with the Multi-Sweep ensemble (see Fig. 9-31).

AC23 =(8*AC22+B23)/9

Y	Z	AA	AB	AC	AD	AE	AF	AG	AH	AI	AJ	AK	AL	AM
				Multi-Sweep Ensemble Average										
									Click:					
									Go To Single-Sweep Average					
					Variances									
				Noiseless	0.201600		Press Function Key F9 for new noise							
				Sweep 1	0.407628									
				Sweep 9	0.270207									
				Multi-Sweep Ensemble Average										
24	25		Data Point	1	2	3	4	5	6	7	8	9	10	11
0	0		Noiseless	0	0	0	0	0	0	0	0	0	0	1
-0.46477	0.024883		Sweep 1	0.991574	0.152329	0.002453	-0.20752	-0.00792	0.130351	-0.04595	0.460175	0.083086	0.098801	0.97634
-0.04889	0.800456		Sweep 2	0.830119	0.298634	0.257897	0.066172	0.312841	0.36467	-0.44899	0.132161	0.248428	0.422151	1.018291
0.29591	-0.29655		Sweep 3	0.342488	0.258637	0.153575	0.130183	-0.11422	-0.06829	-0.10117	0.401974	0.185311	0.276843	1.032561
0.55609	0.049536		Sweep 4	0.242503	0.412538	0.013378	0.162771	-0.03723	-0.00016	0.094814	0.270101	0.292395	-0.00484	1.150131
-0.21318	0.917864		Sweep 5	0.235606	0.396014	-0.15266	-0.0422	-0.19525	-0.10427	0.06026	0.163442	0.042816	-0.10102	1.27992
0.820862	0.767039		Sweep 6	0.092589	0.423418	-0.05212	-0.01502	-0.24654	0.033601	0.18597	0.062569	0.109545	-0.10241	1.261276
0.111728	-0.48526		Sweep 7	0.20268	0.431042	-0.11132	-0.10143	-0.11385	0.092409	0.133154	-0.00899	0.235182	0.0229	1.351515
-0.30071	0.650481		Sweep 8	0.201985	0.492117	-0.02771	-0.07245	0.004592	-0.01081	0.109175	-0.05105	0.13814	-0.07882	1.320864
-0.83519	0.793274		Sweep 9	0.210606	0.465196	0.048834	-0.09613	0.013536	0.035167	0.114446	-0.13648	0.095974	-0.17839	1.283961
-0.00868	0.357969													

Figure 9-31. Multi-Sweep ensemble average screen of the ENSEMBLE workbook. Click on the hyperlink to go back to the Home screen. Note use of the VARP worksheet function to compute the variances.

In the ENSEMBLE workbook, click on the tab named SingleSweep and you will see a worksheet with 25 records. Note the improved reduction in variance compared with 9 records.

9.11 Inserting an EXCEL worksheet in Microsoft WORD

When you write a laboratory report you can include a small worksheet in the text. This is better than an ordinary Table because you can do calculations in it. Open a new file in Microsoft WORD. On the top menu bar click on the icon labeled Insert Microsoft Excel Worksheet (this icon is between the icon for Insert Table and the icon for Columns.) You can select the number of rows and columns to display. Figure 9-32 shows a 5-row, 5-column worksheet inserted.

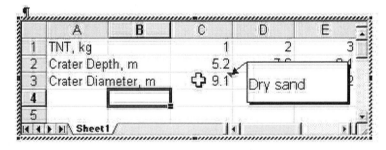

Figure 9-32. An active worksheet inserted in a Microsoft WORD document.

TNT, kg		1	2	3
Crater Depth, m		5.2		
Crater Diameter, m		9.1	Dry sand	

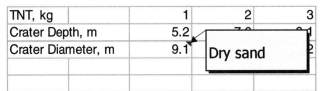

Figure 9-33. The worksheet looks like this in your Microsoft WORD document while you are not editing it. Cell C3 is commented. You have an option of showing or hiding comments.

When you have completed the worksheet move the mouse pointer into the text part of the document and do one left-click. The worksheet transforms into a neat-looking Table without the cell addresses, as shown in Fig. 9-33. To edit the worksheet, just double click on the Table.

9.12 Embed a movie clip in your worksheet

Photographs and drawings are often useful in explaining what your worksheet is about. Movie clips are even more useful when motion is described by your worksheet. Video is more than decoration, however. You can make quantitative measurements on movie clips by including a digital clock and a meter stick (or grid) in the movie, and moving the pointer on the Media Player (described below) so that you see stopped motion, that is, one frame at a time. For measurements on robot motion it is often necessary to include angular measurement.

It is easy to embed a movie clip. Open a new workbook, click on [Insert][Object] and you will see the dialog box in Fig. 9-34. Select the movie type, Movie Clip (AVI) or QuickTime Movie, for example.

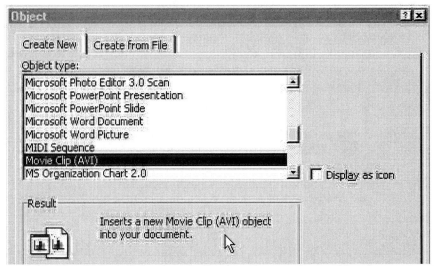

Figure 9-34. The Object dialog box in the Insert menu is used to place a movie clip in your worksheet. Scroll down for QuickTime Movie object.

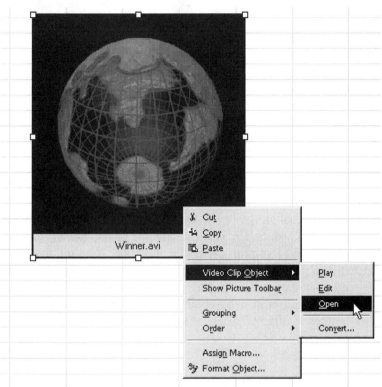

Figure 9-35. A right-click brings up the menu. Select Play or Open. Click on the AVI photo to pop up the menu.

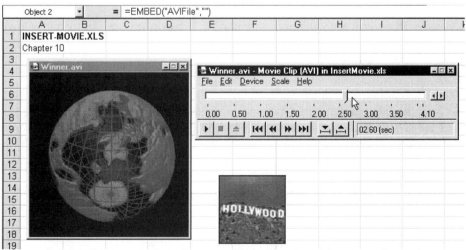

Figure 9-36. When you select Open you bring up the video control panel.

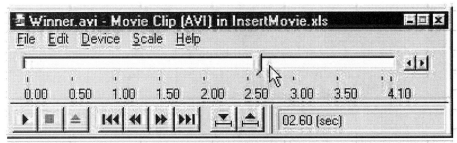

Figure 9-37. This is the control panel that pops up when you select [Video Clip Object][Open]. Open the INSERT-MOVIE workbook and explore the menus on your computer.

The video control panel works like a VCR. You can play, stop, fast forward and rewind, and so on. Even better, you can use the mouse pointer to move the time pointer backward and forward, one frame at a time. Note the time indicator in Figs. 9-36 and 9-37; it reads out as 02.60 (sec). If your video was made at 30 frames per second your data will have pretty good time resolution. For example, you can measure the position of a baseball at each frame time to determine the trajectory. Use numerical differentiation of the position data to obtain the velocity components. Differentiate the velocity components to obtain the acceleration components. (See Chapter 5.)

Some sources for lab software and hardware interfaces

Make your own USB interface:
"A Universal Serial Bus interface for electronics projects and instruments," T. Z. Fullem and C. D. Spencer, *American Journal of Physics* **70** (9), 972–974 (2002).

DATAQ Instruments
Versatile, inexpensive acquisition and playback hardware and software; a free download of the WINDAQ program is available.
http://www.dataq.com

Marlin P. Jones & Associates
8412-KT Analog parallel port 8-bit data sampler $23.21.
8418-KT 12-bit data acquisition system $55.00.
http://www.mpja.com

National Instruments
Laboratory-grade hardware and associated software
http://www.ni.com
If you do not have a licensed copy of MEASURE you should download the MEASURE demo from http://www.ni.com.

PASCO Scientific
Educational hardware and software; Biology, Chemistry, and Physics
http://www.pasco.com

TAL Technologies, Inc.
WinWedge imports data from any RS-232 instrument into EXCEL.
http://www.taltech.com/

TEL-Atomic
Educational hardware and software
http://www.telatomic.com

Vernier Software
Educational hardware and software; Biology, Chemistry, and Physics
http://www.vernier.com

What's next?

Chapter 10 will show you how to use the complex operators and functions in EXCEL. This Chapter is on the CD. Double-click on the file named Chapter-10 and it will appear on your monitor. Note: there is an error in the Acrobat file for Chapter 10 on the CD. The line under Equation (10-2) should read:

Note that Eq. (10-2) implies $z^n = r^n \cos(n\theta) + i\, r^n \sin(n\theta) = r^n\, e^{in\theta}$.

Complex functions are required in Chapters 11 and 12. Chapter 11 will show you how to use the Fourier Transform tool in the Analysis ToolPak. This is EXCEL's version of the Fast Fourier Transform (or FFT), the most powerful tool in the spreadsheet. The FFTs in many laboratory software packages are good for a quick look at spectra, but you can get much more information, and more accurate information, by importing time-domain data into EXCEL and using the methods of the next chapter. Chapter 11 is on the CD. Chapter 12 shows engineering and scientific applications of the FFT.

References

R. Stephens, *Advanced Visual Basic Techniques*, (Wiley, New York, 1997).

The *Microsoft Office/Visual Basic Programmer's Guide* teaches those who understand the fundamentals of Visual Basic how to create concise and efficient code with the powerful programming language used in Microsoft Office. The book teaches readers how to become more productive with Visual Basic for Applications by customizing and adapting tools for specific needs, including how to create custom commands, menus, dialog boxes, messages, and buttons as well as how to show custom Help for all these elements.

You can obtain the *Microsoft Office/Visual Basic Programmer's Guide* at bookstores, computer stores, and direct from Microsoft Press. To order the *Programmer's Guide* (ISBN: 1-57231-340-4) direct, call (800) MSPRESS in the United States or (800) 667-1115 in Canada. For more information, go to the Microsoft web site http://www.microsoft.com/. (You will also find some free downloads at this web site.)

Also, go to http://www.amazon.com and http://www.barnesandnoble.com/ for the latest books on VBA.

Test your skills

1. Importing data. Open a new workbook using [File][New]. Follow the instructions on page 200 and import the text file named OZONE.txt. This file is on the CD in the folder named POLLUTION.

2. Insert a movie in your worksheet. (This is Number 2 on The Top Ten List of Ways to Impress Your Laboratory Instructor.) Open the INSERT-MOVIE workbook. You will see two methods of inserting a movie. Method 1 uses the [Insert][Object] menu to insert an icon for the Movie Clip (AVI) that you will see on the list in the dialog box. Method 2 inserts a photo of the first frame of the movie clip. You can play the movie clip by two methods: (1) Double-click on the icon or the photo. (2) Use one right-click to open the pop-up menu. Select "Video Clip Object" and then select "Play". Now, close the workbook and click on [File][New]. Use the [Insert][Object] menu to insert a movie clip from the CD into your new worksheet. Test the worksheet to be sure it plays correctly.

3. Record a macro to do a Moving Average. Open a new workbook in EXCEL, import the data file named DAMP-MASS.txt located in the folder named Data Files. Follow the instructions in Section 9.2 to create a macro that will perform a 3-point moving average on the Force data using the Moving Average tool in the Analysis ToolPak. Select Chart Output.

4. For Exercise 3, use the VARP worksheet function to compute the variances of the raw Force data and the 3-point Moving Average Force data.

5. Single-sweep ensemble average. Open a new workbook in EXCEL and import the data file named ENSEMBLE-OSC.txt located in the folder named Data Files. Compose a single-sweep ensemble average of the four records. Compute the population variances of the ensemble average and the individual records.

6. Multi-sweep ensemble average. Open a new workbook in EXCEL and import the data file named ENSEMBLE-OSC.txt located in the folder named Data Files.

Compose a multi-sweep ensemble average of the four records. Compute the population variances of the ensemble average and the individual records.

7. Random noise and SNR. Open the NOISE workbook. Use various values of noise amplitude and observe results of variance and SNR. Use your mouse to explore the formulas and composition of the worksheet.

8. ✪ Electromechanical detection of viruses and bacteria. Vibrating electrome-chanical devices can be used for rapid detection of the presence of specific types of microbial forms. For more information go to http://www.akubio.com. Also do an Internet search for akubio, using the Google search engine, for example. De-tection is based on the acceleration (or g) associated with particular microbes when they break from their host cell. The maximum g experienced by jet pilots is 7 to 8. Recall, one g is the acceleration of gravity on Earth, 9.8 m/s². It may be surprising that an electromechanical device can detect something as small as a virus or a bacterium, but recall that the first *atomic force microscope* was based on the bending of a piece of ordinary kitchen-quality aluminum foil.

First, review Section 7.4, page 152. For acceleration, use Eq. (7-22) in the form,

$$\frac{d^2 x}{dt^2} = -\omega_o^2 \, x.$$

Remember, $\omega = 2\pi f$ where ω has units of rad/s and f has units of Hz. Use the maximum amplitude for x.

Compose a workbook to compute the acceleration in m/s² and the corre-sponding g for a quartz crystal vibrating at various frequencies and amplitudes. Let the frequency vary from 1 to 20 MHz in steps of 1 MHz, and let the ampli-tude vary from 5×10^{-7} to 1×10^{-5} m in steps of 10^{-7} m. Graph your results in g vs. frequency, g vs. amplitude, and on a 3-D graph using frequency and ampli-tude for the x and y axes, and g for the z-axis.

You may be astonished at the values of g. The big question is, why didn't people think of this simple idea years ago?

Note: When you import text files you may need to experiment with choosing tab delimited, space delimited, and so on to achieve desired results.

Movie files on the CD use the Codec named "Indeo Video Interactive R4.1 by Intel". This is probably installed on your PC. Click on Control Panel, then click on Multimedia, and click on the Advanced tab. Next, click on the "+box" by Video Compression Codecs. You should see the Codec on the list (Fig. 9-38). If it is not there, download it from the http://www.intel.com web site or from your Windows installation CD. (Codec is an acronym for Compressor-Decompressor.)

This URL will take you directly to the Indeo Codecs:
http://support.intel.com/support/technologies/multimedia/indeo/enduser/index.htm

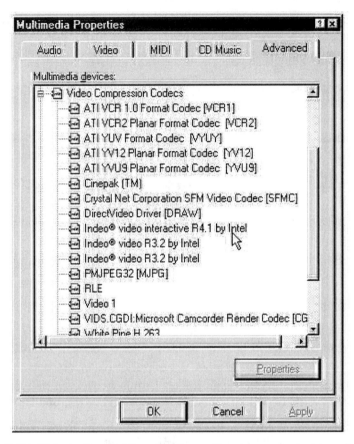

Figure 9-38. This is the Multimedia Properties box selected by clicking on the Multimedia icon in the Windows Control Panel. You may have a different list of Video Compression Codecs.

For the latest information on multimedia technologies from Microsoft, go to: http://www.microsoft.com.

HyperCam is powerful, inexpensive video capture software that records AVI movies (screencam) directly from your monitor, for software presentations, software training, demos, tutorials, and fun. The new version will operate in Windows XP. You can download a free trial version. HyperCam supports text annotations, sound, and screen notes (great for creating lab reports and automated software demos.). You can also select Frame Rate and Compression Quality prior to video capture. Go to: http://www.hyperionics.com/

Appendix 1
Workbooks

Workbooks on the disk

This Appendix contains a list of workbooks and data files on the CD. Some workbooks in this Appendix are supplementary to workbooks in the main text, and some workbooks are associated with end-of-chapter problems.

Some workbooks in this Appendix are not explained in the text. These workbooks are to be used for "reverse engineering" or "forensic engineering" to learn what the workbook does and how it is done. This type of exercise is typical of real life. You may need to use a workbook that someone composed, and you may find it has inadequate documentation. Your task is to document the workbook so you and other people can understand it. Use EXCEL comments (see pages 26 and 27), and write instructions in narrative form on a separate sheet in the workbook.

For updates and downloads go to http://sylvanbloch.hypermart.net/ .

Chapter 1 Getting Started	
Workbook Name	Description
BASEBALL	Tutorial workbook illustrating various techniques
MY WORKBOOK	Introduction to the EXCEL workbook

Chapter 3 Graphing Data	
Workbook Name	Description
EXP-POLAR	Polar graph example, function of a function
GRAVITY	Log-Log graph and use of Trendline in graph
IDEAL-GAS	Pressure-volume relation, constant T
OBJECT DETECTOR	Sensor detects moving objects at various positions. This is used to demonstrate EXCEL's 3-D surface graph.
OLYMPIC	Trendline example using Olympic swim records
PLANETS	Graphing planetary data for solar system

POLAR	Polar graph
ROCKET SCIENCE	Rocket with variable mass, Tsiolkovskii's equation
SINE-SUM	Sum of 2 sine waves. Demonstrates IF function
SURFACE	3D surface graph
SWIM-50	50-meter free-style swimming records, by age group
THIN-LENS	Image and object distances
TWO-Y	Left and right Y axes
XY-EXAMPLE	XY or scatter graph

Chapter 4 Quick-Start Math	
Workbook Name	Description
FOURIER	Fourier series, synthesis of square wave
INCLINE	Object on inclined plane with friction

Chapter 5 Differentiation and Integration	
Workbook Name	Description
DERIVATIVE	Backward, Forward, and Central derivatives
EXP-SMOOTH	EXCEL's Exponential Smoothing tool
INTEGRATION	Rectangular, Trapezoidal, and Simpson's 1/3 Rule
INTEGRATION-101	Comparison of Left-Rectangular, Right-Rectangular, and Trapezoidal integration with selectable step size
MOMENTS	Center of mass and moments of inertia
MOVE-AVG	EXCEL's Moving Average tool
SinXoverX	Numerical integration example
SMOOTH	Sliding window integrators, noiseless test
SMOOTH-2	Sliding window integrators, noisy data
SMOOTH-2A	Adjustable weight FIR and Savitsky-Golay smoothing
SUNSPOTS	Historical data of sunspots, used for data smoothing
TRAPEZOID	Example of trapezoidal and rectangular integration
TREND-INTEGRAL	EXCEL's Trendline tool used for integrating noisy data

Chapter 6 EXCEL's Engineering Functions	
Workbook Name	Description
ATWOOD	Solving simultaneous algebraic equations using matrix methods for Atwood's machine
BESSEL	Bessel functions
ENTROPY	Entropy tutorial using EXCEL's COMBIN function
ENTROPY-2	Entropy of a binary system (coin toss)
MATRIX	EXCEL's matrix operations
ROTATE	Rotation of coordinates using matrix methods
VECTOR ALGEBRA	Sum, difference, dot and cross products, magnitude, angle

Chapter 7 Differential Equations	
Workbook Name	Description
Drag-Force-1	Motion with viscous drag force
EULER	Euler methods tutorial
EXP-D-K-2	Comparison of numerical and analytical solutions
FREE-FALL	Experimental data for analysis
LAPLACE	Laplace's equation in two dimensions using FEM
QUANTUM	Schrödinger's equation for a square-well potential
TEMPERATURE	Introduction to the finite element method (FEM)
VECTORS	Vector algebra in 3 dimensions
VIBRATIONS	Simple harmonic vibrations with adjustable damping

Chapter 8 Analysis ToolPak	
Workbook Name	Description
CORRELATION	EXCEL's Correlation tool
COVARIANCE	EXCEL's Covariance tool
EXP-AVG	EXCEL's Exponential Smoothing tool
HISTOGRAM	EXCEL's Histogram tool
MOVING AVERAGE	EXCEL's Moving Average tool
RANDOM	EXCEL's Random Number tool
REGRESSION	EXCEL's Regression tool

Chapter 9 EXCEL in the Lab	
Workbook Name	Description
DATA-INPUT	How to use Text Import Wizard
EKG	Experimental EKG data
FREE-FALL	Experimental data on free-falling object
HYPERLINK	Use of hyperlinks in a workbook
ENSEMBLE	Ensemble averaging, single and multi
INSERT-MOVIE	How to insert a video clip in EXCEL
INSERT-MOVIE2	How to insert a video clip in EXCEL
MICRO-TUTOR	Tutorial on single-sweep and multi-sweep ensemble averaging
NOISE	Random noise data. Compute average and r.m.s.
PASCO-EXCEL	PASCO experimental data imported into EXCEL
RADIOACTIVE	Using TrendLine tool to estimate half-life of isotope
TITRATION	Regression Tool applied to titration of NaOH and HCl

Chapter 10 Complex Math	
Workbook Name	Description
COMPLEX	Shows use of several of EXCEL's complex operations

Chapter 11 Analysis ToolPak: Fast Fourier Transform	
Workbook Name	Description
ALIAS-DATA	Sampling and aliasing effects, Nyquist frequency
COLLISION	Collision between magnets. Shows use of IF and MAX worksheet functions, and FFT
DATA WINDOWS	Data windows tutorial
EKG	Electrocardiograph data
EKG-2	Electrocardiogram data
FFT-IFFT	FFT and IFFT tutorial
FFT-TEST	Testing EXCEL's FFT
FORCE SENSOR	Force sensor measures time-dependent force due to moving objects. The power spectral density is computed.
FREQUENCY SCALING	How to set the frequency scale in Hz, using sampling frequency and number of samples. Parseval's theorem
PSD	Power spectral density tutorial; Parseval's theorem

Chapter 12 Analysis ToolPak: FFT Applications	
Workbook Name	Description
COHERENCE	Coherence function and SNR function
CONVOLTIME	Convolution tutorial, without FFT
CONVOLVE	Convolution tutorial using FFT
CORRELTIME	Cross-correlation function tutorial, without FFT
CROSSCORR	Cross-correlation function using FFT
DECONVOLVE	Deconvolution using FFT
DECONVOLVE-2	Deconvolution using FFT
RC-CIRCUIT-FFT	RC circuit analyzed using FFT and IFFT
RC-CIRCUIT-2	RC circuit
SYSTEM-I-D	System identification using FFT
SYSTEM-FUN	System function and impulse response

Appendix 3 TrendLine Equations	
Workbook Name	Description
TRENDLINE	Use of TrendLine tool in EXCEL's graphing wizard

Data files on the CD

These files are in ASCII text format in the folder named Data Files. They can be used as exercises in importing raw data into EXCEL for analysis and graphing.

Data File Name	File Size, kB	Description
DAMP-MASS	14	Mass on spring, oscillating in water
EKG	20	Electrocardiogram data
ENSEMBLE-OSC	9	Noisy records of a mass on a spring
OSC-DATA	3	Mass on spring, oscillating in air
POLLUTION	43	File Folder with ozone data
PV-GAS	1	Pressure and volume data for gas
RADIOACTIVE DK	10	Radioactive decay, counts/s
SOUNDWAVE	5	Sound recorded with microphone
SUNSPOTS	5	Historical sunspot records

Note:
More exercises for each chapter are on the CD.

Appendix 2
Internet Links

The Internet contains a vast array of useful resources. It's like having a hard disk with ten million gigabytes in your computer. The following is a small selection of cool URLs. Each one has links to many other sites. For your convenience, this Appendix is also on the CD inside the front cover of this book, in Adobe Acrobat format (Internet Links.pdf.) and HTML format. Use your web browser to open the HTML file. After you bring up this Appendix on your computer, you can click on a URL (underlined) and you will be connected to the selected site on the Internet, if your modem or similar Internet connection is working.

The Internet is constantly changing, so some of these URLs may no longer be available. This Appendix is also in ASCII format on the disk, in the file named `apdx-2.txt.`

Alternative connection to the Internet sites:
Dial up your Internet connection and have your web browser running.
Type in the URL of the desired site and press Enter↵.
Instead of typing, you can use the Copy operation. Copy an address from the list below and click on your browser to Paste it in the address line in your web browser. Then press Enter↵.

http://www.microsoft.com/Office/archive/xl97brch/default.htm
   Keep informed with the latest information, and archives, about EXCEL.

http://www.microsoft.com/downloads/search.asp
   Free downloads for enhancing Microsoft products.

http://officeupdate.microsoft.com/downloadCatalog/dldExcel.htm
   Lots of free downloads specifically for EXCEL. Included are the EXCEL Internet Assistant (instantly convert spreadsheets to HTML), EXCEL Viewer (share spreadsheets with people who don't have EXCEL), add new spreadsheet functions, and so on.

http://www.microsoft.com/mspress/default.asp
  Microsoft Press home page. This has books about Microsoft products and some free downloads.

http://www.spreadsheetworld.com/
  Home page of Spreadsheet World. Lots of links to spreadsheet information.

On July 27, 1999, Microsoft became aware of a security issue involving the ODBC database driver that is installed as a part of EXCEL 97. It is possible that a malicious coder could create an EXCEL 97 spreadsheet that exploits a vulnerability in this database driver to delete files and perform other malicious acts. A user could encounter this problem by opening a spreadsheet attached to an e-mail message or linked from a Web site.
  In the course of producing the solution to this security issue, Microsoft testing became aware of a separate vulnerability in the ODBC database driver that may affect Excel 2000 users. This vulnerability is related to the IISAM component of the ODBC database driver and could be exploited using an EXCEL 2000 query to perform malicious acts similar to those described in EXCEL 97 "ODBC Driver" Vulnerability. Microsoft has produced a solution to this specific vulnerability and incorporated it into an update.
  Now available for download, the following update addresses the EXCEL "ODBC Driver" Vulnerability:
    http://officeupdate.microsoft.com/Articles/mdac_typ.htm
At this URL you will see your download options in the Table of Contents area of the page.

http://www.dataq.com/windaq.htm
  Free download of WINDAQ playback and analysis software that reads spreadsheet files, among others. WINDAQ is quite powerful (see Chapter 9). Dataq Instruments also provides a very inexpensive RS-232 serial data acquisition device, and USB devices.

http://www.senn.com/
  Science and Engineering Network News. A great site with many links and an excellent guide to Internet resources for engineers and scientists.

http://lcweb.loc.gov/homepage/lchp.html
  This is the home page of the Library of Congress. Use its search engine to access the vast information resources of this Library.

http://www.tc.cornell.edu/Edu/MathSciGateway/
  The Cornell Theory Center Math and Science Gateway. Links to almost everything.

http://archives.math.utk.edu/calculus/crol.html
  Calculus resources on-line.

http://euclid.math.fsu.edu/Science/math.html
  The Florida State University Mathematics Department's links to math resources on the net.

http://www.maa.org/
  This is the home page of the Mathematical Association of America.

http://www-sci.lib.uci.edu/HSG/Ref.html
  Engineering Center, Science Tables & Databases, Bioscience Center, Chemistry Center, Mathematics Center, Physics Center, Space & Astrophysics Center, and more.

http://www.ieee.org/
  This is the home page of IEEE, the Institute of Electrical and Electronics Engineers, Inc.

http://www.ieee.org/society/index.html
  This home page has links to the following IEEE technical societies.
  IEEE Aerospace and Electronic Systems Society
  IEEE Antennas and Propagation Society
  IEEE Broadcast Technology Society
  IEEE Circuits and Systems Society
  IEEE Communications Society
  IEEE Components, Packaging, and Manufacturing Technology Society
  IEEE Computer Society
  IEEE Consumer Electronics Society
  IEEE Control Systems Society
  IEEE Dielectrics and Electrical Insulation Society
  IEEE Education Society
  IEEE Electromagnetic Compatibility Society
  IEEE Electron Devices Society
  IEEE Engineering in Medicine and Biology Society
  IEEE Engineering Management Society
  IEEE Geoscience and Remote Sensing Society
  IEEE Industrial Electronics Society
  IEEE Industry Applications Society
  IEEE Information Theory Society
  IEEE Instrumentation and Measurement Society
  IEEE Lasers and Electro-Optics Society
  IEEE Magnetics Society

IEEE Microwave Theory and Techniques Society
IEEE Neural Networks Council
IEEE Nuclear and Plasma Sciences Society
IEEE Oceanic Engineering Society
IEEE Power Electronics Society
IEEE Power Engineering Society
IEEE Professional Communication Society
IEEE Reliability Society
IEEE Robotics and Automation Society
IEEE Signal Processing Society
IEEE Social Implications of Technology Society
IEEE Solid-State Circuits Council/Society
IEEE Systems, Man and Cybernetics Society
IEEE Ultrasonics, Ferroelectrics and Frequency Control Society
IEEE Vehicular Technology Society

http://www.asme.org
The home page of the American Society of Mechanical Engineers. Check out the student page at http://www.asme.org/students/

http://www.asce.org/
This is the home page of the American Society of Civil Engineers (ASCE)

http://www.acs.org/
This is the home page of the American Chemical Society (ACS). Check out the student page at   http://www.acs.org/edugen2/education/stu_aff/sa.htm

http://clogp.pomona.edu/medchem/chem/index.html
Chemistry resources on the Internet

http://www.liv.ac.uk/Chemistry/Links/links.html
Huge collection of chemistry links from the University of Liverpool.

http://www.aibs.org
This is the home page of the American Institute of Biological Sciences. It has links to all of the member societies.

http://www.orst.edu/~ahernk/biochemlinks.html
Biotechnology Software and Internet Journal.

http://www.mpae.gwdg.de/EGS/EGS.html
Home page of the European Geophysical Society.

http://www.agu.org/
   Home page of the American Geophysical Union (AGU). It has more than 35,000 members in 115 countries.

http://physicsweb.org/TIPTOP/
   The Internet Pilot To Physics (TIPTOP). Check out the worldwide collection of cool Java applets in the Virtual Laboratory. You could learn a lot here.

http://www.psrc-online.org/
   Physical Science Resource Center at American Association of Physics Teachers.

http://www.phys.washington.edu/groups/peg/
   Center for Physics Education at University of Washington.

http://www.physics.umd.edu/deptinfo/facilities/lecdem/
   Physics Demonstration Lab at University of Maryland.

http://www2.ncsu.edu/ncsu/pams/physics/Physics_Ed/
   Physics Education Research and Development at North Carolina State University

http://mazur-www.harvard.edu/Education/EducationMenu.html
   Science Education Research at Harvard, Eric Mazur Group.

http://www.me.umn.edu/
   Department of Mechanical Engineering at the University of Minnesota, Twin Cities Campus

http://www.unl.edu/physics/Education.html
   Physics Education Research at University of Nebraska at Lincoln.

http://www.nsf.gov/home/ehr/start.htm
   Undergraduate MSE&T Education Program, National Science Foundation.

http://www.usafa.af.mil/dfp/
   Physics Department at the U. S. Air Force Academy.

http://webphysics.iupui.edu/152_251_mainpage.html
   Just-in-Time Teaching of Physics at IUPUI.

http://www.aip.org/pt/

This is the home page of PHYSICS TODAY. Check this out for the latest news, interesting articles, and Web Watch.

http://www.aas.org/
   American Astronomical Society (AAS).

http://earth.agu.org/
   American Geophysical Union (AGU).

http://www.aapt.org/
   American Association of Physics Teachers – AAPT. The web site for the American Journal of Physics is http://www.kzoo.edu/ajp .You can search by author, title, and subject in the database at http://ojps.aip.org/ajp/

http://www.aip.org/
   American Institute of Physics (AIP).

http://aps.org/
   American Physical Society (APS).

http://www.anl.gov/
   Argonne National Laboratory.

http://www.bnl.gov/bnl.html
   Brookhaven National Laboratory.

http://www.cebaf.gov/
   The Thomas Jefferson National Accelerator Facility, or Jefferson Lab, is a basic research laboratory built to probe the nucleus of the atom the quark structure of matter.

http://www.fnal.gov/
   Fermi National Accelerator Laboratory.

http://www.llnl.gov/
   Lawrence Livermore National Laboratory (LLNL). LLNL is operated by the University of California under a contract with the US Department of Energy.

http://www-phys.llnl.gov/
   Lawrence Livermore National Laboratory, Physics and Space Technology.

http://www.lanl.gov/external/

Los Alamos National Laboratory.

http://www.nas.edu/
National Academy of Sciences. This home page also links to the National Academy of Engineering, the Institute of Medicine, and their principal operating agency, the National Research Council.

http://www.nasa.gov/
The home page of NASA. Prepare to spend a day at this web site.

http://www.jpl.nasa.gov/
NASA/Jet Propulsion Laboratory.

http://www.gsfc.nasa.gov/GSFC_orgpage.html
NASA/Goddard Space Flight Center.

http://ltpwww.gsfc.nasa.gov/
NASA/Goddard Space Flight Center, Laboratory for Terrestrial Physics.

http://www.ornl.gov/home.html
Oak Ridge National Laboratory.

http://www.pnl.gov:2080/
Pacific Northwest Laboratory.

http://www.sandia.gov/
Sandia National Laboratories.

http://www.slac.stanford.edu/
Stanford Linear Accelerator Center.

http://www.ioppublishing.com/
The Institute of Physics (United Kingdom).

http://nobelprizes.com/
The Nobel Prizes. This has a searchable database. Women have won Nobel Prizes in all fields except economics. This web site discusses several theories about the lack of a Nobel Prize in mathematics.

http://www.ibm.com/
The home page of IBM.

http://www.intel.com/

The home page of Intel.

http://telerobot.mech.uwa.edu.au/
Australian telerobot site. Operate a telerobot on the web. Links to other telero-bots, including a cute little robot in the EE Department at Mississippi State University: http://spaceghost.ece.msstate.edu/telerobot.html

http://www.usno.navy.mil
The U.S. Naval Observatory performs an essential scientific role for the Navy, for the Department of Defense and for the United States. Its mission is to determine the positions and motions of celestial objects, to provide astronomical data, to measure the Earth's rotation and to maintain the Master Clock.

http://tycho.usno.navy.mil/
The Time Service Department of the U.S. Naval Observatory is the official source of time used in the United States. This web site has several fascinating sections, including the Global Positioning System and a way to set your PC's clock to the Master Atomic Clock.

http://physics.nist.gov/GenInt/Time/time.html
The National Institute of Standards and Technology presents *A Walk Through Time.*

http://http.ee.queensu.ca:8000/www/dept/courses/elec331/eleclink.htm
Electrical Engineering Software and Reference Materials at Queen's University, Canada.

http://tycho.usno.navy.mil/gps.html
The Global Positioning System (GPS).

http://www.its.bldrdoc.gov/fs-1037/
Glossary of Telecommunication Terms, U.S. Federal Standard 1037C.

http://www.bldrdoc.gov/
Home page of the National Institute of Standards and Technology Boulder, Colorado Laboratories.

http://bul.eecs.umich.edu/uffc/uffc_fc.html
Clocks and time
The comprehensive listing of horological sites on the internet
Glossary of Time and Frequency Control Terms
GPS Internet Connections
NIST Time and Frequency activities (continued next page)

Time signals and frequency standards emissions, List of ITU-R Recommendations

UFFC Sensors and Actuators Section

http://www.slac.stanford.edu/library/nobel.html
Nobel Prize winners related to frequency control and timekeeping: Rabi, Ramsey, Dehmelt, Paul, Chu, Cohen-Tannoudji and Phillips.

http://www.patent-inf.tu-ilmenau.de/links/patinfo-eng.html
Patent Information. See the IBM site for all U. S. patents since 1971.

http://www.patents.ibm.com/
The IBM site for U. S. patents since 1971. This is a searchable database.

http://physics.nist.gov/funcon.html
Fundamental Physical Constants, courtesy of National Institute of Standards and Technology Physics Laboratory.

http://bul.eecs.umich.edu/uffc/uffc_fc.html
Frequency control, University of Michigan.

http://bul.eecs.umich.edu/uffc/quartz/vig/vigtoc.htm
So, you think you know all about crystal oscillators? (Fort Monmouth)

http://www.npl.co.uk/
National Physical Laboratory, Queens Road, Teddington, Middlesex, United Kingdom.

http://www.Colorado.EDU/physics/2000/
University of Colorado at Boulder; excellent interactive Java applets.

http://www.wiley.com/
Western hemisphere home page of John Wiley & Sons, Inc. publishers since 1807. For Europe, go to http://www.wiley.co.uk/ for faster operation. For Australia and the western Pacific area, go to http://www.jacwiley.com.au.

http://www.aaii.org/dloads/sprsheets/

http://home.gvi.net/~cpearson/excel/pivots.htm
PivotTable tutorial

http://home.gvi.net/~cpearson/excel/topic.htm
EXCEL topic index

Appendix 3
Trendline Equations

Here are the equations that EXCEL uses to calculate trendlines in charts. (See Section 3.6 and the Figures showing Add Trendline dialog boxes.) When you select a particular trendline type it is calculated automatically using your data.

To use trendlines effectively you need to understand what you are selecting. A good fit of noisy data with a trendline often reveals things about the process that generated the data. In general, you need to experiment with different types of trendlines and different parameters to find the best fit.

Linear

This selection calculates the least squares fit to your data by a straight line,

$$y = mx + b .$$
$$\text{(A3-1)}$$

Where m is the slope and b is the y-intercept.

Polynomial

A polynomial least squares fit to data is calculated by,

$$y = b + c_1 x + c_2 x^2 + c_3 x^3 + \cdots + c_6 x^6$$
$$\text{(A3-2)}$$

where b and the c_n are constants that you choose. You cannot use a higher polynomial than x^6 but that should be enough for most cases.

Logarithmic

A logarithmic least squares fit for your data is done by the equation,

$$y = c \ln(x) + b$$
$$\text{(A3-3)}$$

where c and b are constants and $\ln(x)$ is the natural log of x.

Exponential

An exponential least squares fit to your data is calculated by,

$$y = c\, e^{bx} \tag{A3-4}$$

where c and b are constants.

Power

A power least squares fits your data by,

$$y = c\, x^{b} \tag{A3-5}$$

where c and b are constants.

R-squared value

The R-squared value is a measure of goodness of fit, that is, how well the calculated trendline fits the data. A perfect fit is 1 and the worst fit is 0. The R-squared value is calculated by,

$$R^2 = 1 - \frac{SSE}{SST} \tag{A3-5}$$

where SSE is the *sum of squared errors*,

$$SSE = \sum (Y_j - \hat{Y}_j)^2 \tag{A3-6}$$

and SST is the *sum of the squared deviations from the mean*,

$$SST = \left(\sum Y_j^2\right) - \frac{1}{n}\left(\sum Y_j\right)^2. \tag{A3-7}$$

In Eq. (A3-6), Y_j is a data point and $\hat{Y}_j$ is the corresponding point in the model for the trendline.

Note: in other works, SST is named SSY and is defined as,

$$SSY = \sum (Y_i - \bar{Y})^2 \tag{A3-8}$$

where $\bar{Y}$ is the mean. For example, see the second reference at the end of this Appendix.

Moving Average

The moving average trendline in EXCEL is calculated by,

$$F_t = \frac{1}{n}(A_t + A_{t-1} + \cdots + A_{t-n+1}).\qquad\text{(A3-7)}$$

Note that the number of points in a moving average trendline equals the total number of points in the series, minus the number of points that you choose for the averaging period. For example, if you have 128 points in a series and you choose a 3-point moving average, the trendline will have 125 points. In EXCEL the maximum number of points you can use in an averaging period is 20.

Trendline example

Open the TRENDLINE workbook and you should see something like Fig. A3-1. This worksheet has a data set consisting of voltage measurements in column A and current measurements in column B. The current measurements are noisy, and we would like to see what sort of quantitative relation exists between voltage and current. From the data it is clear that as voltage increases, current tends to increase most of the time but random errors make the current fluctuate around the general tendency to increase.

Press Function Key F9 to change the noise and see the equation and R-squared value change. Enter a new value for noise amplitude in cell E2. Press Function Key F9 repeatedly for new noise samples. Another sample is shown in Fig. A3-2.

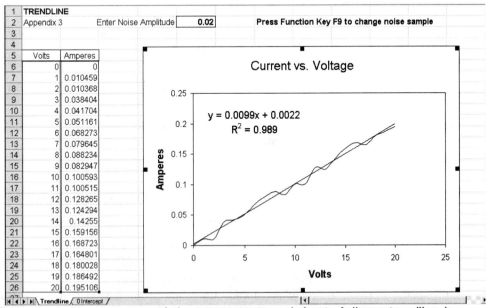

Figure A3-1. Home screen of the TRENDLINE worksheet. A linear trendline is computed automatically, with its equation and R-squared value displayed. According to the R-squared value, a linear fit is pretty good.

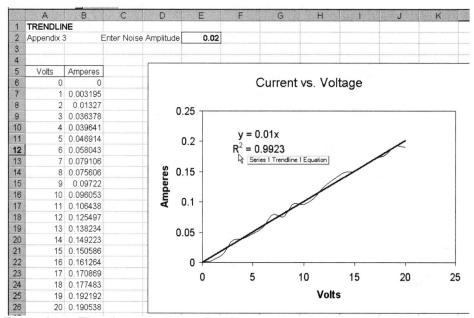

Figure A3-2. This shows another noisy data set based on the same physical system shown in Fig. A3-1. Here the Option has been checked to set the trendline y-intercept to 0. Compare the trendline equations and R-squared values.

The value of *y*-intercept should be zero because no current should flow if the voltage is zero. So, for this noisy data set the trendline tells us with about 99 percent confidence that the resistance *R* of the system is

$$R = \frac{x}{y} = \frac{V}{I} = \frac{1}{.01} = 100 \, \Omega. \tag{A3-8}$$

Try a polynomial trendline with the data in this worksheet. You'll see that the coefficients of powers of *x* greater than 1 are very small. Clearly, a linear fit is the best for this data set.

Related EXCEL tools

As you have seen, the trendline tool operates in the chart mode and is easy to use. EXCEL has some related tools, LINEST, LOGEST, and REGRESSION, that can be used on worksheet data without invoking the chart operation.

These are rather powerful tools and they require some knowledge of statistics in order to apply them effectively. LINEST is used to produce a linear best fit; LOGEST is similar, but it is used for an exponential best fit. See Chapter 9 for REGRESSION.

LINEST

Calculates the statistics for a line by using the least squares method to calculate a straight line that best fits your data, and returns an array that describes the line. Because this function returns an array of values, it must be entered as an array formula. See Help for more information about array formulas. The equation for the line is:

$y = mx + b$
or if there are multiple ranges of x-values (x1, x2, x3. . .this becomes

$y = m1x1 + m2x2 + ... + b$

where the dependent y-value is a function of the independent x-values. The m-values are coefficients corresponding to each x-value, and b is a constant value. Note that y, x, and m can be vectors. The array that LINEST returns is {mn,mn-1,...,m1,b}. LINEST can also return additional regression statistics.

Syntax

LINEST(known_y's,known_x's,const,stats)
Known_y's   is the set of y-values you already know in the relationship $y = mx + b$.

- If the array known_y's is in a single column, then each column of known_x's is interpreted as a separate variable.

- If the array known_y's is in a single row, then each row of known_x's is interpreted as a separate variable.

- Known_x's   is an optional set of x-values that you may already know in the relationship $y = mx + b$.

- The array known_x's can include one or more sets of variables. If only one variable is used, known_y's and known_x's can be ranges of any shape, as long as they have equal dimensions. If more than one variable is used, known_y's must be a vector (that is, a range with a height of one row or a width of one column).

- If known_x's is omitted, it is assumed to be the array {1,2,3,...} that is the same size as known_y's.

- Const   is a logical value specifying whether to force the constant b to equal 0.

- If const is TRUE or omitted, b is calculated normally.

- If const is FALSE, b is set equal to 0 and the m-values are adjusted to fit $y = mx$.

- Stats is a logical value specifying whether or not to return additional regression statistics.

If stats is TRUE, LINEST returns the additional regression statistics, so the returned array is {mn,mn-1,...,m1,b;sen,sen-1,...,se1,seb;r2,sey;F,df;ssreg,ssresid}. If stats is FALSE or omitted, LINEST returns only the m-coefficients and the constant b.

See EXCEL Help for additional information on Statistics and examples of using LINEST.

References

H. Skala, "Will the real best fit curve please stand up?", *College Mathematics Journal* **27** (3), 220–223 (1996).

B. Rossa, D. Pulskamp, and D. Otero, "Remarks on fitting functions to data", *Primus* **8** (4), 289–304 (1998).

Appendix 4
Goal Seek, Solver
and Lookup Wizard

What is the difference between Goal Seek, Solver and Lookup?

You can use the Goal Seek operation when you know the desired result of a single formula but you do not know the input value that the formula needs to determine the result. When goal-seeking, EXCEL varies the value in *one specific cell* until a formula that depends on that cell returns the result you want.

With Solver you can determine the value of a cell when you need to change the values in *more than one cell* and have *multiple constraints for those values*. When you use Solver, the cells you want to work with must be related through formulas on the worksheet. Solver uses sophisticated algorithms to achieve results. The Lookup Wizard is used for *empirical data* when no formula is known.

Look on the CD for more examples and exercises for Goal Seek and Solver.

A4.1 Goal Seek

How to find a specific result for a cell by adjusting the value of one other cell

1. On the Tools menu, click Goal Seek.
2. In the Set Cell box, enter the reference for the cell that contains the formula you want to resolve. See Fig. A4-1.
3. In the To Value box, type the result you want.
4. In the By Changing Cell box, enter the reference for the cell that contains the value you want to adjust.

Micro-tutorial on Goal Seek

Figure A4-1 shows a micro-tutorial on Goal Seek. In this problem, the initial values of cells B1, B2, and B3 are given. Cell B4 is related to these cells by the formula shown. Our goal is to change the cell B4 to 63 by changing cell B1.

Figure A4-1. Goal Seek is set to try to change the value in cell B1 to a value that will make cell B4 equal to 63, consistent with the formula in cell B4 shown in the cell editing box `=B1^2+ln(B2)-sin((degrees(B3))`.

Select [Tools][Goal Seek] and enter our goal of 63 as shown in Fig. A4-1. When you click on OK, Goal Seek changes the value of cell B1 to the new value 7.89296 and cell B4 is now 63.00010315.

After you click OK you will see the result shown in Fig. A4-2. Note that Goal Seek could not achieve an exact result of 63. This is due to the natural logarithm and the sine function in the formula that make it impossible to obtain an integer (63) for a result.

Caution: For some formulas Goal Seek cannot achieve a requested result because of mathematical impossibility. For example, it is not possible to find the logarithm of a negative number.

Here is an exercise that is not impossible. Try this with Goal Seek:

In cell A1, enter 4.

In cell A2, enter 16.

In cell A3, enter 1.

In cell A4, enter the formula $= (-A2+SQRT(A2^2-4*A1*A3))/(2*A1)$.

In cell A5 your should see the result, –0.06351.

Use Goal Seek to set cell A5 to the value –0.5 by changing cell A3.

Figure A4-2. Goal Seek Status reports that it has found an approximate solution.

A4.2 Solver

You can use Solver to determine the maximum or minimum value of one cell by changing other cells. For example, suppose you want to know the maximum volume of a rectangular box that you can generate by changing lengths of the sides, subject to some maximum or minimum constraints on their lengths. The cells you select *must be related through formulas* on the worksheet. If they are not related, changing one cell will not change the others.

Solver is a powerful tool that you can use immediately for simple problems. For more advanced applications you need to explore Solver's full capabilities. A complete discussion would require several chapters, but you can learn by doing instead of reading. The CD has more information on using Solver.

After a brief introduction to Solver we will do the previous problem that we did with Goal Seek, and you can compare the results. This example will not show the full powers of Solver, but you will see how to get started using it.

✪ EXCEL's Solver uses the Generalized Reduced Gradient (GRG2) nonlinear optimization code developed by Leon Lasdon (University of Texas at Austin) and Allan Waren (Cleveland State University). For linear and integer problems, Solver uses the simplex method with bounds on the variables, and the branch-and-bound method, implemented by John Watson and Dan Fylstra of Frontline Systems, Inc. For more information on the internal solution process used by Solver, go to the web site http://www.solver.com. You will also find a tutorial here on advanced linear and nonlinear optimization.

How to set Solver solution time and iterations
1. On the Tools menu, click Solver.
2. Click Options.
3. In the Max Time box, type the number of seconds that you want to allow for the solution time. See Fig. A4-8, to be discussed later.
4. In the Iterations box, enter the maximum number of iterations that you want to allow. See Fig. A4-8.

Note: If the solution process reaches the maximum time or number of iterations before Solver finds a solution, then Solver displays the Show Trial Solution dialog box. For more information about options in the Show Trial Solution dialog box, press Function Key F1 or see Help.

Figure A4-3 shows the Solver Parameters dialog box and a simple worksheet. Cells A1, A2, and A3 contain the values 4, 16 and 1, respectively. The formula connecting the data is shown in the formula editing box. This formula is the standard quadratic equation formula,

$$=(-A2+SQRT(A2^2-4*A1*A3))/(2*A1).$$

The Target Cell is A4, and you can set the Target Cell to <u>Max</u>, <u>Min</u>, or choose <u>Value Of</u> and enter the value in the box.

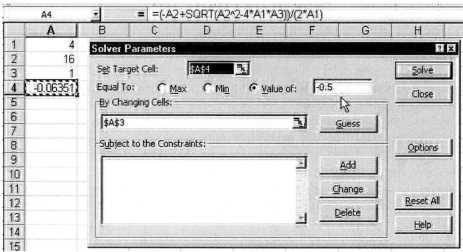

Figure A4-3. The Solver Parameters dialog box. Cell A4 is related to cells A1, A2, and A3 by the formula shown in the dialog box. We want to set cell A4 (Target Cell) to the value of −0.5 by changing cell A3.

Compose the worksheet in Fig. A4-3 on your computer so you can follow the procedure. Notice the Options button at center-right in Fig. A4-3. We will return to this after we see the results of pressing Solve at upper-right. Our solution is shown in Fig. A4-4.

In Fig. A4-4 notice the Reports box. You can request reports on Answer, Sensitivity and Limits. These reports are shown in Figs. A4-5, A4-6 and A4-7.

Also, notice the Save Scenario button at the bottom of the dialog box. Click this if you want to use it again. What is a scenario? A scenario is a set of values you use to forecast the outcome of a worksheet model. You can create and save different groups of values on a worksheet and then switch to any of these new scenarios to view different results.

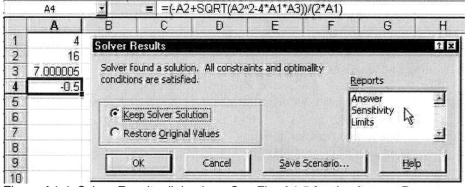

Figure A4-4. Solver Results dialog box. See Fig. A4-5 for the Answer Report.

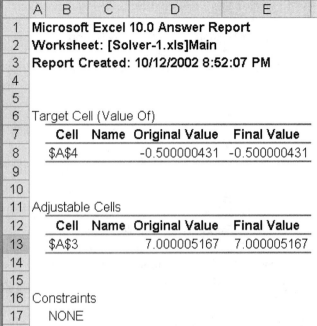

Figure A4-5. This is the Answer Report for our simple example. Compare the Final Value for cells A3 and A4 with the values obtained for the same problem using Goal Seek.

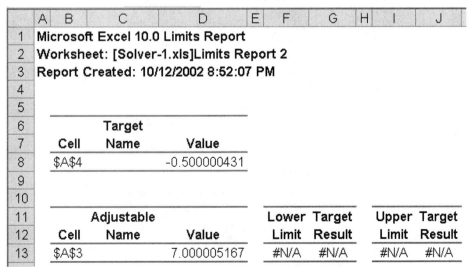

Figure A4-6. This is the Limits Report box. The limits are not applicable to our simple problem. Note automatic adjustment of column widths.

	A	B	C	D	E
1	Microsoft Excel 10.0 Sensitivity Report					
2	Worksheet: [Solver-1.xls]Main					
3	Report Created: 10/12/2002 8:52:07 PM					
4					
5					
6	Adjustable Cells				
7				Final	Reduced
8		Cell	Name	Value	Gradient
9		$A$3		7.00000517	0
10					
11	Constraints				
12		NONE			

Figure A4-7. The Sensitivity Report is applicable to more complicated problems.

Now that you have done a simple example, let's see what options are available in Solver to handle more advanced solutions.

About the Solver Options dialog box

You can control advanced features of the solution process, load or save problem definitions, and define parameters for both linear and nonlinear problems. Each option has a default setting that is appropriate for most problems.

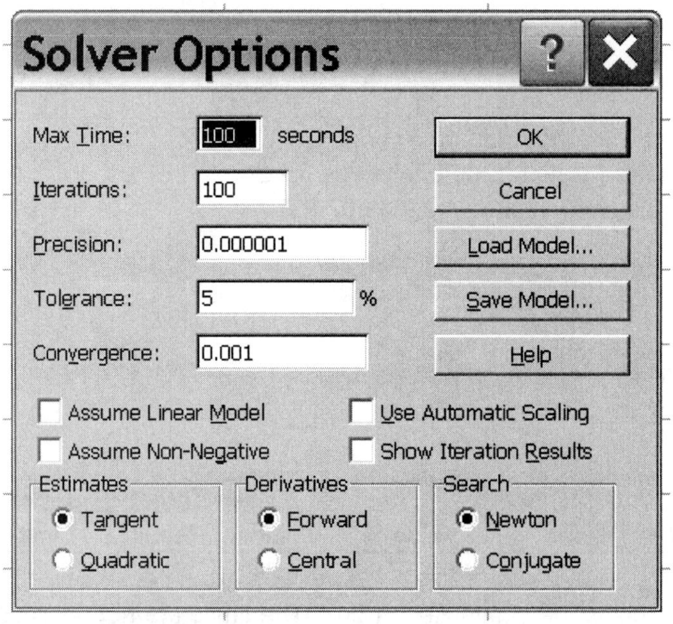

Figure A4-8. The Solver Options dialog box. This gives you complete control of the options available in Solver's algorithms.

Max time

This limits the time allowed for the solution process. While you can enter a value as high as 32,767, the default value of 100 (seconds) is adequate for most small problems.

Iterations

The Iterations choice limits the time taken by the solution process by limiting the number of interim calculations. While you can enter a value as high as 32,767, the default value of 100 is adequate for most small problems.

Precision

This controls the precision of solutions by using the number you enter to determine whether the value of a constraint cell meets a target or satisfies a lower or upper bound. Precision must be indicated by a fractional number between 0 (zero) and 1. Higher precision is indicated when the number you enter has more decimal places. For example, 0.0001 is higher precision than 0.01. The higher the precision, the more time it takes to reach a solution.

Tolerance

Tolerance is the percentage by which the target cell of a solution satisfying the integer constraints can differ from the true optimal value and still be considered acceptable. This option applies only to problems with integer constraints. A higher tolerance tends to speed up the solution process.

Convergence

Solver stops when the relative change in the target cell value is less than the number in the Convergence box for the last five iterations. Convergence applies only to nonlinear problems and must be indicated by a fractional number between 0 (zero) and 1. A smaller convergence is indicated when the number you enter has more decimal places. For example, 0.0001 is less relative change than 0.01. The smaller the convergence value, the more time Solver takes to reach a solution.

Assume Linear Model

Select this to speed the solution process when all relationships in the model are linear and you want to solve either a linear optimization problem or a linear approximation to a nonlinear problem. Be careful when you use results of a linear approximation to a system that you know is nonlinear.

Show Iteration Results

Select this to have Solver pause to show the results of each iteration.

Use Automatic Scaling

Select this to use automatic scaling when inputs and outputs have large differences in magnitude, for example, when maximizing the percentage of profit based on your latest million-dollar investment.

Assume Non-Negative
Choose this to make Solver assume a lower limit of 0 (zero) for all adjustable cells for which you have not set a lower limit in the Constraint box in the Add Constraint dialog box.

Estimates
This specifies the approach used to obtain initial estimates of the basic variables in each one-dimensional search.

Tangent
Tangent uses linear extrapolation from a tangent vector.

Quadratic
Quadratic uses quadratic extrapolation, which can improve the results on highly nonlinear problems.

Derivatives
This specifies the difference method used to estimate partial derivatives of the objective and constraint functions (See Section 5.1).

Forward
Use Forward for most problems in which the constraint values change relatively slowly (See Section 5.1).

Central
Use Central for problems in which the constraints change rapidly, especially near the limits. Although this option requires more calculations, it might help when Solver returns a message that it could not improve the solution (See Section 5.1).

Search
This specifies the algorithm used at each iteration to determine the direction in which to search.

Newton
This uses a quasi-Newton method that typically requires more memory but fewer iterations than the Conjugate gradient method.

Conjugate
Conjugate requires less memory than the Newton method but typically needs more iterations to reach a particular level of accuracy. Use this option when you have a large problem and memory usage is a concern, or when stepping through iterations reveals slow progress. Use and compare Conjugate and Newton on the same problem to see the difference.

Load Model
This displays the Load Model dialog box, where you can specify the reference for the model you want to load.

Save Model

This displays the Save Model dialog box, where you can specify where to save the model. Click only when you want to save more than one model with a worksheet. The first model is automatically saved.

Download more Solver workbooks from http://sylvanbloch.hypermart.net.

A4.3 Lookup Wizard

Goal Seek and Solver compute values based on formulas. Often, experimental data are collected in the form of a Table in which no formula is known. This is *empirical* data. The Lookup Wizard is a great convenience when you need to find an experimental result in a large table of data. We will demonstrate the use of the Lookup Wizard with a simple example.

Click on [Tools][Wizard][Lookup] and you will see Fig. A4-9. The Lookup Wizard will guide you in finding the desired result and the Wizard will write a formula in the formula editing box. In Step 1 of 4 you select the cell range to search. Use your mouse to select the row and column range. In Fig. A4-9 the entire Table has been selected.

After you have selected the desired range, click on Next and you will see Fig. A4-10. If you change your mind about your selection in later steps, click on Back.

	A	B	C	D	E	F
1	Depth (m)	Gauge Pressure (N/m^2)			Water, 4 degrees C	
2	0	0				
3	1	9800				
4	2	19600				
5	3	29400				
6	4	39200				
7	5	49000				
8	6	58800				
9	7	68600				
10	8	78400				
11	9	88200				
12	10	98000				

Lookup Wizard - Step 1 of 4

The Lookup Wizard helps you write a formula that finds the value at the intersection of a column and a row.

	2/15/94	10/10/94	7/25/95
8:45	5.31	30	51.55
10:15	10.84	13	84.87
15:30	12.83	66	83.87
18:45	15.98	16.89	95.02

Where is the range to search, including the row and column labels?

Sheet1!$A$1:$B$32

Cancel | < Back | Next > | Finish

Figure A4-9. Step 1 of 4 in the Lookup Wizard. In this simple example we will find the gauge pressure corresponding to a depth of 11 m in water at 4 degrees C. Of course, in this two-column Table you could just look in column A for the depth, but in a large multi-column Table it would be a tedious task to find a desired value.

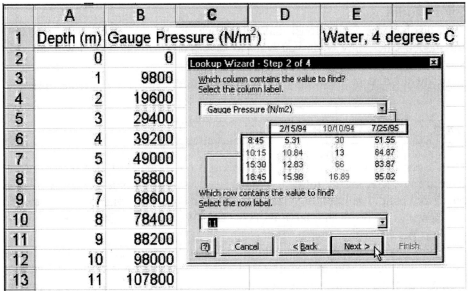

	A	B	C	D	E	F
1	Depth (m)	Gauge Pressure (N/m^2)			Water, 4 degrees C	
2	0	0				
3	1	9800				
4	2	19600				
5	3	29400				
6	4	39200				
7	5	49000				
8	6	58800				
9	7	68600				
10	8	78400				
11	9	88200				
12	10	98000				
13	11	107800				

Figure A4-10. Step 2 of 4 in the Lookup Wizard. In the upper box, select the column label for the value you want to find. In the lower box, select the row label (the input value in this example).

After selecting the column and row, click on Next and you will see Fig. A4-11. You can choose to copy just the formula, or copy the formula and lookup parameters.

	A	B	C	D	E	F
1	Depth (m)	Gauge Pressure (N/m^2)			Water, 4 degrees C	
2	0	0				
3	1	9800				
4	2	19600				
5	3	29400				
6	4	39200				
7	5	49000				
8	6	58800				
9	7	68600				
10	8	78400				
11	9	88200				
12	10	98000				
13	11	107800				

Figure A4-11. Step 3 of 4 of the Lookup Wizard. Select one of the two options.

D5	▼		=	=INDEX($A$1:$B$32, MATCH(D4,$A$1:$A$32,), MATCH(D3,$A$1:$B$1,))

	A	B	C	D	E	F
1	Depth (m)	Gauge Pressure (N/m²)			Water, 4 degrees C	
2	0	0				
3	1	9800		Gauge Pressure (N/m2)		
4	2	19600		11		
5	3	29400		107800		
6	4	39200				

Figure A4-12. Cells D3:D5 contain the output of the Lookup Wizard. The formula in the cell editing box was written automatically by the Wizard.

The final result of the Lookup Wizard is shown in Fig. A4-12. In this example, the output was placed in three cells of one column (D3:D5) but you can select any locations you want. Notice the use of the worksheet function MATCH in the formula generated by the Wizard. For information about MATCH press Function Key F1 or look in Help.

References

For the latest information on Solver from Frontline Systems Inc. go to:
   http://www.solver.com/

For a beginner's tutorial go to: http://www.solver.com/tutorial.htm

This tutorial is also on the CD with your book. It answers the questions:
   What are Solvers Good For?
   What Must I Do to Use a Solver?
   How Do I Define a Model?
   What Kind of Solution Can I Expect?
   What Makes a Model Hard to Solve?
   Can You Show Me Step by Step?

After completing the beginner's tutorial you can learn more about topics such as linearity versus nonlinearity and sparsity in optimization models by going to the Advanced Tutorial: http://www.solver.com/tutorialadv.htm

The advance tutorial is also on the CD with your book. The Advanced Tutorial covers several concepts that underlie all optimization problems:
   Derivatives, Gradients, and the Jacobian
   Linearity, Nonlinearity, and Non-Smoothness
   Mixed Linear and Nonlinear Functions and Terms
   Using the LP Coefficient Matrix Directly

Appendix 5
PivotTable Wizard, Internet Assistant Wizard

A5.1 PivotTable

Who needs it and what does it do?

You need a PivotTable if you want an *interactive* table that quickly summarizes, or cross-tabulates, large amounts of data. You can rotate its rows and columns to see different summaries of the source data, filter the data by displaying different pages, or display the details for areas of interest.

The PivotTable summarizes data by using a summary function that you specify, such as Sum, Count, or Average. You can include subtotals and grand totals automatically, or use your own formulas by adding calculated fields and items. For more, go to http://home.gvi.net/~cpearson/excel/pivots.htm .

What goes in a PivotTable?

You can create a PivotTable from an EXCEL list or database, an external database, multiple EXCEL worksheets, or another PivotTable. A PivotTable contains fields, each of which summarizes multiple rows of information from the source data.

What is a field button and what does it do?

By dragging a field button to another part of the PivotTable, you can view your data in different ways. For example, you can view the names of CPU manufacturers and the speeds of their chips either down the rows or across the columns.

How do I start a PivotTable?

EXCEL makes this easy. Use the PivotTable Wizard as a guide to locate and arrange the data you want to analyze. To begin, click PivotTable Report on the Data menu.

Creating a PivotTable from a Microsoft Excel list or database

1. Click a cell in your list before running the PivotTable Wizard. In the Pivot-Table Wizard – Step 2 of 4 dialog box – the wizard fills in the reference to the list for you.
2. EXCEL ignores any filters you have applied to a list by using the commands on the Filter submenu of the Data menu. The PivotTable automatically includes all data in the list.

To create a PivotTable from filtered data, use the Advanced Filter command to extract a range of data to another worksheet location, and base the PivotTable on the extracted range. For information about advanced filtering, see Help.
3. EXCEL automatically creates grand totals and subtotals in the PivotTable. If the source list contains automatic grand totals and subtotals, remove them before you create the PivotTable.
4. Because EXCEL uses the data in the first row of the list for the field names in the PivotTable, the source list or database must contain column labels. For list formatting guidelines, see Help.

Tip
To make the PivotTable easier to refresh and update when the source list or database changes, name the source range and use the name when you create the PivotTable. If the named range expands to include more data, you can refresh the PivotTable to include the new data.

How to use totals and subtotals in a PivotTable
You can include grand totals for data in PivotTable (see Appendix 5) rows and columns, calculated by using the same default summary function as the data fields being totaled.

EXCEL automatically displays subtotals for the outermost row or column field when you create two or more row or column fields in a PivotTable. For inner row or column fields, EXCEL displays subtotals only if you add them. You can specify the summary function to use for subtotals.

How to show or hide grand totals in a PivotTable
1. Select a cell in the PivotTable.
2. On the PivotTable toolbar, click Options on the PivotTable menu.
3. To display grand totals, under Format options, select the Grand totals for columns check box, the Grand totals for rows check box, or both.
To hide grand totals, clear either or both check boxes.

How to add or remove subtotals in a PivotTable

1. Double-click the field button for which you want to display or remove subtotals.

2. To display subtotals if the field is an outer row or column field, click Automatic under Subtotals.

To display subtotals if the field is an inner row or column field, click Custom under Subtotals, and then click a summary function in the box to the right.

To remove subtotals, click None under Subtotals.

3. To use a different summary function or to display more than one type of subtotal, click the summary functions you want to use in the box to the right of Custom. For a description of the available summary functions, see Help.

Note: EXCEL adds one subtotal line for each summary function that you select.

To include hidden page field items in the subtotals, click Options on the PivotTable menu of the PivotTable toolbar, and select the Subtotal hidden page items check box under Format options.

How to change the summary function used to calculate PivotTable subtotals

1. Double-click the field button for which you want to change the subtotal summary function.

2. Under Subtotals, click one or more of the summary functions. For information about the summary functions that you can specify for subtotal types, see Help.

Note: To add subtotals to inner row or column fields, or to use two or more types of subtotals (such as Sum and Average) on a selected PivotTable field, click Custom.

A5.2 Internet Assistant Wizard

You can use EXCEL to open workbooks on your local Web or intranet. If you have a connection to the Internet, you can also open workbooks on Internet sites such as FTP (File Transfer Protocol) and HTTP (Hypertext Transfer Protocol) servers. You can also use EXCEL to open Web files stored in HTML (Hypertext Markup Language), the format used on the World Wide Web.

Click on [Tools][Add-ins] and examine the list to be certain that the Internet Assistant Wizard is installed (see Fig. A5-1).

Use the Web toolbar to move among files. You can jump forward or backward among the workbooks and other files you've visited and add the ones you want to return to frequently to a "favorites" list.

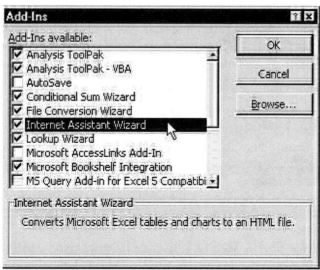

Figure A5-1. The Internet Assistant Wizard is checked to make it available in the Add-Ins dialog box.

Hyperlinks are shortcuts that provide a quick way to jump to other workbooks and files. You can jump to files on your own computer, your network, and the Internet and World Wide Web. You can create hyperlinks from cell text or graphic objects, such as shapes and pictures. The hyperlink button is on the top tool bar next to the Web button. See Fig. A5-2.

To jump to another workbook or file, point to a hyperlink, and then click it when the pointer changes to a hand. Hyperlink text is blue and underlined. When you return to the workbook after visiting another file by clicking a hyperlink, the hyperlink color changes to purple.

You can make your EXCEL data available to users on your intranet or the World Wide Web so that anyone who has a Web browser can view it. Use the Internet Assistant Wizard add-in program to convert worksheet data or charts to HTML Web pages that you can post on the World Wide Web.

If you want to gather information submitted by Web users, you can design a form in EXCEL to collect the data and then use the Web Form Wizard to set up a database system on your Web server.

Figure A5-2. The Insert Hyperlink button is by the Web button. The Web tool bar is visible on the bottom row.

How to add worksheet data or a chart to an existing Web page

The Save As HTML command should appear on the File menu in EXCEL, shown in Fig. A5-3. If the Save As HTML command is not available you need to install the Internet Assistant Wizard add-in program. (See Help or press Function Key F1.)

1. Using your Web browser or a text editor, edit the source code for your existing HTML Web page. For example, in Microsoft INTERNET EXPLORER, you could click the Open command on the File menu and then click Open File to open the .htm file. Click the file with the right mouse button, and then click View Source on the shortcut menu.

2. In the location where you want the additional worksheet data to appear, insert a new blank line, and then type the following on the new line:

<!--##Table##-->

For example, if you have a Web page that was previously created with the Microsoft EXCEL Internet Assistant, you could add the new line following the line in the .htm file that contains </Table>.

3. Save the edited HTML Web page. For example, in Microsoft INTERNET EXPLORER, you could click Save As on the File menu, and then enter the name of the .htm file.

4. In EXCEL, click a cell in the data that you want to add to the Web page.

5. On the File menu, click Save As HTML.

6. Follow the instructions in the Internet Assistant Wizard.

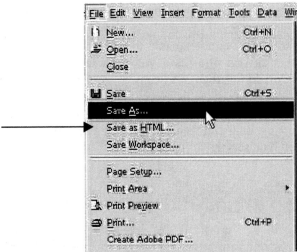

Figure A5-3. The Save as HTML command should be visible in the File menu, just below the Save As command.

How to create a Web page from worksheet data or a chart

If the Save As HTML command does not appear on the File menu in EXCEL, you need to install the Internet Assistant add-in program. For more information, see Help. To create a Web page:

1. Click a cell in the data that you want to convert to a Web page.
2. On the File menu, click Save As HTML.
3. Follow the instructions in the Internet Assistant.

A5.3 Web page programs

There are several programs that make it even easier to create Web pages. Among the most popular are Microsoft FRONTPAGE, Macromedia DREAMWEAVER and Adobe GOLIVE. FRONTPAGE is available as a stand-alone program, and it is also included as a component of Microsoft OFFICE 2000 and 2002. Adobe GOLIVE runs on the Apple MACINTOSH operating system. (http://www.adobe.com)

A short list of references for web page design can be found at http://www.macromedia.com/support/dreamweaver/ts/documents/dreamweaver_books.htm

Bibliography

Books

E. J. Billo, *Excel for Chemists: A Comprehensive Guide* (John Wiley & Sons, Inc., New York, 1997).

S. C. Bloch, *Excel per Ingegneri*, (Apogeo, Turino, Italia, 2001). http://www.apogeonline.com/libri/00827/scheda

S. C. Bloch, *Spreadsheet Analysis for Engineers and Scientists* (John Wiley & Sons, Inc., New York, 1995).

S. C. Bloch, *SSP, The Spreadsheet Signal Processor* (Prentice Hall, Englewood Cliffs, New Jersey, 1992).

S. C. Bloch, *Introduction to Classical and Quantum Harmonic Oscillators* (John Wiley & Sons, Inc., New York, 1997).

D. Diamond and V. C. A. Hanratty, *Spreadsheet Applications in Chemistry Using Microsoft Excel* (Wiley, New York, 1997).

B. S. Gottfried, *Spreadsheet Tools for Engineers* (WCB/McGraw-Hill, New York, 1998).

B. V. Liengme, *A Guide to Microsoft Excel for Scientists and Engineers* (John Wiley & Sons, Inc., New York, 1997).

W. J. Orvis, *Excel for Scientists and Engineers* (SYBEX, Alameda, CA, 1996).

G. E. Forsythe and W. R. Wasow, *Finite-Difference Methods for Partial Differential Equations* (John Wiley & Sons, Inc., New York, 1960), pp. 242-283.

Microsoft has books on several versions of EXCEL: http://www.microsoft.com

274

Papers

Kyle Forniash and Raymond Wisman, "Simple Internet data collection for physics laboratories," *American Journal of Physics* 70 (4), 458–461 (2002).

K. R. Morison and P. J. Jordan, "Spreadsheet documentation for students and engineers," *International Journal of Engineering Education* **16**, No. 6, 509–515 (2000)

S. C. Bloch and R. Dressler, "Statistical estimation of π using random vectors," *American Journal of Physics* **67**(4), 298–303 (1999).

L. N. Long and H. Weiss "The Velocity Dependence of Aerodynamic Drag: A Primer for Mathematicians," *American Mathematical Monthly*, **106**, 127 – 133 (February 1999)

T. A. Moore and D. V. Schroeder, "A different approach to introducing statistical mechanics," *American Journal of Physics* **65**(1), 26–36 (1997).

S. C. Bloch, "Fine-tune sliding-window integrators in a spreadsheet before processing real-world signals," *Personal Engineering and Instrumentation News* **10**(5), 46–52 (1993).

S. C. Bloch, "Compression of wavelets," *American Journal of Physics* **61**(9), 789–798 (1993).

S. C. Bloch, "Spreadsheet implements scalar ensemble averaging for dramatic yet simple noise reduction," *Personal Engineering and Instrumentation News* **9**(11), 45–52 (1992).

S. C. Bloch, "Spreadsheet implements easy, cost effective matched filters," *Personal Engineering and Instrumentation* News **9**(8), 39–44 (1992).

R. Smith, "Spreadsheets as a mathematical tool," *Journal on Excellence in College Teaching*, **3**, 131–149 (1992).

F. X. Hart, "Validating spreadsheet solutions to Laplace's equation," *American Journal of Physics* **57**(11), 1027–1034 (1989).

R. L. Bowman, "Electronic spreadsheets for physics students' use," *American Journal of Physics* **56**, 184–185 (1988).

W. H. Lockyear, "Spreadsheets cut finite-difference computing costs," *Microwaves & RF*, 99–108, November (1988).

F. X. Hart, "Software for introductory physics," *American Journal of Physics* **55**, 200–201 (1987).

T. T. Crow, "Solutions to Laplace's equation using spreadsheets on a personal computer," *American Journal of Physics* **55**, 817–823 (1987).

J. M. Crowley, "Electrostatic fields on PC spreadsheets," *J. Electrostat.* **19**, 137–149 (1987).

R. Feinberg and M. Knittel, "Microcomputer spreadsheet programs in the physics laboratory," *American Journal of Physics* **53**, 631–634 (1985).

J. F. Hoburg and J. L. Davis, *IEEE Trans. Education*, vol. **E-26**, 138 (1983).

J. L. Friar, "A note on the roundoff error in the Numerov algorithm," *J. Computational Phys.* **28**, 426 (1978).

Software

Statistical Add-Ins for Excel

NAG's add-ins are functions, not macros, so your results are updated automatically when data are revised. There are more than 50 statistical algorithms in this package. The algorithms are organized into four books: basic statistics, multivariate methods, time series analyses, and analysis of variance and generalized linear models.

http://www.nag.com/
http://www.nag.co.uk/
Numerical Algorithms Group, Inc.
1400 Opus Place, Suite 200
Downers Grove, Illinois 60515-5702

ESIM Monte Carlo Simulation for Microsoft Excel 2000

This download supports Excel 97 and Excel 2000. Support for earlier versions is available. Monte Carlo methods generate thousands of random inputs while tracking the range of uncertain outputs. Results are displayed graphically with histograms and cumulative distributions.

Two chapters from Dr. Sam Savage's book are included for a tutorial guide. Example files are included. A free download is available at the URL:

http://officeupdate.microsoft.com/2000/downloadDetails/esim50.htm

Also, go to AnalyCorp's web site for more information and free downloads:

http://www.analycorp.com/

Index

Bold numbers **10**, **11** and **12** refer to chapter numbers on the CD.